THE TROUBLE WITH NORMAL:
POSTWAR YOUTH AND THE MAKING OF HETEROSEXUALITY

In the years after the Second World War, economic and social factors combined to produce an intense concern over the sexual development and behaviour of young people. In a context where heterosexuality and 'normality' were understood to be synonymous and assumed to be necessary for social and national stability, teenagers were the target of a range of materials and practices meant to turn young people into proper heterosexuals.

In this study, Mary Louise Adams explores discourses about youth and their place in the production and reproduction of heterosexual norms. She examines debates over juvenile delinquency, indecent literature, and sex education to show not *why* heterosexuality became a peculiar obsession in English Canada after the Second World War, as much as *how* it came to hold such sway. Drawing on feminist theory, cultural studies, and lesbian/gay studies, *The Trouble with Normal* is the first Canadian study of 'youth' as a sexual and moral category. Adams looks not only at sexual material aimed at teenagers but also at sexual discourses generally, for what they had to say about young people and for the ways in which 'youth,' as a concept, made those discourses work. She argues that postwar insecurities about young people narrowed the sexual possibilities for both young people and adults.

While much of the recent history of sexuality examines sexuality 'from the margins,' *The Trouble with Normal* is firmly committed to examining the 'centre,' to unpacking normality itself. As the first book-length study of the history of sexuality in postwar Canada, it will make an important contribution to the growing international literature on sexual regulation.

MARY LOUISE ADAMS is an assistant professor in the School of Physical and Health Education at Queen's University.

STUDIES IN GENDER AND HISTORY

General editors: Franca Iacovetta and Craig Heron

MARY LOUISE ADAMS

The Trouble with Normal: Postwar Youth and the Making of Heterosexuality

UNIVERSITY OF TORONTO PRESS
Toronto Buffalo London

© University of Toronto Press Incorporated 1997
Toronto Buffalo London
Printed in Canada

ISBN 0-8020-4202-3 (cloth)
ISBN 0-8020-8057-X (paper)

∞

Printed on acid-free paper

Canadian Cataloguing in Publication Data

Adams, Mary Louise, 1960–
    The trouble with normal: postwar youth and the making of heterosexuality

(Studies in gender and history series)
Includes index.
ISBN 0-8020-4202-3 (bound) ISBN 0-8020-8057-X (pbk.)

1. Heterosexuality.   2. Young adults – Canada – Sexual behavior.
3. Youth – Canada – Sexual behavior.   4. Youth – Canada – Social
conditions.   5. Canada – Social conditions – 1945–   I. Title.   II. Series.

HQ27.A32 1997   306.76'4'09710945   C97-931083-0

This book has been published with the help of a grant from the Humanities
and Social Sciences Federation of Canada, using funds provided by the Social
Sciences and Humanities Research Council of Canada.

University of Toronto Press acknowledges the financial assistance to its publishing program of the Canada Council for the Arts and the Ontario Arts
Council.

Contents

ACKNOWLEDGMENTS   vii

1 Introduction   3

2 Sexuality and the Postwar Domestic 'Revival'   18

3 Hope for the Future or Repercussions of the Past: Discursive
  Constructions of Youth   39

4 Youth Gone Bad: The Sexual Meaning of Delinquency   53

5 'Why Can't I Be Normal?': Sex Advice for Teens   83

6 Sex Goes to School: Debates over Sex Education in Toronto
  Schools   107

7 Manipulating Innocence: Corruptibility, Youth, and the Case
  against Obscenity   136

8 Conclusion   166

NOTES   173
SOURCES   197
ILLUSTRATION CREDITS   215
INDEX   217

Acknowledgments

The Trouble with Normal began life as a doctoral dissertation at the Ontario Institute for Studies in Education. The early stages of the project were punctuated by the AIDS-related deaths of two close friends. Peter McGehee died at the age of thirty-five, in the fall of 1991. His lover, Doug Wilson, died at the age of forty-one, exactly one year later. In some way these two events are part of this book and, for me, Doug and Peter's memories will always be tied to it.

During the years I worked on the dissertation, I was fortunate to be immersed in a supportive and challenging community of feminist academics and activists – one that I now fear I took too much for granted at the time. In particular I want to thank the members of the sex/history study group who 'pushed' this and many of my other productions over the years: Debi Brock, Karen Dubinsky, Julie Guard, Margaret Little, Becki Ross, and Carolyn Strange. Thanks also to members of the women's history group, many of whom made comments on early bits of the manuscript and from whom I learned much about the writing of history: Himani Bannerji, Chris Burr, Karen Dubinsky, Franca Iacovetta, Maureen McCarthy, Janice Newton, Susan Prentice, Tori Smith, Carolyn Strange, Mariana Valverde, and Cynthia Wright. And, thanks to the members of the thesis-writing group organized by Kari Dehli in the Department of Sociology at OISE.

The book, of course, would not exist were it not for the generosity and support of friends and family. My mother, Betty Adams, shared with me her recollections of Toronto in the 1940s. Her stories were part of the original motivation for the project. Karen Dubinsky answered questions, from the theoretically complex to the plain silly, and helped me keep the writing in perspective. She lent books, copied articles, and supplied me with gossip in those weeks when I wasn't getting out enough. Kate McKenna was a good neighbour and a reassuring sounding board at critical moments. Eric Mykhalovskiy read drafts of early chapters, and they are better now for his having done so. Steven Maynard, Rob Champagne, and Cynthia Wright offered advice and references. Daintry Norman helped me procrastinate and made sure I continued to talk about things other than the history of sexuality.

This project benefited greatly from the intellectual guidance of my supervisor, Kari Dehli. I am especially thankful for her encouragement, pragmatism, and organizational talents, both during and after the dissertation. The other members of what grew to be a very large dissertation committee – James Heap, Ruth Roach Pierson, Kathy Peiss, David Rayside, Roger Simon, and Mariana Valverde – contributed insightful comments and helpful criticisms that proved invaluable as I was preparing the manuscript for the book. I also would like to thank the ten people who agreed to be interviewed during the initial stages of my research. Their memories and insights helped to determine the direction the project would eventually take.

At the University of Toronto Press, Franca Iacovetta provided useful comments on early revisions of the manuscript. Gerald Hallowell's enthusiasm for the project and his sound logistical and editorial advice made it a pleasure to work with him. Emily Andrew's efficiency and gentle nudging – at always the right time – helped to keep me on track. Margaret Allen's excellent copy-editing has made this book more user-friendly.

My research was made possible by the collections and the work of archivists at the City of Toronto Archives, the Metro Toronto Archives, the Toronto Board of Education Archives, the Toronto Harbour Commission Archives, the Archives of Ontario, and the National Archives of Canada. In particular, I would like to thank John Choules and Stormie Stewart at the Archives of Ontario and Rick Prelinger, of Prelinger and Associates, for giving me access to an amazing collection of educational films. The Social Sciences and Humanities Research Council provided much-needed financial support.

Finally, I want to thank Helen Humphreys for living with me and the book, in all its incarnations, and for helping us both to be much better than we would have been without her.

THE TROUBLE WITH NORMAL

1

Introduction

In the Bruce Cockburn song from which I borrowed the title of this book, 'the trouble with normal is it always gets worse.'[1] In this study, the trouble with normal is its taken-for-grantedness and its power as a regulatory sexual category. In the 1940s and 1950s, the difference between definitions of normal and abnormal sexuality operated as a profound space of social marginalization and exclusion. As a powerful organizer of everyday life, the imperative to be normal limited possibility in people's lives; certainly it limited the forms of sexual expression and identity available to them.

This book investigates the constitution of sexual normality in postwar English Canada. In particular, it explores the role played by discourses about young people in the production and reproduction of heterosexual norms. It explores the relationship between dominant sexual discourses and a variety of practices meant to turn teenagers into 'proper' heterosexuals. I argue that social conditions particular to the postwar period combined to put notions about youth and adolescence at the centre of sexual discourses. Moreover, notions about youth and adolescence helped to shape the general meanings ascribed to sexuality in the period.

Present-day sexual conservatives like to remember the 1950s as a lost era of family values and solid, 'traditional' morals. In contemporary sexual politics, the 1950s are the standard against which some conservatives measure changes in the organization of sexuality. The mores of that decade sit as a kind of benchmark, a symbol of how far North Americans have travelled since morality was 'as it should be,' with clear gender roles in every household and heterosexual conjugal monogamy as the primary form of sexual partnership.[2] That this portrait is an idealized version of fifties norms does not decrease its effectiveness in contributing to present-day anxieties about changing sexual behaviours and identities. A study of the late 1940s and 1950s makes apparent the ideological underpinnings of the nostalgia that currently runs counter to the gains made by feminists, gay men, and lesbians over the past two decades.

Ironically, this project on heterosexuality grew from an interest in lesbian and gay history. My research was motivated by a desire to document the social meanings of homosexuality in the years prior to gay liberation. I wanted to get a sense of the context of lesbian and gay lives, of the distance people would have had to travel through mainstream discourses to identify themselves as homosexual in the postwar period. This study, therefore, is less about the sexual margins to which homosexuality was relegated than it is about the sexual centre that gave those margins their shape. I am concerned with the processes through which particular forms of heterosexuality were constructed as normal, and therefore socially desirable, in the postwar period in English Canada. Without an understanding of the dominant sexual culture, it is impossible to understand the depth of the resistance engaged in by lesbians, gay men, and others who were unwilling or unable to conform to prevailing definitions of sexual normality. In this vein, *The Trouble with Normal* provides contextual grounding to the growing field of Canadian lesbian and gay history.[3]

To gain access to the dominant sexual discourses that are my primary concern in this book, I focused my research on discourses about youth and adolescents. During the postwar years, young people were the targets of a range of formal and informal sex-education materials through which mainstream sexual norms were both reproduced and constituted. But the importance of young people to sexual discourses did not lie solely in their position as targets of knowledge; they were also important to the construction of that knowledge. Assumptions about the corruptibility of young people, about their need for protection from moral harm, and about their role as representatives of the future helped to set boundaries for how sexuality, in a general sense, could be understood. This study, then, looks not only at sexual material aimed at teenagers; it looks at sexual discourses generally – including discussions of obscenity, homosexuality, sexual perversions, and delinquency – both for what they had to say about young people and for the ways that 'youth,' as a concept, made those discourses work.

Discourse as Social Geography

Let me state at the beginning that, because this is a study of dominant discourses, the 'English Canada' I refer to is not a representative one. It is an English Canada constructed in mainstream national discourses that were produced, for the most part, in Toronto. Originally, this study had a specific focus on Toronto, and this focus remains in two of the chapters that follow – about debates over sex education at the Toronto Board of Education, and discussions of juvenile delinquency as one of the city's most pressing postwar problems. But, generally, the discourses I investigate here are not easily described as 'Toronto discourses.' The problems defined through these discourses, even as they circulated within organizations specific to Toronto, were not constructed as local problems; their solutions were not limited to the city. Discourses like those on indecent literature, for instance, were constructed and responded to as if they were of national concern.

Of course, so-called national discourses of this type did not operate in similar ways across the country – the range of practices and institutions to which, and by which, they were articulated varied regionally, between rural and urban areas, and among class, racial, ethnic, and age groups. They were, nevertheless, frequently put into circulation by way of practices and institutions located in Toronto – by the CBC, for instance, which began television broadcasts in the early 1950s, or by magazines like *Maclean's* or *Chatelaine*. In the postwar period, Toronto was the centre of English-language publishing, broadcasting, and cultural production, a position that contributed to the publicizing of urban issues and Toronto-based perspectives across the country. In representing itself through national media, Toronto became entwined with the definition of the 'national culture.' The process was facilitated by national media outlets and by the fact that Toronto was home to many organizations, from the YWCA to the Health League, that claimed to be national in scope and to represent the interests of 'all Canadians.'

What distinguished Toronto's grip on the 'national' culture in the postwar period was its conspicuousness. While present-day CBC announcers make at least some effort to downplay the Toronto-centredness of the public broadcaster (in spite of current management strategies that do not), writers and journalists in the 1940s and 1950s showed little evidence that the hegemony they represented was even an issue. Thus, when CBC television put together a panel of youth, chances were they came from Toronto high schools. In part, this tendency was as much a product of limited technology and resources as it was of political perspective. But it also reflected postwar notions that 'the nation,' however represented, was a desirable entity. French-English conflict notwithstanding, the idea of 'the nation' as a unified collective was the object of far less scrutiny, in the English part of the country, than it is today. In some senses, the shared experiences of the Depression and the Second World War gave Canadians a common point of reference. And the expansion of the welfare state at war's end meant that all Canadians had something to gain from an identification with the nation and from the marking of national interests.

It's ironic, then, that the postwar period was also a time when many Canadians thought the interests of the nation were best served by falling into line behind the United States. By the early 1960s, Canadian intellectuals looked back on the preceding decade and decried the 'Americanization' of Canada.[4] J.M. Bumsted argues that the 1950s produced one of the least virulent strains of anti-Americanism in Canadian history. 'Almost without exception,' he writes, 'Canadians accepted the role of the United States as moral and military leader of the western democracies.'[5] National discourses, therefore, were not without their international attachments.

A brief note on discourse as a tool of analysis: The notion of discourse I use here is a Foucauldian one and refers to organized systems of knowledge that make possible what can be spoken about and how one may speak about it. At their most fundamental level, these 'systems' are about the production of meaning, a process that is not without its material effects. Discourses, according to Foucault, 'crystallize into institutions, they inform individual behaviour, they act as grids for the perception and evaluation of things.'[6] They are not, as some have suggested, unrelated to the material aspects of our world. Indeed, material factors – printing presses, institutional resources, money – are what allow certain discourses to become more powerful than others. The task of discourse analysis is to determine which discourses are operating when and how and in what configurations. What possibilities for the construction of meaning arise through their circulation? In analysing discourses one investigates the various processes – language and social practices – which make possible the statement of the 'truths' that order our social world[7] – for instance, the claim that heterosexuality is the most (or, in some versions the only) natural form of sexual expression. The intent is not to prove the veracity of such claims or their alternatives, but to understand how it is that they have come to be made.

Heterosexuality as Subject of Investigation

'Heterosexuality is not natural, just common'
– T-shirt slogan, 1993

In the late 1800s, sexologists across Europe and North America compiled vast lists of strange and unusual sexual 'types' and sexual behaviours. These ranged from various forms of bestiality and sado-masochism to auto-eroticism, fetishism, and a wide array of what were assumed to be neurotic distortions of the 'sex instinct.' Given this history, it is interesting that out of all these possibilities, the most profound sexual-social division in present-day Western culture is the one between straight and gay, although the divide between homo- and heterosexualities is perhaps more a linguistic construction than a reflection of the sociosexual landscape. Clunky and inefficient in an analytic sense, this divide works politically to obscure the diversity of experience and allegiance among those who participate in same-sex sexual activity – a diversity that makes it impossible to construct a firm boundary around the proper subject matter of specifically lesbian and gay or specifically heterosexual research. As long as homosexualities and heterosexualities are dichotomized, it is difficult to understand either side of the dichotomy without also considering its so-called opposite. As an analytic category, sexuality – like race, like gender, like class – is relational. There can be no homosexuality without a heterosexuality from which to differentiate it. Thus, it makes sense for those of us interested in the social meanings of the former to engage in research on the latter.

As a means of categorizing and regulating particular types of behaviour and people, both homo- and heterosexuality are relative latecomers to everyday discourse. The term 'homosexuality' was coined in 1868 by German sodomy-law reformer Karl Maria Kertbeny. In his usage, the term referred not to sexual object choice, as it does now, but to gender inversion, that is to effeminacy exhibited by men and masculine demeanour exhibited by women.[8] According to gay historian Jonathan Ned Katz, in his important book *The Invention of Heterosexuality*, this new category of homosexuality was initially counterposed not to heterosexuality, which did not yet exist as either a word or a concept, but to a narrowly defined reproductive sexuality. Katz says that it wasn't until 1880 that Kertbeny's new word 'heterosexuality' went public – in a published defence of homosexuality.[9] Twelve years later, an American doctor named James Kiernan used the new term to refer to those who were sexually inclined towards both sexes.[10] A 1901 medical dictionary, cited by Katz, gave a more narrow definition: 'Abnormal or perverted appetite toward the opposite sex.'[11]

The equation of heterosexuality with perversion reflected the centrality of reproduction to pre-twentieth-century sexual systems. It was not until the beginning of this century that the criteria for classifying sexual behaviours shifted from their reproductive to their erotic possibilities. Katz argues that the emergence of the homosexual/heterosexual opposition was part of this shift away from reproductive norms and towards what he calls a 'different-sex erotic norm.'[12] The work of Viennese sexologist Richard von Krafft-Ebing helped to crystallize this binary as well as the notion of heterosexuality as a non-pathological predisposition to different-sex erotic feelings and behaviour. In his book *Psychopathia Sexualis*, which first appeared in English in 1893, the erotically normal heterosexual is counterposed to the abnormal homosexual, thus setting the groundwork for the hierarchical organization of sexuality that we continue to face today.[13]

It took some time, however, for the homosexual/heterosexual binarism to be widely adopted as a form of classifying erotic attraction. George Chauncey argues that in male working-class communities in New York City, for instance, 'homosexual behaviour per se became the primary basis for the labelling and self-identification of men as "queer" only around the middle of the twentieth century.' Prior to that time, 'queerness' had been attributed to a man's inability to fit into normative gender roles, not to the sex of the people he chose to have sex with. Thus, masculine men who had sex with effeminate men – 'fairies' – had not been considered to be abnormal or homosexual. It wasn't until the 1930s, 1940s, and 1950s, says Chauncey, that 'the now-conventional division of men into "homosexuals" and "heterosexuals," based on the sex of their sexual partners, replace[d] the division of men into "fairies" and "normal men,"' a distinction that had been based on their display of accepted gender attributes. For white, middle-class men in New York, the importance of erotic inclination and the division between homo- and heterosexuality had become a way of marking normality two generations earlier.[14]

Chauncey says that the increasing importance of heterosexuality to the middle class reflected the reorganization of gender relations in the early part of the twentieth century. New corporate forms of work, the growing participation of women in the public sphere, and perceptions that modern life was 'softening' the male character had led to a crisis of middle-class masculinity. Widespread fear of effeminacy – crystallized around the public image of the fairy – translated into a fear of homosexuality, thereby making heterosexuality a route for the demonstration of manliness. Exclusive erotic desire for women came to be a mark of being a man, while gender identity and sexual identity came to be an inseparable pair.[15]

This coupling of gender and sexual identities helped to transform the place of sex in North American cultures. Victorian discourses about the need for sexual control and about women's sexual passivity and passionlessness were, increasingly, being questioned by young women and men and by political and sexual radicals. Christina Simmons says that by the 1920s in the United States, the 'predominant tone' about sex was one of 'liberal reform.'[16] Simmons writes that the 'new' thinkers argued for less distance between husband and wife, especially in terms of sex. They claimed that 'denying sexual urges made marriage itself less stable'; hence they argued for companionate marriages based on emotional intimacy and sexual satisfaction for both women and men.[17] This became the model of heterosexuality in the 1920s and 1930s, although, as Simmons makes clear, it did not go uncontested by those, especially women, who felt that the new sexualized marriages diminished female power. In previous middle-class arrangements, women had held a moral power that enabled them to determine the shape of their sexual relationships. In companionate marriages, women's role became a responsive one. Women were counselled to follow men's sexual lead; to withdraw from sex was to threaten the marriage, to treat a husband unfairly. Sex was the glue that was to hold these marriages together. Gender-based roles under male control were the prescription for making sex work. Heterosexuality itself became synonymous with gender hierarchy.

By the 1940s, companionate forms of heterosexual marriage had achieved dominance as *the* way of organizing erotic, emotional, and reproductive life. The 'revival of domesticity' after the war helped to entrench the strict gender dichotomies that held up these forms of marriage, while efforts to control extramarital sex contributed to their sexualization, a process that was seen as one route to family harmony and domestic stability. The increasing influence of psychoanalytic theories in the postwar period also meant that heterosexuality was not simply a means of organizing relationships between women and men; rather, it came to be seen as essential to the expression of 'maturity,' and it determined one's ability to make claims on normality, that most important of postwar social classifications.

It was not until the postwar period that the process of developing a proper heterosexual identity came to be understood as something that took place before marriage. Not only was teenage sexuality acknowledged – in dozens of advice books and magazine articles on petting and necking – but it was watched and nurtured and guided in socially appropriate directions by sex educators, concerned parents, various civic bodies, and voluntary organizations. Following Freud, heterosexual development was seen as a fragile process, one open to corruption. Adult heterosexuality was not taken to be an inevitability; it was an achievement, a marker of safe passage through adolescence.

What I want to stress in sketching how the notion of heterosexuality developed is both its only recent emergence as an articulated concept and the fact that it has, over the last 100 years, changed considerably as an idea and a practice. As an important sexual category that is too often taken for granted, it requires historical and sociological investigation. Such scrutiny is especially important in light of present-day popular wisdom about so-called family values, in which nothing is seen as more natural and universal than heterosexuality and the nuclear families many people build around it.

To say that homo- and heterosexuality are only recent concepts is, of course, not to say that people in earlier eras did not engage in activities which today we would think of as homo- or heterosexual. Nor is it to suggest that forms of sexual expression were not, previously, subjected to processes of differentiation and regulation. The point is that over the course of several decades, sexual desire and behaviours came to be seen in a new light, as central to identity, as keys to the personality of the individual, and, most importantly for this study, to his or her claim on normality.

While there exist many studies in which the centrality of heterosexual identities or behaviours is implicit – for instance, historical and sociological explorations of marriage, or of the modern nuclear family – it is only quite recently that researchers and writers have been foregrounding heterosexualities as a problematic in their work. In failing to question the 'naturalness' of heterosexual identities and practices, research supports the ideological formation which allows heterosexuality to be seen as the dominant and only acceptable form of sexual expression, the one from which homosexualities (and other forms of sexual expression) deviate.

In this study, I begin from the premise that this hierarchical organization needs constantly to be questioned and brought into view as socially constructed rather than biologically 'natural' or socially self-evident.

Gay historian Jonathan Ned Katz has been the first to undertake a systematic historical study of 'the idea' of heterosexuality. In his recent book, *The Invention of Heterosexuality*, Katz challenges the notion that heterosexuality 'just is' by detailing its short but complex history, from its beginnings as a category of deviance to its current position of contested but dominant form of eroticism and fundamental organizer of social relationships. Katz locates the beginning of his project in the lesbian and gay liberation movements of the early 1970s which proclaimed the abolition of the homosexual/heterosexual distinction as an important goal. Similar demands were made by women's liberation groups as they developed powerful critiques of heterosexual ideologies as mechanisms for the social regulation of women.[18] But, as Katz says, questioning the dominant position of heterosexuality was not the same thing as unpacking its history. It would take a decade of research into gay and lesbian and feminist history before the possibility of such an analysis would crystallize. It still remains rare for heterosexualities to be the central focus of social research.[19]

In feminist circles, Adrienne Rich's important 1980 article on 'compulsory heterosexuality' remains the most often-cited source on the subject (even though Rich's own position on the issue has changed).[20] In that article, Rich correctly rejects notions that 'most women are innately heterosexual'; however, she then goes on to suggest that women's nature may, in fact, tend towards lesbianism. The implicit suggestion in Rich's argument is that heterosexuality is an imposed system of control that keeps women from acting on their more 'natural' inclination for sexual and emotional relationships with other women. Using examples as wide-ranging as foot-binding and clitoridectomy, the South Asian practice of suttee, and the modern Western trade in pornography, Rich constructs heterosexuality as a pervasive and almost inescapable system through which men control women.

In this formulation, heterosexuality is a given category, constant across time and place. While Rich claims that heterosexuality has always been resisted by some women, she does not seem to see this resistance as having had transformative effects. I agree with Rich when she argues that heterosexuality must be analysed as '*a political institution*' (her emphasis), as a factor in male dominance over women, but it needs to be analysed on other levels besides this. As Karen Dubinsky has persuasively argued in her book on heterosexual conflict in turn-of-the-century Ontario, heterosexuality has not only been lived as a site of coercion or violence or dependency for women.[21] Heterosexual relations have also been entered into by women as a site of pleasure and a route to independence from controlling parents and stifling families. To claim that the social and political effects of the 'heterosexual' relations analysed by Dubinsky are the same as those between men and women who lived in other time periods or on other continents is to essentialize a category that is more usefully investigated as a product of changing historical and cultural circumstances. While I do not dispute that heterosexuality has been implicated in men's dominance over women, Rich's presentation of dominance as a singular achievement leaves little room for either critical understanding of how that dominance was constructed or social optimism for how it might be dismantled. In contrast, I argue for the importance of analysing heterosexual dominance as it is constantly being reproduced, negotiated, and subverted.

Sexual Discourses and Normalization

To argue that sexuality is socially constructed, that it changes across time and place, is not to say that we experience it that way. Certainly, as Foucault and others have pointed out, people in Western cultures have not done so over the last two centuries during which sexological, medical, and psychoanalytic discourses have all, in various ways, come to place sexuality at the centre of our personal identities. To say that sexuality is socially constructed is not to say that it is not real right now, in the late 1990s, that it is a trivial force in our lives, or that it is easily changed. Rather, it is to suggest the importance of questioning the way we think about sexuality, how it is organized and regulated. Why is it that we categorize ourselves and others by our sexual behaviours and identities? Why has sexuality come to be so 'personal'? Why is it assumed to hold the key to our development as individuals?

For Foucault, sexual discourses are conduits through which power gains access to human bodies and where it is expressed by them at the most fundamental level: 'When I think of the mechanics of power, I think of its capillary form of existence, of the extent to which power seeps into the very grain of individuals, reaches right into their bodies, permeates their gestures, their posture, what they say, how they learn to live and work with other people.'[22] This particular understanding of the relationship between sexuality and power and the framing of power as something which operates within and through the individual is immensely important to contemporary notions of sexuality as one of the primary defining features of the individual. It is also critical to the study of the construction of norms and the processes of normalization which I have undertaken in this book.

As a concept, normalization draws our attention to discourses and practices that produce subjects who are 'normal,' who live 'normality,' and, most importantly, who find it hard to imagine anything different. These discourses and practices work to delineate possible forms of expression, sexual or otherwise, as legitimate, while others are left to exist beyond the limits of acceptability. As Cathy Urwin describes it, normalization operates as a type of deviance-prevention mechanism.[23] Individuals are encouraged, through a variety of discursive and institutional practices, to meet normative standards, and they come to desire the rewards that meeting those standards makes possible. In this way individuals become self-regulating. While repressive mechanisms may be tied to this process, as in the criminalization of homosexual behaviours in the 1950s, their effects are far outweighed by the power of the original 'encouragement.'

What makes normalization such an effective exercise of power is the way it operates at the level of the individual, the way, as Foucault says, it uses its subjects. As a form of social regulation, normalization defines and limits the choices that are available to us. Julian Henriques and colleagues write that norms form the 'conditions of [our] desire.'[24] The point is not that we simply try to meet social norms, it's that we *want* to. In the 1950s, this tendency to conformity was lauded and derided by social critics; many thought it was one of the defining features of the period.[25]

While there is definitely a relationship between social norms and various scientific and professional constructions of 'normality,' these two categories are not entirely synonymous. Norms are not always based on what's normal. Normal, as Ian Hacking points out, can refer simply to what's usual or typical, a definition which may approximate the norm or may not.[26] To simplify Hacking's argument, the notion of normal as what is usual comes from medicine where, in the 1820s, it evolved as an empirical category counterposed to the pathological. In this sense 'normal' was descriptive; however, it also had a positive value, as in 'healthy.' This normal/pathological opposition eventually moved from medical fields to sociological and political ones. As social systems were perceived to be in an unhealthy state, normal conditions were what these systems had deviated from – normal conditions were seen as 'the good ones.' Here, normal does match 'the norm' in the sense of how 'things ought to be.'[27]

Both of these senses of the word – normal as description, normal as desirable – differ from more recent connotations of normality as a statistical category. In this usage, normal is not necessarily desirable; it is 'mediocre,' as Hacking puts it, following Francis Galton. Normal is the point from which we deviate, for better or worse. It is perhaps not a coincidence that 'the normal curve,' the bell curve, was developed in 1893, at the same time that sexologists were detailing and defining the 'normal' sexual type known as heterosexuality.[28] While these two modes of determining normality were different, they both helped contribute to notions of its importance as a social marker, a means of measuring difference.

It is when this measure of difference goes to work through moral discourses that it becomes a norm, a regulatory standard of behaviour, an expression of disciplinary power. In detailing the competing means of defining normal, Hacking makes clear that this progression is not inevitable. Nevertheless, what I want to suggest here is that sexual and moral discourses were so tightly connected in the post–Second World War period that definitions of 'normal sexuality' – as defined, for instance, in sex education manuals, in films for teenagers, or in magazine articles – and social/sexual norms were interchangeable. Furthermore, definitions of what is normal and what isn't – whether those definitions are based on statistical evidence or on notions of typicalness – are influenced by social-sexual norms and the moral discourses through which they are produced. It's for this reason that Alfred Kinsey, in his statistical studies of sexual behaviours, tried to avoid using 'normal' as a category. In the present study, the relationship between definitions of normality and social norms is often a circular one.

Historical sociologists Philip Corrigan and Derek Sayer identify the power of the norm and the process of normalization as an important aspect of what they call moral regulation – the social and political project of rendering 'natural' the perspectives and ideologies of hegemonic interests.[29] Their idea of moral regulation shares certain features with the forms of disciplinary power, the self-regulatory processes described by Foucault in *The History of Sexuality* and elsewhere.[30] Like Foucault, Corrigan and Sayer are concerned with the ways that discourses come to work through us so that we become not only easily regulated, but self-regulating. But Corrigan and Sayer, more than Foucault, tend to focus on the fact that only certain discourses seem to gain this power. There are powerful and less powerful discourses, a distinction that has much to do with the material relationships within which they are grounded. The effects of even the 'positive,' 'productive' exercise of power are related to material circumstances through, for instance, the means by which discourses are circulated, whether that be printed materials, television and radio broadcasts, public school lessons, or any of a multitude of other means. Such attention to the inequities in the distribution of power is crucial to an analysis of sexuality, where the realities of subordination and domination are longstanding and impossible to ignore.

Corrigan and Sayer suggest that moral regulation works by limiting the forms of expression available to us – in part, by masking difference under an illusion of social unity. It homogenizes. What we take to be 'normal' are, for the most part, representations of dominant interests. Moral regulation helps establish dominant modes of being as not only legitimate, but desirable. Thus, as individuals, we become embedded in and embrace the very processes which restrict possibility in our lives and which diminish our abilities to make sense of ourselves and the world around us. If, for instance, heterosexuality is revered and validated while same-sex sex is punishable by law, by social ostracism, or by its definition as abnormal, it can be difficult for young people who feel they are homosexual to reconcile their sexual and social desires. Fears of punishment, or of not fitting in, can inhibit their ability to express themselves in a manner of their own choosing. It's in this most insidious way that moral regulation limits the number of acceptable or possible social identities that we can take on, all the while making this situation of reduced opportunity appear natural.

It is because the various procedures and regulatory techniques of normalization are directed towards the formation of appropriate kinds of persons that discussions of moral regulation, and the normalization that accomplishes it, are by necessity discussions about subjectivity and about the construction of social subjects. Here, subjectivity is to be understood as both the conscious and unconscious aspects of the individual. It refers to the way we understand who we are in the world and how we take our place in it. We make this knowledge 'ours,' not through the revelations of our 'true selves,' but via our negotiations through and within discourse – regulated systems of what can be expressed or said. Our discursive attachments let us bring meaning to the world around us and to our place within it. They offer us subject positions through which we come to understand who and what we are. Our location at the confluence of a variety of discourses makes possible the range of ways we have of expressing ourselves, as well as the meanings we assign to our expressions. It makes it possible to resist what some have called 'discourse-determinism.'

The production of subjectivity is an ongoing and contested process, not something that occurs once and for all. In terms of the marginalization of homosexualities, for instance, we need to question how such a process of differentiation is accomplished, and how difference comes to be known (and respected or resisted) by people on either side of it. How is 'queerness,' for instance, positioned by the discourses and practices which contribute to dominant heterosexual norms? The point is, as Richard Johnston writes, that subjectivities – even the most normal and heterosexual ones – are 'produced and not given and are therefore the objects of inquiry, not the premises or starting points.'[31]

This book outlines some of the conditions of possibility within which postwar sexual subjectivities were produced. What were the systems of sexual meaning available to adults and teenagers, through which identity could be expressed and understood? While I talk very little about the subjectivities of specific individuals, I am interested in the different subject positions produced in and made available by various discursive formations, in the way discourses position both those who speak through them and those of whom they speak. It is through the negotiation of multiple, often contradictory subject positions that subjectivity is produced. In this light, it is the 'preconditions' of subjectivity that I am concerned with here. How were specific subject positions – the juvenile delinquent, the pervert, the nice girl, the sissy, the promiscuous teen – organized through discourse? What was their relationship to the 'normal heterosexual'?

In my research I looked at a variety of sites through which the postwar social-sexual order was constructed and maintained: schools, courtrooms, social-work agencies, municipal bureaucracies, popular advice literature, and mainstream social comment. The result of these investigations is not a cohesive, chronological, historical narrative. Sexuality is far too slippery a concept to lend itself to either tidy forms of research or tidy forms of writing. Instead, this text moves back and forth, across the time period and across discourses and social locations, as it points to instances where we can see the different ways discourses about youth and sexuality were important to the constitution of heterosexual normality.

What Foucault calls 'the putting into discourse of sex'[32] is not coterminous with the production of what we might easily identify as 'sexual discourses.' Sexuality is typically displaced onto other social categories. While Foucault may be right that our era suffers from an explosion of sexual discourse,[33] it is not always easy to identify or classify the debris. What we might want to call the sexual realm is not easily defined.[34] Banking regulations, zoning by-laws, hospital visiting policies – none of these is immediately identified as a sexual 'thing.' Nevertheless, each of these has promoted and protected heterosexual marriage. The point is that 'sexuality' is not always a self-evident category, a fact which greatly complicates research about it.

Wherever possible I have used Canadian materials in this research. There are, however, several instances in this book, particularly in discussions of popular cultural material, where the use of American sources was unavoidable. As J.M Bumsted has written about the 1950s, 'Canada failed dismally to prevent the United States from gaining a veritable stranglehold within Canada over popular culture.'[35] Even the Massey Commission, set up in 1949 to develop a national cultural strategy, left popular cultural forms almost entirely in the hands of the Americans. According to Bumsted, the assumption was that mass culture was, by definition, not Canadian.[36] But Canadian or not, it was consumed in this country, in great quantities: in the mid-1950s, English-Canadian television stations drew 53 per cent of their programming from the United States;[37] by 1959, *Time* and *Reader's Digest* alone were taking forty cents out of every dollar spent on magazines in Canada.[38] This incursion of American products into the Canadian cultural marketplace creates difficulties for Canadian researchers interested in Canadian discourses. But one may still make an argument that Canadians 'read' American popular culture in a Canadian way and that issues of prominence in both countries – juvenile delinquency, obscenity – were negotiated differently in each national context. That said, the American sources that appear in this book do so because they helped to shape Canadian discourses about youth and sexuality.

This book identifies a variety of processes involved in the normalization of particular forms of heterosexuality in the postwar period. What I have paid most attention to are those points where discourses about youth and discourses about sexuality became intertwined. I argue that each of these two sets of discourses is critical to the way we take meaning from the other. Furthermore, the relationship between them has had a significant influence on both popular and expert ideas about 'normal' forms of sexual expression.

2

Sexuality and the Postwar Domestic 'Revival'

In present-day popular culture, the postwar period is routinely depicted by a predictable mix of Ozzie and Harriet, suburban bungalows, and rock 'n' roll teen culture. On the one hand, the period has come to represent a lost era of family values for which many now yearn; on the other hand, it is seen as a time of unceasing conformity, repression, and blandness, broken only by the tyrannies of McCarthyist anti-Communism. In Canada, any of a number of recent studies – Doug Owram's *Born at the Right Time*, Franca Iacovetta's *Such Hardworking People*, and Reg Whitaker and Gary Marcuse's *Cold War Canada*, among others – is capable of shattering these simplistic views.[1] While the postwar period was a time when social conformity was valued by many and when popular culture frequently traded in images of smiling suburban housewives, it was also a period that saw tremendous changes on the social landscape – such as a steady increase in the numbers of working women and huge increases in the numbers of immigrants coming to Canada from southern and eastern European countries.

Canadian sociologists and historians have dealt constructively with this contradictory image, avoiding the false polarization that has characterized some postwar scholarship in the United States: Was the period a time of repression or a time of social change? In her recent anthology, *Not June Cleaver*, American historian Joanne Meyerowitz takes other feminist historians to task for focusing too much attention on the conservatism of the postwar years and not enough on women's resistance. Her argument seems to be directed primarily at Elaine Tyler May's book, *Homeward Bound*, which discusses the links between United States foreign policy during the cold war and prevailing ideologies of gender and domesticity. While recognizing the era's conservatism, Meyerowitz claims that the emphasis on the constraints women encountered in the period 'tends to downplay women's agency and to portray women primarily as victims. It obscures the complexity of postwar culture and the significant social and economic changes of the postwar era ... the sustained focus on the white middle-class domestic ideal ... sometimes renders other ideals and other women invisible.'[2] But surely it is not a matter of either/or, or that researchers need to give priority to one of these projects over the other. The point of studying dominant cultural discourses – mainstream ideals – as May has done, is that we all have to negotiate them, whether we subscribe to them, are marginalized by them, or actively resist them. There can be no understanding of agency – the resistance Meyerowitz wants to reclaim – without an understanding of the context within which it occurs.

Domesticity and Security in Postwar Canada

While the term 'postwar' is a convenient way of marking a time period, it cannot be emphasized enough that it refers to the specific social configurations that arose as six years of war came to an end. So, for instance, when we talk about postwar prosperity we need to remember that this prosperity arose in the wake of tremendous loss and disruption.

In 1945, the Canadian domestic economy underwent substantial change as both public and private sectors shifted production and services away from military requirements. While peace was obviously welcomed, many Canadians feared the type of economic downturn that had followed the First World War; would the economy collapse with the end of military production? Such postwar concerns about economic security were complicated by the emotional and social upheavals that resulted from attempts to reintegrate into civilian life the million men and women who had been in the armed forces. More than 40,000 Canadians had been killed during the war, and thousands more had been injured either physically or mentally.[3] It is not surprising, then, that homecomings did not always provide a happy ending to long and difficult separations.

As victory celebrations subsided, Canadians struggled with the changes the war had brought to the home front. War work had introduced thousands of women and teenagers to relatively lucrative industrial jobs. Many children and teenagers had been free of adult supervision, with fathers in the military and mothers doing war work. Workers of all ages who had migrated to cities in search of wartime jobs experienced for the first time the freedom of living in communities away from their relatives. Further demographic changes occurred as tens of thousands of immigrants and refugees arrived from Europe, many from countries and ethnic/religious backgrounds not widely represented (or forcefully kept out) in previous waves of immigration: Jews, Czechs, Poles, Hungarians, Ukrainians, Russians, Yugoslavians, Italians. The degree to which these and other social changes would, or could, be integrated into the fabric of postwar life was open to considerable debate – as, for instance, in the widespread discussions about the place and acceptability of married women workers in the peacetime labour market, or those about the desirability of having Jews and southern and eastern Europeans enter the country.[4]

According to historian Doug Owram, the physical and emotional disruptions caused by the war, and the significant social changes it motivated, oriented Canadians towards home, family, and stability to a degree unparalleled in other historical periods in this country. Owram suggests that giving precedence to home and family was a primary value of the postwar era and is central to any understanding of the economy, gender relations, politics, or other aspects of those years.[5] As represented by married, middle-class, heterosexual couples and their legitimate offspring, the ideal family was at once seen as a source of affectional relationships, the basis of a consumer economy, a defence against Communism, and a salient metaphor for various forms of social organization, from the nation to the high-school class. In the 1940s and 1950s, writes Joy Parr, 'Domestic metaphors ... proclaimed the promise of peace.'[6]

During the Depression of the 1930s, fears about security and the future were easily attributed to material deprivation and the social disruptions that followed from it. But after the Second World War, discourses about an uncertain future existed in spite of considerably improved material circumstances across North America. While 25 per cent of the Canadian population continued to live in poverty into the 1960s, this figure was down substantially from the 50 per cent that had been the average during the interwar years.[7] During the postwar period, the United States and Canada had the highest and second-highest standards of living in the world. Total industrial output rose by 50 per cent in the 1950s. Canadian manufacturing wages doubled between 1945 and 1956 while prices rose only slightly. Unemployment remained between 2.8 and 5.9 per cent, depending on the region, until the mid-1950s.[8] In contrast, the 1933 national unemployment rate had been 20 per cent.[9]

Between 1948 and 1961, a decades-old housing crisis began to reverse as building boomed and home ownership jumped from just over 30 per cent to 60 per cent. Clearly, many Canadians were better off than they had been. Still, speech-makers and journalists referred to a collective distrust of the future.

In a 1952 editorial, *Chatelaine* editor Lotta Dempsey tried to put this unease into words. Writing of a cross-Canada train trip, she noted prosperous-looking people at 'every station' and found herself remarking on the difference a single decade could make:

I listen to conversations of well-fed, well-dressed people enjoying the ease and luxury of modern trains and planes. They seem to have everything ... everything except some indefinable inner security ... and faith. Some sense of certain strength to hold and maintain this largesse.

Perhaps we know that the borders of our peaceful land grow thinner as the turmoil of the outside world increases.[10]

After fifteen years of domestic uncertainty, Canadians were confronted with the cold war and they were nervous about 'the outside world,' the unknown, the other. In the face of such a nebulous threat, there seemed little that an individual could do, and Dempsey counselled her readers to have faith in God.

In the 1950s, Christianity remained a profoundly important discourse in both popular and official media. Certainly, Christian values underlay recurring arguments that placed the heterosexual nuclear family at the centre of a secure future for both individuals and the nation.[11] In 1946, for instance, a Toronto mayor promoted good citizenship by declaring 'Christian Family Week.' An ad in the *Toronto Daily Star* read: 'If our country is to fulfil its destiny, family life, founded on Christian ideals and principles, must be preserved.'[12]

Domesticity as Cold-War Strategy

In magazines, school board curricula, and instructional films, an idealized image of the nuclear family was promoted as the first line of defence against the perceived insecurity of the cold-war years.[13] Family life would shield Canada from the threat of 'outside turmoil.' As both Canadian and American historians have shown, in this age of prosperity both international and domestic affairs were suffused by familial discourse and, thus, contributed to the need North Americans expressed for control on a personal level. As American historian Elaine May puts it, the postwar family was located firmly 'within the larger political culture, not outside it,'[14] although contemporary representations of the family usually portrayed the opposite.

Cold-war rhetoric and the activities that followed from it were not the same in Canada as they were in the States, as Reg Whitaker and Gary Marcuse have shown.[15] Nevertheless, few Canadians could have escaped the American cold-war hype that infused the popular culture of the era – from the predominantly U.S. films and television shows that came across the border to the U.S. magazines that, by 1954, occupied 80 per cent of Canadian newsstand space.[16] At the very least, Canadians and Americans shared both a fear of and a fascination with the bomb. In 1946, the Toronto Board of Education proclaimed the theme of Education Week to be 'Education for the Atomic Age,'[17] marking the bomb and nuclear energy as the harbingers of a new era. Four years later, a *Chatelaine* editorial identified the bomb as the 'biggest thing in our new half century.' Noting the fear that the bomb inspired in many people, the editorial carefully refrained from mentioning the potential of such an invention to cause mind-boggling harm, referring instead to that fear as 'man's [sic] reaction to his own creative powers.' *Chatelaine* readers were encouraged to focus on the good that could come of this creativity, to 'help abolish those Atom Bomb blues!'[18] *Chatelaine* was nothing if not optimistic; hence the claim that atomic energy might one day provide for 'a fantastic new way of life,' one with 'luxury and security for all.'[19] Ironically, a feature on the same page acknowledged that most nuclear research at the time was going into 'making bigger and better bombs,' not domestic innovations.[20] And while the feature writer didn't mention it, her readers knew what stood in the way of the hoped-for luxury and security, knew why military rather than other forms of research were necessary: Western democracies were on the alert against the threat of Communism.

In Canada, the East-West conflict that eventually came to be known as the cold war started in 1945 when Igor Gouzenko, a cypher clerk in the Soviet embassy in Ottawa, defected and claimed that the Soviets had been running a spy ring in Canada.[21] Investigations into his allegations focused national attention on the need for internal defences against Communism. According to Len Scher, in his book on the Canadian cold war, an unsuccessful search for spy rings gave way to efforts to track 'domestic dissidents.'[22] Between October 1950 and June 1951, the Royal Canadian Mounted Police (RCMP) dealt with 54,000 requests to screen both civil servants and private-sector workers.[23] Those who were most likely to be put under surveillance included labour organizers, members of Communist and socialist organizations, peace activists, and homosexuals. Deviance from any number of mainstream norms, writes Philip Girard, 'represented an independence of mind that could no longer be tolerated' during the cold war. In such a climate, 'the unknown' – homosexuals, for instance – 'represented a triune denial of God, family, and (implicitly or potentially) country at a time when departing from any one of these norms was immediately suspect.'[24] Deviance also precluded the homogenization that was seen to be central to Canada's strength as a nation. The conformity that is so often identified as a primary aspect of postwar social life wasn't simply a characteristic of increased consumerism and/or the centralization of popular culture and entertainment industries. It was also produced by an approach to citizenship that demanded a willingness to participate in social consensus, to adopt a shared set of behavioural standards and mores.

Democracy and Moral Standards

In 1946, an interdepartmental Security Panel (National Defence, External Affairs, and the RCMP) was established to check on federal civil servants who had been identified by the RCMP as security risks. As Larry Hannant writes, this was not the first time the RCMP had initiated security screening; however, it was the first time the effort had received formal government approval.[25] In the first three months of the panel's operation, the RCMP offered panel officials 5466 names. Checks on these individuals resulted in 213 'adverse reports,' although only 27 of the people in question were determined to be bona-fide security risks – possible spies. The remainder had been included on the original list because of 'moral' failings or 'character' weaknesses, a category that included homosexuals, and parents of illegitimate children, among others.[26] To security officials, these character weaknesses suggested an inability to do the right thing, a tendency to compromise, an impairment of moral fibre. These were the characteristics of someone who might be influenced by Communists or, worse, who might be a Communist. Normal sexual and moral development signalled maturity and an ability to assume responsibility. By contrast, those who transgressed sexual and moral norms were assumed to be immature, trapped in adolescence. How could they be counted on to safeguard their country?

Despite the overenthusiasm of RCMP security checks, writer John

Sawatsky claims that Canadian officials abhorred the McCarthyism that swept through the American military and the government bureaucracy.[27] In Canada, the search for the red menace was conducted more quietly, was more 'gentlemanly,' says Erich Koch, who worked with the CBC International Service in Montreal after the war.[28] There were no televised proceedings, and there was little publicity. People were either fired quickly or were never hired in the first place. Communist sympathies were the original source of concern, but this quickly translated into a fear of anyone who could potentially be blackmailed by a Communist spy: alcoholics, gamblers, and people who visited prostitutes or who had affairs. Also on this list were homosexuals, and though they were no more blackmailable than any of the others, the RCMP formed a special unit, A-3, to root out homosexuals from the civil service. Eventually, writes Sawatsky, the Mounties had files on 3000 people, including members not only of the civil service but of the general public as well.[29]

In 1952, Canada's immigration law was quietly changed to keep homosexuals out of the country.[30] In the late 1950s and early 1960s, attempts to construct homosexuals as security risks led the RCMP and the Security Panel to recruit psychologists and psychiatrists to assist in the ousting of 'perverts' from the civil service. The experts' cooperation culminated in a research project to develop what they called the Fruit Machine, an instrument that would confirm an individual's homosexuality by measuring his reaction to homoerotic imagery. (Men were the primary target of the purge. Lesbians, according to Sawatsky, refused to disclose the names of friends and colleagues, thus limiting the investigations of their networks by the mostly male Mounties.) The effort was, not surprisingly, unsuccessful, and stands as a stunning example of the use of science to support moral regulatory practices.[31]

That homosexuals were identified as particularly dangerous by the guardians of national security suggests the importance of normative sexuality in the social and political landscape of postwar Canada. Certainly the vilification of sexual deviants did much to shore up the primary position of the heterosexual nuclear family as the only legitimate site of sexual expression. But the links made between sexuality and national security also suggest the way that sexuality worked as a site for the displacement of general social and political anxieties. In official discourses, homosexuality was constructed not simply as the tragic fate of particular individuals but as a force so menacing it carried the potential to undermine the strength of the nation. In the face of the cold war, Communists and spies and those with mysterious and questionable sex habits or morals were almost equal threats to the security of the Dominion.

In this context, having a family became an important marker of social belonging, of conformity to prevailing standards. It was a sign of maturity and adulthood, of one's ability to take on responsibility. The social positions of mother/wife and father/husband defined individuals as contributors to their community and their country. As a psychiatrist argued in *Chatelaine*, the formation of families and the raising of children was, at root, a patriotic obligation. In becoming parents, men and women were 'giving to the best of their ability.'[32] Thus, the nuclear family came to operate as a symbol of safety – not just on the individual level, but on the national level as well.

Discourses about shared values, common goals, and mutual goodwill among Canada's citizens helped to construct an image of the Dominion itself as a family, as Annalee Gölz has argued.[33] In this frame, Communists and sex deviates were disruptions to the larger domestic order. By protecting the borders against perverts, the state was protecting the 'home,' safeguarding those under its charge. After the war, with the expansion of the welfare state, the government was increasingly positioned as concerned parent of its citizens. Attempts to purge the country of 'perverts' and 'Commies' suggest that the state, as 'head of the family,' was attending to more than the material well-being of Canadians. Policies and practices that targeted deviants were an effort to protect and foster moral standards, a primary task of any 'concerned parent.'

The Family

In a Canadian Youth Commission pamphlet called 'Speak Your Peace,' the family was identified as 'the chief support of the new world.'[34] Certainly, as the crucible of consumption, the middle-class family was the chief support of the postwar economy. Essential to the nurturing of workers and the buying of goods, the nuclear family was also understood to be the primary site of moral education and the training ground for the democracy that, in part, was thought to define the age.[35] Hence the anxiety created when various expert voices claimed that 'the family' was threatened in the postwar world. If the family failed, would democracy – and, by implication, Canada – fail too? The fact that families were being formed by more people more often than at any other time in this century did little to counter a pervasive sense that 'the family' as a social institution was under threat.

As evidence of the family's decline, social critics were most likely to cite figures about divorce rates. At the end of the Second World War, the divorce rate in Canada tripled, 'from 56.2 divorces per 100,000 married persons 15 years of age and over in 1941 to 131.9 in 1946.' After 1946, the rate fell off, but then it 'rose steadily from 1951 to 1968 (88.9 to 124.3).'[36] Most of the early rise was attributable to hastily considered wartime weddings, although increasing opportunities for women to achieve some measure of economic independence may also have been an important factor. The divorce rate served to bolster a protectionist stance towards the family and to justify its ideological fortification by way of, for instance, television programs, school health curricula, and moral panics over sex crime. The state of the family was a central – if not *the* central – concern of postwar life.

For the most part, the image of 'the family' that was used to represent the ideal was drawn from urban, white, Anglo-Saxon, middle-class and upper-middle-class communities. The authors of the massive *Crestwood Heights*, a 1956 study of Toronto's 'internal suburb' of Forest Hill, offered the following description:

In infinite variety, yet with an eternal sameness, [such a community] flashes on the movie screen, in one of those neat comedies about the upper middle class family which Hollywood delights to repeat again and again as nurture for the American Dream. It fills the pages of glossy magazines devoted to the current best in architecture, house decoration, food, dress, and social behaviour. The innumerable service occupations bred of an urban culture will think anxiously about people in such a community in terms of what 'they' will buy or use this year. Any authority in the field of art, literature, or science, probably at some time has had, or will have, its name on a lecture itinerary. A teacher will consider it a privilege to serve in its schools. For those thousands of North Americans who struggle to translate the promise of America into a concrete reality for themselves, and even more important, for their children, it is in some sense a Mecca.[37]

The authors of *Crestwood Heights* argued that upper-middle-class families were a marker of 'what life is *coming to be* more and more like in North America – at least in the middle classes.' In this sense, they wrote, a community like Crestwood Heights '*is* normative, or "typical," not in the sense of the average of an aggregate of such communities, but in the sense of representing the norm to which middle-class community life tends now to move.'[38] While I agree with their point, that society tends 'to move' in such a direction, it bears remembering that it does not necessarily arrive. The experience of the 'ideal family' – breadwinner father, stay-at-home mother, and well-adjusted children – was not available to everyone.

If divorce was considered to be the main threat to this idealized image of the nuclear family, working mothers and immigrant families were also serious – and related – challenges to its claim on the Canadian imagination. As many historians have noted, the numbers of married women in the workforce increased rapidly in the postwar period. In the early 1940s, one in twenty women worked outside the home; in 1951 that figure had risen to one in ten, only to rise again, to one in five, by 1961. As Joan Sangster writes, concerns about increases in the numbers of married women working for pay masked class and race biases; the labour participation rates of recent immigrants, women in some ethnic and racial communities, and women who were poor had not changed.[39]

Between 1946 and 1954, Canada admitted almost a million immigrants.[40] That not all of the new arrivals organized their families in accordance with Canadian middle-class norms led to concerns that 'New Canadians' would disrupt postwar efforts to shore up the family as an institution. Settlement services and advocacy groups encouraged immigrants to abandon their own family structures in favour of those thought to be essential to the moral strength of the nation: single-family households, presided over by breadwinner fathers and stay-at-home mothers. Franca Iacovetta says that the cold war gave social workers an opportunity to frame such assimilationist rhetoric as a matter of national urgency 'by equating the predominance of respectable, middle-class, family values with the superiority of Western democracies such as Canada.'[41] That Canadian family norms were neither desirable for many immigrants, who had their own ways of doing things, nor attainable for those facing the hardship of arrival in a new country, did not deter Canadian experts from labelling immigrant families as 'deviant' and a threat to both 'Canadianization' and the institution of the family itself.[42]

An emphasis on the family was not a new phenomenon in Canada. However, this emphasis took a new shape in the postwar period. Whereas the primary focus of many earlier family discourses had been on women, motherhood, and the development of proper femininity,[43] postwar discourses about the family tended to show (and construct) most concern for the development of properly adjusted – normal – children. Certainly these strands of concern are closely tied together, but what is important here is the way their relationship was characterized. In postwar discourses the construction of appropriate forms of femininity – and masculinity – were seen as the means to the nobler goal of childrearing. In Crestwood Heights, the production of the future Crestwood adult was *the* focus of the community's institutions.[44]

According to the Crestwood authors, the upper-middle-class families they studied were relatively isolated social units with limited connection to a wider network of kin. In contrast to 'the usual Victorian family,' or, presumably, working-class or immigrant families, Crestwood families were units of consumption, rather than production. And, importantly, they allowed 'more individuality and freedom' to their members than had earlier forms.[45] These modern families, though not as religious as their predecessors, drew heavily on Judaeo-Christian ethics, 'democratic practice,' and the advice of 'child-rearing experts.' Deviation from prevailing norms could result in a family's being defined by such experts as malfunctioning and likely to produce 'disturbed' children.[46]

Present-day writers have also noted this tendency of postwar middle-class families to be relatively self-contained.[47] While 1990s conservatives nostalgically recall the postwar family as a link to earlier times, and as exemplifying enduring 'traditional' values, Elaine May claims that 'the legendary family of the 1950s ... represented something new. It was not, as common wisdom tells us, the last gasp of traditional family life with roots deep in the past. Rather, it was the first whole-hearted effort to create a home that would fulfil virtually all its members' personal needs through an energized and expressive personal life.'[48]

The extent to which the ideal family had come to be constructed in popular discourse as a set of relationships, a source of affectional and material needs, is evident in a 1950s educational film for adolescents called *A Date with Your Family*. In the film, a teenaged boy and girl arrive home from school full of excitement because they have 'an important date ... dinner with the family,' which to them 'is a special occasion.' Sister changes her clothes to 'something more festive' because 'the women in this family seem to feel that they owe it to the men of the family to look relaxed, rested and attractive at dinnertime.' Brother studies while sister sets the table. Then he gets Junior ready for dinner. Sister makes a centrepiece of flowers for the dining table. Father comes through the door, and the boys greet him enthusiastically, before Mother calls them all to the dining-room where 'they converse pleasantly' over their meal. Brother compliments Mother 'and maybe sis' on the food because 'it makes them want to continue pleasing you.' The whole event is a 'time of pleasure, charm, relaxation ...'[49] For the non-cinematic families who failed to meet this ideal of civility and gratification, it was, nevertheless, a modern standard by which they would be measured, one that took material comforts for granted. It assumed a strict sexual division of labour and a public life in which troubles were manageable enough to be either left at the door or assuaged by family harmony. Certainly this picture of the 'united happy family'[50] was distinct from earlier versions in which affectional needs came second to economic ones and expectations for emotional fulfilment were considerably lower.

In part, idealized images of the postwar family were a consequence of the economic changes and prosperity that favoured consumerism over mutual dependence, suburban bungalows over farms and crowded downtown apartments. But the constitution of the notion of nuclear-family-as-island was also related to postwar desires for individual satisfaction and needs for social stability. Middle-class families were frequently portrayed as offering refuge from the turmoil of the outside world. That they could actually engender isolation and alienation, as we now know from numerous articles in *Chatelaine* and from books like Betty Friedan's *The Feminine Mystique*, was not widely discussed.[51] Nor was the fact that many Canadians, by choice or circumstance, lived in families that bore little resemblance to the middle-class nuclear ideal.

In 1956, *Maclean's* published a special report on 'the family' by Eric Hutton. Noting 'the comeback of the Canadian family,' Hutton characterized it as a resilient but basically unchanging entity, although he also told his readers 'the family way of life has changed out of recognition in half a century.'[52] It had taken on a particularly modern guise as Canadian young people married at younger ages, gave birth to more children, and, like the parents in *A Date with Your Family*, had more expectations of the whole package than had the generations before them. As Doug Owram writes, 'the young adults of the 1940s were the most domestically oriented generation of the twentieth-century.'[53]

In 1941, the average age of first marriage for women was 25.4 years of age. By 1961 that figure had dropped to 22 years of age. Between 1937 and 1954, the marriage rate for women between the ages of 15 and 19 doubled from 30 per 1000 to 62 per 1000.[54] Once married, these women had more children, more quickly, than their mothers did. Between 1937 and 1947, the number of births per 1000 of the population rose from 20.1 to 28.9, and it continued to rise until 1956. Much of this increase was accounted for by mothers under 25 years of age and by families with three or more children. In 1956, almost 50 per cent of live births in Canada were third or later children.[55]

Maclean's accounted for the popularity of babies and families in a number of ways: large families, Hutton said, provided security in an insecure world; the baby bonus (established in 1945) and an overall prosperity made them easier to afford; maternal and child health had improved; television encouraged families to spend their leisure time together at home; Princess Elizabeth and Princess Grace of Monaco had made maternity fashionable; and parents – even fathers – had come to realize that children could be fun. According to the Provost of Trinity College at the University of Toronto, 'the family is returning to favour because so many men are making the discovery that it's the pleasantest company they're ever likely to have in a world that is full of competition and unpleasant episodes.'[56] That fathers were under heavy pressure from psychological experts to participate to a greater extent in the life of their children, especially to prevent the abnormal sexual and emotional development of their sons, is not discussed in Hutton's article. Without adequate fathering, some experts said, a boy might become delinquent, turn into a homosexual, or suffer 'untold mental distress.'[57]

What is also not mentioned in Hutton's article about the comeback of the family is that there was tremendous pressure applied to anyone who failed to follow the trend, as evidenced by the RCMP crackdown on homosexuals. But that episode was only the most obvious aspect of a more widespread trend. In an American survey conducted after the war, only 9 per cent of those questioned believed that single people could be happy.[58] Toronto gynaecologist and author Marion Hilliard (who was herself not married) counterposed single women and married women in ways that made them seem almost like different species. Single women, she said, could only be 'out of place at a gathering of married couples.' And single women and married women could 'only, unwittingly, hurt one another.'[59] Even young divorcees and widows, Hilliard wrote pityingly, 'fit in nowhere.'[60] Single men, in the 1950s, risked being seen as homosexuals, a group whose social currency was nonexistent. From her reading of postwar American sociology, Barbara Ehrenreich says that experts claimed a number of reasons why men might not marry: 'Some were simply misfortunes, such as "poor health or deviant physical characteristics," "unattractiveness" and extreme geographical isolation. But high on the list for men were homosexuality, emotional fixation on parent(s) and unwillingness to assume responsibility.'[61]

But simply getting married was not enough to satisfy postwar social expectations. Married couples without children were also subject to disapproval and admonishments for not doing their duty to their country.[62] A *Chatelaine* article featured an infertile couple who received constant ribbing from their friends: 'How come you two are leading such selfish lives?'; 'Aren't you going to prove yourself a man? What are we supposed to think, eh?'[63] Another *Chatelaine* story, a first-person account by a woman who chose not to have children, was roundly denounced in the letters column of two subsequent issues.[64] A reader from Ontario wrote: 'That writer who is "not going to have any" [children] has aroused my indignation to such a point that I must answer, in the face of such malformed humanity ... I am mother of nine ... Such a woman is denying herself the greatest of all love and satisfaction, that of mothering a child, and giving life the purpose of your being, the purpose of your Creator, great and true.' After a number of similar comments, *Chatelaine* editors intervened on the letters page to set things right: 'One moment please! The Editors are happy to announce, for all such readers' peace of mind, that the anonymous writer in question has just telephoned to say Hurray, she *is* going to have one!'[65]

While this particular exchange can be read as little more than a rally of individual opinions, the importance of postwar professionals in constructing this kind of discussion cannot be overstated. In magazines, on the radio, and in newspapers, experts were increasingly evident as mediators of everyday life and as primary participants in the construction of boundaries between normality and deviance. For instance, the *Chatelaine* letters about the woman's decision not to have a baby appeared exactly one year after the magazine published an article by a psychiatrist criticizing those who chose not to have children, suggesting that they were immature and unpatriotic.[66] The point is not that the letter writers were directly influenced by the earlier article; rather, their comments were part of a larger discourse that was, in part, constructed via expert commentary.

While the middle class often consulted experts voluntarily, or sought out their ideas in print, working-class and immigrant families were likely to encounter these professionals in any number of institutional settings – such as schools, the courts, or social service offices.[67] But even as the general category of 'the expert' was gaining prominence, some experts were more revered than others. Psychologists and psychiatrists had a particular appeal in a social system that was based more and more on individualism. Part of the appeal of the mental-health professionals stemmed from the influence they had wielded during the war. Their contribution to the screening and rehabilitation of the troops had increased public awareness of their work,[68] and widely circulating discourses about the importance of mental hygiene validated their concerns. But sociologists and medical doctors were also routinely called upon to diagnose social trends, to make pronouncements on behaviours or identities, and to lend legitimacy to certain positions.

It was the increasing influence of psychiatry in postwar North America that constituted babies as evidence of their parents' 'normal,' gendered, sexual and emotional development – of their having achieved maturity. Babies were a public sign of married sexuality and, in theory, of marital harmony. Babies could also be seen to signal acceptance of community norms and to confirm that men and women were performing their respective normative gender roles (whether, in fact, they were or not) and assuming the responsibility that came with them.

Those seen to be outside the family, from runaway youths to homosexuals, were anomalies. Hard to classify, they were often the objects of scorn or pity. Discourses about life in the middle-class nuclear family made available a variety of subject positions (albeit gendered and restrictive ones) – parent, sexual being, responsible citizen, consumer – that either were not available or were available in limited ways to adults who were single. Families, narrowly defined – monogamous, heterosexual marriages and the children produced within them – provided an important way of making sense of one's position in the postwar social structure.

Marriage: Site of Legitimate Sex

One of the primary defining factors of the postwar nuclear family was an emphasis on the sexual compatibility between husband and wife and the importance of sex in a conjugal union. According to Steven Seidman, the eroticization of romantic relationships was a trend that had been building throughout the twentieth century.[69] Certainly, reproduction continued to be a primary goal of marital sexual activity, but sex had come to be understood as entailing more than this. In the postwar period, sex was meant to be a source of pleasure and emotional fulfilment for both men and women.[70] In this framework, women's sexuality was, in theory if not in practice, as important as men's.[71] Sex was also perceived to be a 'natural' part of a healthy life, even if it wasn't engaged in for the sole purpose of producing babies.

Isolated within their families, away from kin or other members of the community, the ideal postwar couple were meant to draw their support primarily from each other. In some popular constructions of marriage, even close friends were to be shunned in order to protect the sanctity and privacy of the heterosexual bond. One article in *Chatelaine* goes so far as to suggest that 'The [wife's] girl friend is a danger signal, a clear alarm that the marriage is sick and in need of loving attention ...'[72] In the same article, a psychiatrist argues that the 'primary rule of married life' was 'that nothing of intimate consequence be discussed with friends.' Marriage was drawn as the most important, indeed as the only important, relationship between adults. Husbands and wives were to gain their 'basic sense of belonging, of well-being, of fulfilment' from each other. Sex was the glue that would hold them together. As Steven Seidman argues, sex was *the* sphere upon which rested the success of the marital bond.[73]

While the role of sex within marriage may have been clear, the role of men and women in that same relationship was seen to be in an incredible state of flux. Once glued together by their sexual attraction, it was not always clear how men and women were to perform their non-sexual conjugal duties. The presence of married women in the labour force – rates rose from 12.7 per cent of all women in paid employment in 1941, to 30 per cent in 1951, to 49.8 per cent in 1961[74] – suggested to some people that the difference between gender roles was diminishing. While this could have been looked upon as a positive gain for women, it was interpreted by many as a demasculinization of men. It was also seen to spell trouble for heterosexual relationships, based as they were on an assumption of essential difference between men and women. In 1954, *Chatelaine* printed this advice to young brides from a Protestant minister:

Wives you can unman your husband by taking his place. If you are going to go to work, you should work only for a few years ... While working you should still live on your husband's income ... Within one or two years, depending upon your ages, you should quit work and let him support you and live on what he can make ...

The wife should also take pride in being good at her wifely job. In our day it is sometimes difficult for women to adjust themselves to this fact ...

... Make the man act his part. Do not start to be the man yourself.[75]

Women's advances in the workplace, slim as they were, and new forms of corporate organization contributed to what some contemporary writers have called a postwar crisis of middle-class masculinity.[76] Corporate culture demanded a personality concerned with the thoughts of others, tuned to the needs of others. It was the antithesis of the 'rugged individualism' that grounded the versions of white, middle-class masculinity available in popular culture. In his study of conformity in (male) middle-class America, sociologist David Reisman, author of *The Lonely Crowd*, called this the 'other-directed' personality.[77] Its characteristics, he said, were more closely matched to a traditional feminine identity than to a traditional masculine one. In robbing men of their 'individuality,' 'other-direction' feminized men.

On top of this, changes in the structure of the economy and the increasing importance of consumption as a family-based activity shifted men's place of importance in the household. As Barbara Ehrenreich points out in her study of (male and female) middle-class America, men might have earned the money, but women were the ones who spent the bulk of it. Consumption was women's work. Men's paid employment certainly made it possible, but it did not necessarily give men control over it: 'In the temple of consumption which was the suburban home, women were priestesses and men mere altar boys.'[78]

These transformations in the organization of gender contributed to a stressful negotiation of the relationship between husband and wife. Both women and men were under a tremendous strain to build what *Chatelaine* called 'modern marriages': 'a new kind of joint-ownership marriage ... which may beat any earlier model back to Adam and Eve.' As one psychologist put it, 'We are moving from dictatorship to equality in marriage, from the day when the husband's word was law to a time when the wife shares equally in the family decisions. And the working wife is probably doing more for the partnership idea than anything else.'[79] Indeed, it was middle-class assumptions about the lack of equality in the marriages of some working-class immigrants that led social workers to label those marriages deviant and in need of 'Canadianizing.'[80] The popular assumption was that gender roles in marriage were relaxing, but not too far. Expectations remained that women would be responsible for domestic life and men for 'breadwinning.' In a 1955 investigation of marriage, *Chatelaine* encouraged women to give more rather than less to their homes and families: 'And the siren-wife-mother who realizes the once simple business of being a married woman has become a complex and fulltime career in itself is at least halfway to licking these [aforementioned] problems'[81] – problems like confusion over roles, loneliness, and boredom.

As Wini Breines writes, despite discourses about 'modern marriages' and the 'age of equality,' men and women continued to experience gender as a deep-rooted site of social difference. While there were more options for white, Anglo-Saxon, middle-class women than there had been in previous decades, few women were encouraged to pursue them. Middle-class women's social worth continued to be measured by their success in raising children and providing a comfortable home for their husbands. Marriage continued to be an inevitability rather than a choice. At the same time, middle-class men were being told to participate more in the affectional life of the family while having to give themselves over to a corporate culture that was constructed on the assumption of their freedom from domestic responsibilities. For both men and women, frustration seemed an inevitable consequence of a relationship that was supposed to reflect 'new' forms of gender organization without giving up the old ones. That this package of contradictions was supposed both to inspire and to sustain sexual attraction and pleasure was just one more strain on a relationship that, nevertheless, maintained remarkable levels of popularity right up until the late 1950s.

The Kinsey Reports and the Sexual Climate

Although marriage remained the only legitimate site of sexual activity between adults throughout the late 1940s and the 1950s, postwar sexual discourses did preserve some of the liberalization that had been fostered by the war.[82] Popular culture, especially, became increasingly sexualized by way of sexy movie stars, the so-called 'sex appeal' of advertisements, and sexually explicit books and magazines. Divorce rates increased.[83] Some Protestant churches supported the need for sex education and were even prepared to accept its limited introduction into the schools.[84] And, though the birth-control movement was hardly at its peak in the 1950s, interest in the pill, which would be released in 1961, was high.[85] Lesbians and gay men in urban centres gained access to limited but important public spaces.[86] Single mothers in Ontario were eligible for the first time to receive mother's allowance. While these and other changes were significant, they existed alongside a more familiar reticence about matters pertaining to sexuality. Thus, even the mention of sex in the public realm continued to elicit reactions of strong disapproval from some people. *Chatelaine* readers, for instance, regularly chastised the editors for succumbing to so-called prurient interests. Questionable material included an article about menstruation for teenage girls, cover illustrations that showed too much leg, and self-help-type features that focused on psychiatric explanations (perceived to be inherently sexual explanations) for emotional and relationship problems.[87]

Nothing crystallizes the various strains of postwar sexual discourse like public response to the Kinsey reports, *Sexual Behavior in the Human Male* (SBHM, 1948) and *Sexual Behavior in the Human Female* (SBHF, 1953). When the first volume appeared, in an 800-page, hardcover edition, published by a little-known scientific publishing house, it sold a total of 200,000 copies in its first six months. Even the publishers were unaware of the impact the book would have and originally planned to print only 10,000 copies, 'one of the more spectacular publishing mistakes of the decade,' says Kinsey's associate Wardell Pomeroy.[88] Within a month, Kinsey had received more than 1000 letters, only six of which, Pomeroy claims, were negative.[89] When the female volume was about to come out in 1953, more than 150 magazines and major newspapers wanted pre-release access to the text. That same year, *Time* declared the sex researcher their man of the year, and Kinsey was, by all accounts, a household name.

In general, reaction to the two books was mixed, and perhaps there-fore suggestive of the various ways that sex was understood to fit into North American culture. According to Pomeroy, reaction to the male volume was largely favourable, with most of the criticism it received focusing on the method of the study. In contrast, reaction to the female volume was significantly more negative and tended to focus on the morality of the findings and on the moral basis of the project itself. Clearly, it was one thing to talk about men's sexual activity and quite another to talk of women's. The uproar over the second book eventually led to the termination of funding (from the Rockefeller Foundation) for Kinsey's research.[90] Still, there were many who appreciated the work that Kinsey had done and the impact it could make, even if they weren't particularly thrilled with what the doctor had found. At the very least, reviewers were impressed by the sheer size of Kinsey's sample. The male volume was based on interviews with 5300 men, the female vol-ume on interviews with 5940 women. Both samples were diversified in terms of class background, age, region and religion, but they dealt almost exclusively with white people, a fact not noted in any of the Canadian commentaries. Reviews in liberal Canadian magazines like *Saturday Night*, *Canadian Forum*, and *Canadian Welfare* were largely posi-tive and took seriously the implications of the research for sexual stan-dards.[91] Even *Chatelaine* sent a reporter to Indiana to interview Kinsey at work.[92] In her article, *Chatelaine* writer Lotta Dempsey took pride in being the first Canadian woman to be part of the sex doctor's sample – as a rule, Kinsey only granted press interviews to those who would agree to be interviewed for his study.

Canadian reviewers made little of the fact that Kinsey's material was American. B.K. Sandwell, in a piece for *Saturday Night*, criticized Kinsey's first volume for succumbing to the familiar American habit of not openly identifying itself as American. But Sandwell also concluded that the difference between Canadian and American males was so slight that the absence of Canadians from the study was of little importance.[93] That Kinsey had identified numerous social factors as having an influence on sexual behaviour (education, religion, class, region), was certainly an opportunity for Canadian critics to speculate on the possible sexual implications of 'Canadian-ness.' But it was an opportunity that seems not to have been taken up.

Before Kinsey, public discussions of sex had taken place in the context of related issues such as birth control, divorce, sexual crime, and venereal disease. While marriage manuals with explicit descriptions of sexual activities had been published throughout the first half of the century, these were not the subject of mainstream, everyday discussion. Certainly, such material was unlikely to find its way into newspapers and magazines. One of Kinsey's main achievements, then, was packaging information about sex in a fashion that could be widely disseminated. In his books, sex was reduced to a series of clean statistics. Kinsey's emphasis on his own scientific background and on the scientific integrity of his study made sex more acceptable as a topic of conversation. In a period when North Americans were enamoured of scientists and experts of all kinds, and were concerned about wartime changes in sexual mores, Kinsey's timing was perfect.

In publishing his findings, Kinsey not only brought sex into public discussion, he brought a lot of different kinds of sex into public discussion: homosexual acts, premarital sex, oral sex, anal sex, and masturbation. In his description of sexual behaviour, heterosexual intercourse was just one of many possible activities in which North Americans engaged to satisfy what Kinsey understood to be a natural need for orgasm. It was this challenge to normative standards of sexual behaviour – to the definition of normal sexuality – that most concerned Kinsey's critics and supporters alike. As Janice Irvine has written, homosexuals and others who wanted to liberalize moral standards used the reports' statistics about sexual diversity to back demands for social tolerance for sexual minorities. On the other hand, 'vigilantes' against such changes used the same figures to show the extent of a moral breakdown, 'to fuel the postwar backlash' against relaxing sexual mores.[94]

A reviewer in *Canadian Forum* wrote that 'what this [diversity of sexual behaviours] does to our concepts of "normal," "excessive" and the like needs no emphasis ...'[95] An editor at *Saturday Night* wrote that there was no problem in the statistics themselves (remarkable as they were); rather, the danger lay in the conclusions people might draw from them. Some people might decide, he said, that 'anything that is done by seven-tenths of the population cannot possibly be wrong – a conclusion which reduces morality to a sort of popular plebiscite.'[96] In another *Saturday Night* article, Perry Hughes questioned even the ethics of applying sta-tistics to sex. Sex, he wrote, is a 'subject that cannot be divorced from its moral and spiritual associations, and which therefore is not a proper subject for statistics at all ... the obligation to behave oneself in a certain manner is not affected by the question whether 90 per cent, or 50 per cent, or only 20 per cent, of one's fellow citizens behave in that man-ner.'[97] Not everyone was as willing as Kinsey was to base moral norms on statistical ones.

In the years following the Second World War, the heterosexual nuclear family was valued as the 'traditional' foundation of the Canadian social structure. The family was reified as a primary stabilizing influence on both individuals and the nation as a whole. Metaphorically and practi-cally, it was assumed to be the basis of the social consensus that was a central part of cold-war discourse and practice. Mainstream discourses suggested that dissent and difference could weaken the face of democ-racy in the ideological fight against Communism. Canadians were called upon to show an impressive social cohesiveness as evidence of their dedication to the superiority of the Western way of life. A commitment to the family was central to the social homogeneity necessitated by this display.

Inherent in the postwar definition of 'the family' was its basis in a sex-ually charged heterosexual marriage. Elaine May argues that marriage operated to 'contain' sexuality, to protect against the social disorder that was thought to be the inevitable result of sex-out-of-control.[98] Certainly, this type of anxiety was evident in the vilification of homosexuals prac-tised by agencies of the Dominion government. As a form of social orga-nization and the only site of legitimate sexual behaviour, the family was integral to the definition of deviance. Those who found themselves on the outside of the family existed beyond the bounds of social legitimacy, and so were denied claim to one of the defining features of normality. It was a lesson that adults would emphasize over and over again in their dealings with postwar youth.

3

Hope for the Future or Repercussions of the Past: Discursive Constructions of Youth

Pause of a moment to consider what the boy or girl of today is confronted with: Countless novels filled with immorality, profanity, and a profound belief in nothing – most of them, hailed as masterpieces by reviewers who don't know a sentence from a group of words; radio programs that in the main get laughs by scoffing at what were once considered sterling virtues; movies that glorify rudeness, riches, power, animal passion, and drinking; a world that cheerfully squanders billions on liquor, cars, tobacco, gambling, sports, chewing gum, and sleeping tablets but protests strenuously at spending a few millions on education, the church, the physically handicapped; an eagerness to honour movie stars, successful speculators, and warriors, and more or less quietly to ignore the great missionaries, peace-makers, preachers, teachers, doctors and artists; a realm in which God is pushed into a back corner and the worship that used to be His lavished wholeheartedly on screen actors and actresses, not to mention money; an age in which unfaithfulness and divorce are coolly taken as a matter of course, and bawdy jokes and speech are too often bandied about even in mixed company; a world that at incredible expense has produced the atomic bomb and now cringes in fear of it; and psychologists who apparently never heard of self-control and patly explain away misconduct by attributing it to sickness or unhappiness or a carry-over from early life.[1]

This postwar version of 'the world's going to hell in a handbasket,' was penned by the principal of Toronto's Palmerston Avenue Public School in 1948. Perhaps longer and more comprehensive than other public expressions of social despair over the state of youth, R.K. Hall's lament on behalf of his students was not, however, new or unusual. Nor was his proposed solution to the problems he had outlined. Hall encouraged the parents of his pupils to give more to family life. In particular, he wanted them to take advantage of the wholesome 'influence of the family dinner table.'

Hall's flagging of an alleged social and moral disintegration and his faith in the calming and rehabilitative powers of domesticity make his plea, which appeared in a school bulletin for parents, emblematic of a strong current of postwar middle-class social comment. Although Hall's professional position shaped his personal concern for young people, and lent him the authority to speak of such matters, references to 'children' and 'youth' were regularly employed by a whole range of social critics as symbolic devices to underline the gravity of problems wrought by changes in the modern world and the need for ameliorative actions.

A brief note on the use of the term 'youth': The word can be used to refer to chronological age, to a stage of life, or to specific individuals, as in: Who are those youths sitting over there? Ostensibly, in this latter sense, 'youth' is an ungendered noun that can refer to people of either sex. In practice, however, the people referred to by the term 'youth' are almost always male. That was the case in the 1940s and 1950s, and it continues to be so today. Nevertheless, I use the term, with reservations, because as articulated in a number of postwar discourses, 'youth' conveys a meaning distinct from either 'adolescent' or 'teenager.' It marks a social problem in a way that 'adolescent,' as the more 'scientific' term, cannot. And while many postwar adults considered teenagers to be a problem, there was no generally articulated 'teenage problem' in the same way that there was a 'youth problem' in the years after the Second World War. Conversely, neither 'teenager' nor 'adolescent' captures the kind of hope in the future that 'youth' was often used to convey. 'Youth' was a term steeped in both anxiety and promise, a contradiction that is emblematic of the position of young people in postwar Canada.

Young People and the Transition from War to Peace

In the postwar period there were a number of competing discourses about youth, some with clear roots in wartime disruptions, others more distinctly tied to postwar prosperity and the 'modern age.' The notion of adolescence as a time of rapid and profound change operated as a funnel for fears about change in the society at large. As the progression of one's adolescence was seen to determine the shape of one's adulthood,[2] so, too, the collective progress of adolescents could indicate the shape society would take in the future; youth operated as metaphor for the development of the society as a whole. It was as if, after two decades of turmoil, the late 1940s and the 1950s presented Canadian society with a 'second chance' to grow up.

For many adolescents, wartime had meant that their supposedly precarious 'transitional years' were spent without a lot of adult supervision, as fathers joined the forces and left home and mothers joined the burgeoning wartime labour force. In 1944, more than 30 per cent of women over the age of fifteen were working outside the home for pay.[3] Teenage girls and boys were also among those who kept the war industries operating. After a decade-long depression it was an easy decision for many adolescents to give up their studies for wartime wages. The combination of teenagers' growing economic independence and the alleged lack of parental supervision lay at the root of a broad-based debate on the inevitability and extent of juvenile delinquency and a more generalized phenomenon that was known simply as the 'youth problem.' Educators, civic officials, and journalists all claimed that the wartime climate had set teenagers upon the path of trouble. The absence of parents (especially mothers) and the assumed emotional turmoil of adolescence were taken by some as a perilous combination that could only ensure a negative outcome in terms of young people's development into mature and responsible citizens.

As Ruth Roach Pierson and Susan Prentice have both argued, the uproar over youth and delinquency in Canada was, in part, constructed through discourses about mothering. After the war there was a concerted effort by government agencies at all levels, by business, and by many civic organizations to push women out of the paid workforce and back into the home. A good part of this struggle was fought on an ideological level. Working women were told it was their patriotic duty to give up their positions in manufacturing plants to returning soldiers. They were also told that their children were suffering from the absence of mothers from their homes, the consequences of which might be the transformation of so-called normal youth into delinquents.[4]

Even after the war, after women's and youth's participation in the labour force had begun to drop, and after fathers had returned home from overseas, there continued to be public expressions of fear, like R.K. Hall's, about the many harmful influences in adolescent lives. If it wasn't the war it was the changing shape of popular culture – television, popular dance music, Hollywood movies, and crime comics. All of these were, at various times, marked as influences capable of corrupting youthful 'innocence' – as threats to young lives, and therefore to the future of the society as a whole. As historian John Gillis has written, both the idea of youthful innocence and the fears of juvenile delinquency that opposed it were the products of a worried middle class: 'The notion of a stage of life freed from all the cares and responsibilities of a troubled civilization was their escapist dream, the vision of juvenile degeneracy their recurring nightmare.'[5] Of course, to middle-class adults who believed that 'juvenile degeneracy' was rooted in the working class, that 'nightmare' was perhaps a recognition of the volatility of class inequalities.

What rendered such fantasies particularly poignant, in the late 1940s and the 1950s, were hopes that, after all the losses of the war and the Depression, not just youth but society as a whole could cease to be troubled. In the midst of prosperity, a tremendous faith in science and the unshakability of democracy gave many white, middle-class North Americans the sense that there could be peace, comfort, and contentment in the world. On the one hand, middle-class adolescents – by their scholastic achievements, the clothes they wore, and the entertainment they pursued – were taken as symbols of the prosperity and potential of their families and their society. On the other hand, potentially delinquent or unruly youth made obvious the limitations of postwar society. Not surprisingly, those young people most likely to be understood as 'problems' came from working-class homes and had the least to gain from middle-class visions of the future.

What differentiated postwar discourses about troubled and troublesome young people from earlier worries about youthful disorder was the changing place of the adolescent in mainstream postwar society and the emergence of a commercialized 'teen culture.' In the 1920s, white, middle-class, high school and college youth had developed their own distinct, peer-regulated youth culture. Based on fashions and fads, this youth culture was in no extensive way nurtured or encouraged by adults.[6] In contrast, in the 1950s, business interests responded to economic and demographic changes by nurturing teen consumerism and targeting youth as a specific market. Teen magazines, rock 'n' roll, teen films, teen columns in newspapers, teen sections in department stores were all products of the 'discovery' of the teenager. While middle-class and working-class young people had unequal access to the products of this market, and would ascribe different meanings to its products, they were all affected by it.

The word 'teenager' was already in use by the early 1940s. American in origin, it was first printed in Toronto newspapers with an apostrophe marking the dropped, numerical prefix, as in 'teen-ager. The apostrophe had disappeared by the end of the decade, but it was not until the 1950s that 'teenage' referred to a cultural perspective as well as an age. Thomas Doherty, in his study of Hollywood teen movies, says that in the 1950s, 'teenager' marked a special 'social status.' He cites the *Dictionary of American Slang*, which suggests that teenagers, as a social category, emerged *circa* 1935. Before that, those between thirteen and nineteen years of age 'were considered young adults and not a special group.'[7] Doherty argues that 'special treatment from Big Business was crucial in establishing and reinforcing the subcultural identity of 50s teenagers.'[8] While his point is well taken, it's important to point out that, enthusiastic media portrayals to the contrary, there was no singular version of the 1950s teen. In Toronto, teenagers were divided along the lines of gender, religion, race/ethnicity, and class.[9] Some of these divisions fell between neighbourhoods or 'parts of town,' some were reflected in the different populations of technical schools and collegiates, public schools and separate schools, or in the chasm between students and teenaged workers.

Certainly other factors besides business contributed to the growth of teen cultures in the 1950s. After the war, many young people were forced to give up their lucrative industrial jobs to returning soldiers. And technological changes were beginning to eliminate many of the unskilled positions still open to them. Hence, teenagers tended to stay in school longer and to spend more years in the company of their peers. Moreover, as long as they were contained within the state-run educational system, they provided research material for inquisitive professionals – including psychologists, psychiatrists, physicians, sociologists, and journalists. Teenagers were new and interesting. Those who took an interest in them created specialized niches for themselves in their various fields of study. So, for instance, psychologists and psychiatrists alike undertook studies to determine the boundaries of normal teenage development, including sexual development. Journalists and sociologists made mileage out of explaining teenagers to their elders, as did educational film houses like the National Film Board. Films like *The Meaning of Adolescence*, *The Teens*, and *Who Is Sylvia?* (about a teenage girl) were intended to be instructional for both adults and teens themselves.[10] While adults were informed about a strange and baffling culture, teens were enlightened about appropriate modes of behaving.

G. Stanley Hall and the 'Discovery' and Study of Adolescence

Twentieth-century scholarly investigations of youth owe much to the massive 1904 study on adolescence conducted by American psychologist G. Stanley Hall.[11] His biographer, Dorothy Ross, claims that Hall's 'concept of adolescence was probably the first systematic portrayal of that stage of life in the modern world,' although, as she acknowledges, it was based on ideas about youth that had been popular in the nineteenth century.[12] Writing in a rapidly urbanizing society, Hall understood adolescence to be a distinct developmental period that began with the process of sexual maturation at puberty and continued into the early twenties. At the centre of his work was a theory of 'recapitulation' which said that the development of the individual paralleled the historical development of the race – a term that variously meant the human race or the white or civilized race. Historian Joseph Kett suggests that recapitulation had roots within and prior to Darwinism, as well as in the romanticism of both Rousseau and various nineteenth-century American writers.[13] It was a theoretical stance with strong eugenic overtones.

Hall 'insisted that the misbehaviour and eccentricities of young people be viewed as normal outgrowths of biological maturation rather than as inexcusable departures from a fixed standard of behaviour.'[14] He described adolescents as being in a 'primitive' state where they were ruled by instinct. While not expressed explicitly by Hall, the racist corollary of this view was that so-called primitive societies could then be said to represent the adolescence of humanity. They could be portrayed as not yet developed, as immature.

Hall firmly believed, as did other eugenicists, that as the biological individual evolved so would society. What made his theory unique, however, was its emphasis on adolescence as the key to racial and cultural betterment. Like Rousseau, he believed that adolescence was a time of second birth. According to Ross, Hall thought that 'The broader and higher development reached in adolescence would be progressively inherited until a higher evolutionary product, the superman of the future, was created.'[15] In Hall's scheme, adolescence was the critical measure of human 'progress.' His perspective lent significant weight to youth's claim on the future and underscored the need to ensure that young people had every advantage.[16]

Clashes between 'primitive' young people and more civilized adults were, according to Hall, what caused the inevitable 'storm and stress' of youth. In fact, he claimed that such stress was necessary to ensure the young person's safe passage to maturity. Hall counselled parents and teachers to give adolescents enough freedom to let nature take its course – in all areas but one. In terms of sexuality, Hall preached the need for control by way of sublimation. He claimed that youthful passions were malleable or 'plastic' and could easily be directed into non-sexual occupations and pursuits like religion, the arts, or athletics.[17] Indeed, Hall wrote that such sublimation was 'vastly easier ... than is often said' – easier because it was motivated by the instinct for social and physical evolution.[18] While Hall was concerned with chastity, he was at least equally concerned with the continual development of civilization, a process he, like Freud and others of his day, thought resulted from the redirection of sexual energies.

Hall's theories were roundly criticized by theorists of various persuasions who followed him. In particular, he was derided for his biologism and his attempts to parallel the development of children and 'the race.' In 1930, sociologist Arthur Wallace Calhoun used Hall to argue against the notion that child development is determined by 'some inward timer.' Hall's recapitulation theory – child development 'from Bushman ... to Babbitt'[19] – was held up as the unfortunate extreme of this kind of thinking. In a 1947 book, sociologist Paul Landis argued bitingly that Hall had made 'a notable contribution to the understanding of adolescents in spite of his theoretical postulate rather than because of it.' Landis worried that Hall's notoriety had helped to keep biological theories in circulation long past the period of their usefulness.[20]

Anthropologist Margaret Mead was perhaps the most well-known of Hall's critics. Indeed, her books on adolescence in South Pacific cultures were based on studies designed to put Hall's theories of 'storm and stress' to the test. His view, she wrote, 'though unsanctioned by the cautious experimentalist, [has] gained wide currency, influenced our educational policy, paralysed our parental efforts.'[21] Mead claimed North American parents and teachers would do well to understand that 'Human nature within a different social form lacks the conflicts which are so often characteristic of adolescence [in the United States].'[22] Mead thought that Hall's views had done much to complicate the relationship between youth and adults in twentieth-century North America. It was but a short step from the idea that adolescence was by nature a turbulent time to common-sense notions that young people were inevitably troublesome, that they constituted a social problem.

Despite his critics, Hall's conceptualization of adolescence as a stressful, instinct-driven, transitional stage between childhood and adulthood has yet to be completely overturned. While his ideas about recapitulation went out of fashion with the eugenic movement that influenced them, his claims about the biological basis of adolescent behaviour still inform both popular and professional discourses about young people. They fit nicely into common-sense discussions of puberty as the grounds of the 'youth problem,' a perspective made evident in the 1940s and 1950s by some of the strategies designed to regulate delinquency, strategies based on efforts to control adolescent sexual energies.

American youth historian Joseph Kett writes that the modern relationship between adolescence and biology owes much to Rousseau. In *Émile*, the onset of puberty and the process of sexual maturation were identified as the roots of adolescent behaviour and personality. Rousseau waxes romantic about the profound emotional and spiritual changes for which puberty is a catalyst.[23] According to Kett, his sentiments were echoed by North American doctors and educators during the mid- to late nineteenth century. Kett quotes one of these, Orson Fowler, who wrote in 1870: 'All his [the pubescent boy's] feelings shoot into rampant growth and vigor ... Before half asleep, how much animation and the highest phase of human vigor he evinces! Desires before tame, now become almost resistless.'[24] Sexual development was thought to fuel the social and psychological transformations attributed to adolescence. Sexual energies were thought to lead to 'a rise in physical, moral and spiritual energy,' although this process had to be watched and protected from corruption. Adolescent sexual development, Kett says, was seen by some nineteenth-century observers as a delicate process that could lead to, among other things, insanity.[25] In this century, the imagery grew more secular, the superlatives became less plentiful, and the potential outcomes less extreme, but the basic correlation between the process of sexual maturation and the course of adolescence persisted.

Hall's turn-of-the-century study did little to interrupt this conflation of adolescence and puberty. Sociologists and anthropologists who came after him went to great lengths to untangle the physical and the social in discussions about teenagers. In his 1949 study, *Elmtown's Youth*, A.B. Hollingshead complained that psychologists, the intellectual descendants of Hall, held especially fast to biological explanations for youthful experiences. He wrote, in particular, about 'a recent summary of the field of adolescent psychology [which] insisted upon the "causal" connection between the physical manifestations of adolescence and social behaviour.'[26] In a footnote, he continued, 'We would agree with Dennis [author of the summary] if he or any other psychologist demonstrated any "causal" connection between the physical phenomenon of puberty and the social behaviour of young people during the adolescent period, irrespective of cultural milieu.'[27] Paul Landis made a similar argument in the 1952 edition of his sociology textbook, *Adolescence and Youth*.[28] He was concerned that few researchers interested in adolescence looked beyond the internal workings of the human organism for explanations of behavioural problems – like delinquency. They neglected the social forces he considered to be of paramount importance to focus, instead, on biology. When talking about youth, 'biology' is easily reduced to pubertal change, to what Havelock Ellis referred to as that gradual combination of 'several factors' that 'constitute what may be properly termed sexuality.'[29]

This overemphasis on puberty as a defining feature of adolescence sexualized youth as a category. That youth and sexuality were both concepts that funnelled postwar social anxieties only increased the weight the two concepts drew from each other. It is because of this semiotic equation that the 'youth problem,' on some level, was imbued with sexual meaning. Conversely, sexual problems, like venereal disease, were understood to be problems of youth. On the postwar landscape, discourses about youth and discourses about sex were not entirely separate.

Youth Trouble

Popular wartime and postwar discussions about youth issues frequently relied on an incongruous mix of biology, psychoanalysis, and sociology. In newspaper and magazine articles, 'wartime conditions,' 'world confusion,' and 'modern times' were proposed, alongside difficult family and emotional circumstances and hormonal change, as the environment which produced troubled youth.[30] Reporters faithfully related non-biological theories on the causes of the youth problem, but these 'expert' positions could hardly compete with the overwrought tone that tended to colour discussions of delinquency. What remained constant from Hall's time to the 1950s – despite the increasing attention given to sociological and psychoanalytic opinion – was a general notion that the biological nature of adolescence – 'all those raging hormones' – made it a constant struggle to keep trouble at bay. According to British cultural critic Dick Hebdige, trouble is what, even now, makes adolescents visible in the broader social scene; and so, Hebdige says, it is no wonder young people act out:

in our society, youth is present only when its presence is a problem, or is regarded as a problem. More precisely, the category 'youth' gets mobilized in official documentary discourse, in concerned or outraged editorials and features, or in the supposedly disinterested tracts emanating from the social sciences at those times when young people make their presence felt by going 'out of bounds,' by resisting through rituals, dressing strangely, striking bizarre attitudes, breaking rules, breaking bottles, windows, heads, issuing rhetorical challenges to the law.[31]

Hebdige suggests that young people's own efforts to transgress (delinquency as resistance) are what set adult discourse about the youth problem in motion. And while I don't disagree with him, his argument obscures a point that is critical to an understanding of the postwar youth problem, namely the importance of biological determinism in discourses about youth. Young people were assumed by some to be, by their very nature, a social problem. Young people didn't need to 'act out' or step out of bounds to get attention; they could be perceived as trouble simply because they were teenagers. The category of having the potential for trouble slipped easily into the category of being trouble. And so in 1950, *Maclean's* could send Sidney Katz out to write a three-part story, not on the delinquent, but on 'the teenager as a national problem.' As Katz writes in the introduction to the first part of his series, 'They are frequently pictured as being irresponsible hoodlums who spend most of their time making a nuisance of themselves. It is often said that the younger generation smokes too much, drinks too much, is ill-mannered, promiscuous and perhaps criminal as well.'[32]

While Katz admits that this is an overgeneralization, the fact remains that his stories were intended as a response to shifting popular discourses about the pervasiveness of the 'youth problem.' The point is not that discourses about troublesome teenagers displaced the discourse about the delinquent or obscured discourses about model postwar teens. Rather, these contradictory discourses came to exist side by side – each shifting the bounds of the others – facilitating and justifying broad-ranging regulatory measures that would circumscribe the activities of all young people, not just the 'bad' ones.

The Teenager as a Problem

Divergent discourses about 'youth' represented ideological and tactical differences among adults as much as they marked adult discomfort with the changing place of youth in North American culture. Between the mid-1940s and the early 1960s, youth behaviour changed dramatically.

Young people, generally, had access to more money than had previous generations. They were courted by advertisers and manufacturers as an important new market. They developed new codes of sexual behaviour and pushed down statistics on the average age of marriage. And, perhaps most important, they came to rely increasingly on their own peer-based institutions which had been fostered by prolonged attendance at school.

For adults who had been raised in different times, the thought that youth – teenagers – comprised a distinct social group was difficult to take. In a rant published in 1950 by *Chatelaine*, Frank Tumpane (columnist for the Toronto *Globe and Mail*) oozed bitter sarcasm as he warned teens what they would find at the end of this period of special treatment:

With all this barrage of propaganda designed to bolster the ego of adolescents, it is little wonder that the young crowd have become pretty firmly attached to the notion that they are very important people indeed ...

... But the chief flaw in being a teen-ager as a professional career is that the life expectancy of the career is so brief. You are petted and courted by adult merchandisers and publishers for the five high-school years. And then what?

You graduate from high school into the cruel, cruel world and suddenly your status has changed to a remarkable degree.[33]

In his 1959 book, *The Vanishing Adolescent*, Edgar Friedenberg claimed that adults' own issues with sexuality were at the bottom of Tumpane's kind of hostility towards teenagers. Friedenberg writes that stereotypes of (male) teens are built upon 'prurient features: the tight, tight jeans; the provocative gait; the conception of the basement fraternity as the scene of copulation so continuous as to defy the laws of nature.'[34] (One could certainly construct a female counterpart to this: tight sweaters, grown-up makeup, that same basement.) Images like these, says Friedenberg, aroused in adults fears about losing control not just of young people but also of themselves. Not surprisingly, such images led to fears about delinquency and to the subsequent regulation by adults of young people's behaviour.

Friedenberg goes on to argue that adolescent males awaken in adult men the latent homosexual feelings the men have carried since their own youth.[35] Adolescents, in the way he describes them, would then come to symbolize to adults their own psychic struggles to maintain normative standards, those potent regulators of social and personal life. According to Friedenberg, such individual psychic responses contributed to the organization of a mean-spirited social consensus: 'The "teen-ager" seems to have replaced the Communist as the appropriate target for public controversy and fore-boding, for discussions designed less to clarify what is going on than to let people vent their fearful or hostile feelings and declare themselves on the side of order and authority.'[36]

While Friedenberg doesn't make the link between Communists and homosexuals, it has been made by many historians of postwar culture.[37] In the cold-war era, Communists represented the external threat to pros-perity and democracy. Homosexuality, in this context, was the threat from within, a destabilizer of families and the sexual/moral order. Some felt that teenagers, open to new experiences and not yet strong of charac-ter, would be vulnerable to both these pernicious influences. Thus, teen-agers could indeed become a threat to social stability.

As long as teenagers as a group were seen to be potentially trouble-some, the perimeters of the space between delinquency and regular teenaged behaviour (whatever that was) were fuzzy. Thus, in 1962, a North Toronto Committee on Juvenile Delinquency decided to focus its attention on 'behaviour standards among teenagers, rather than upon juvenile delinquency per se.' Members of the committee had discussed some of those troublesome standards at a meeting in 1961: 'early dating, going steady, and social drinking.'[38] They acknowledged that it would be a while before North Toronto would be 'plagued by' what they called 'overt delinquency.' Nevertheless, committee members claimed that the area was already under the influence of 'a great deal of hidden juvenile delinquency,' necessitating their vigilance over the 'moral cli-mate and behaviour standards.' In this case, it seems delinquency was less a concrete social problem than a conceptual tool that helped to jus-tify and organize adult surveillance of teenage lives, especially of teen-age sexuality.

Teens as Symbols of the Modern Age

Although some social commentators saw all teenagers as potential delinquents, no matter what their class background, others saw teens and delinquents as two separate, opposing categories, a distinction that was often, but not always, based on class. In 1951, a column in *Saturday Night* claimed that Canadian mothers had no troubles with their teens and that all the hype about the youth problem must have been an Amer-ican import.[39] Many middle-class adults, if not quite so optimistic, per-ceived postwar adolescence as a 'charmed' and special time, a period of security. Certainly it compared favourably with their own Depression-era experiences. In the 1940s and 1950s, the extension of economic dependence well into the teens (and later, for young people who would go on to university or college) was certainly not understood to be in any sense regulating or limiting.[40] Instead, it was taken as a symbol of the importance of youth to postwar North American society. The prolonging of childhood was one of the distinctive markers of the postwar world, a signal that grown-up worries could be kept at bay for a good part of life. Teens were seen by many adults to live a carefree life, without responsibility. They were seen to have greater freedom than their parents had had. That young people were permitted to choose their own courses at school, to date without chaperons, to drive cars, and keep pocket money frequently obscured the fact that, as not-quite-adults, they had little real power in their lives. They were not expected to make any significant decisions or even to be capable of doing so. And, most importantly, their freedoms were contingent upon adult approval. The fact that many postwar adults had been earning full-time wages and, thus, had achieved adult status during their teenage years was never part of such comparative discussions.

In 1955, a feature in *Chatelaine* portrayed teens as friendlier, more frank, and more democratic than previous generations of young people had been. The unsigned article said that 'personalities and attitudes of today's kids' reflected a saner more prosperous world and the 'return to normal family life.'[41] It was in this sense that teenagers, particularly middle-class ones, were held up as the fortunate products of their era. Well-fed and well-brought-up in a time of peace and economic growth, they would, it was assumed, move smoothly into the 1960s. On a symbolic level, postwar teenagers represented the investment in the future that had been made by their parents, men and women who had come of age in more difficult times. That teenagers could 'go bad' when so much was assumed to be right within Canadian society was one contradiction (among many others) that threw optimistic visions of a tranquil, democratic future into question.

In the years after the Second World War, a variety of social and economic factors combined to generate an intense concern for the position and behaviour of young people. Youth came to symbolize both what was 'good' and what was 'bad' about the modern world. While the 'youth problem' existed as a mark of social disarray, teenage confidence and security stood as an emblem of postwar progress. That youth and sexuality were both vehicles for social anxieties meant that these two categories of discourse were frequently entwined. Certainly young people were regularly positioned as targets of and symbols within sexual discourses. That many people understood the tone of adolescence to be set by the physical changes associated with puberty only strengthened the links between youth and sexuality and contributed to the discursive construction of youth as a sexual category. This sexualization of youth was central to public discussions over delinquency, discussions where social anxieties about sex and about the state of young people were tightly entwined.

4

Youth Gone Bad: The Sexual Meanings of Delinquency

In the 1955 film *Blackboard Jungle*, an earnest Second World War veteran takes his first teaching job at a boys' trades school in a large American city. In scene after endless scene, Mr Dadier is exposed to a range of what the film's textual preamble identifies as delinquent behaviour: an attempted rape, destruction of property, robbery, street violence, disobedience in the classroom, and a pronounced unwillingness to respect authority. The audience witnesses Dadier's struggle to get through to both his students and his jaded colleagues. They see him suffer the consequences of juvenile brutality. We watch him question his own ability to effect change. Of course, in the end, the sensitive but firm English teacher wins the boys over. But this victory on behalf of middle-class values and social order wasn't enough to forestall the public outcry that marked the film's release. In Toronto, Board of Education trustees protested about *Blackboard Jungle* to the Ontario Board of Censors.[1] The film was an accessible, visual representation of one of the trustees' greatest fears: youth out of hand, or as the media so frequently put it, 'the youth problem.'

In 1954, the Toronto Board of Education had passed a similar motion of protest against *The Wild One*. In that film a sullen Marlon Brando – clad in the black-leather jacket and jeans that would soon become the uniform of disaffected, urban, male youth (and, much later, the marker of a particular version of cool, urban, especially lesbian and gay, sexuality) – leads a group of bikers into a small California town where they face off against a rival 'gang.' Again, law and order prevail, but not before the bikers rend the tranquillity of the town with a tragic display of masculine aggression. Brando's crowd was the antithesis of the maturity and civic-mindedness the Toronto Board wanted to encourage in its students:

whereas the Toronto Board of Education is responsible for the education of many children and young people of this city. And whereas education in a broad sense comprises not only skills but a sense of values and attitudes to social responsibilities. Therefore be it resolved, that this Board register its disapproval of a motion picture now showing at Shea's Theatre entitled 'The Wild One,' and that the Social Hygiene Committee of the Health League of Canada ... be respectfully requested to view the film and to make such representations to the Honourable, The Premier of Ontario, as may be deemed advisable.[2]

Board of Education trustees were concerned that the film would set an undesirable example for young people and that it might lead to local unrest. Their enlistment of the Social Hygiene Committee suggests the kind of disruption the trustees envisaged. A relic of wartime concerns over venereal disease, the work of the Social Hygiene Committee was focused on sex education and related matters. It seems odd that the board would bow to this external authority while protesting a film that is more about drinking and fighting than about sex. But fears about out-of-control teenage sexuality lay thick beneath public discussions of delinquency. A decade before the movie protests, Abraham Feinberg, public welfare advocate and well-known rabbi of Toronto's Holy Blossom Temple had drawn on this conflation of the 'youth problem' with sex when he declared that 'Juvenile delinquency, not syphilis, is the crucial social disease of our civilization.'[3] In popular parlance, social diseases are not caused by germs, they're caused by certain types of people and certain types of sexual activity.[4] This chapter explores the discursive context that made Feinberg's statement possible, looking at the ways delinquency operated as a sexual category.

Delinquency as a Symbol of Social Change

As a social issue, delinquency was not unique to the years during and after the Second World War. As numerous historians have shown, it had been the focus of intense social concern in Victorian Canada.[5] In a general sense, one can argue that there is a striking continuity to public discourses about delinquency and to the way they connect to social fears about cultural change, particularly in terms of popular media and commercial entertainment. Of course, the specifics of those fears, and the meanings they take on, change. At the turn of the century, delinquency was understood to be a fundamental problem of 'the city.' Industrialization, urbanization, and the many social changes they wrought contributed to the discursive construction of the city as a 'social problem' in its own right; delinquency was just one of its many harmful effects. By the end of the Second World War, the city itself was less likely to be vilified. The process of urbanization had stabilized, and the direction of migration was as likely to be out of cities – to the new suburbs – as it was to be into them – from rural areas or other countries. In this context, urban problems were not seen to be an inevitable consequence of the city's 'unnaturalness.' Instead, they were seen in a more optimistic light, as a series of difficulties that needed to be, and probably could be, rectified. Which is not to say that there was agreement on how these problems originated or on how they might be solved. Urban problems continued to occasion impassioned moral debates, if only because they were perceived as slowing down the transformation of Canada into a modern, affluent society. Certainly this was one perspective on delinquency that emerged in discussions of the perceived problem in Toronto.

During the Second World War, delinquency had often been taken up as a symbol of social fallout from global conflict.[6] After the war, delinquency signified the distance between vision and reality, between hopes for a 'new,' democratic, postwar society and the difficulty of overcoming past inequalities and moral weaknesses. Delinquency was a marker of the limits of postwar optimism and affluence in bringing about social harmony. To many observers in the postwar period, Toronto's delinquency problem was a sign that young people refused to get on board, that they were reneging on their responsibility (indeed their privilege) to help build the new society.[7] To the more liberal-minded, delinquency was 'only one of the many symptoms of a deteriorating and disorganized society and culture.'[8] Either way, evidence of delinquency dampened discourses about the possibility of postwar progress. Certainly it disrupted the social homogenization – the smoothing over and 'declassing' – that was promoted as a feature of North American postwar society.

In popular media, delinquency was routinely constructed as a national problem. Nevertheless, it was a problem that was negotiated primarily on the local level. Local organizations such as the Big Brothers and the Children's Aid Society took responsibility for documenting the problem in their regions and for proposing solutions. Many of the institutions that were seen as integral to the fight lay within municipal jurisdictions: schools, juvenile and family courts, parks and recreation departments. The focus of this chapter is on Toronto; there, because of its relationship to national media, its position as 'home' to national civic organizations, and its modern aspirations, delinquency was a popular cause. Indeed, it was so popular that committees were formed to eradicate it in neighbourhoods where it did not yet exist.[9]

It is important to note that discourses about delinquency were not simply limited to legal/judicial decisions or to discussions about the behaviour of individual young people. Delinquency, as it was constructed in discourses of social concern had ramifications that extended far beyond the corridors of the juvenile court (which is not to minimize the effects legal and judicial actions had on the lives of young people and their families). Thus, decreases in the actual numbers of legally defined delinquents had little impact on public discussions of the issue. While both the total number of offences and the number of children committing them dropped after the war, public concern as expressed by the media did not diminish.[10] It is for this reason that the postwar response to delinquency is best categorized as a moral panic. 'When the official reaction to a person, groups of persons or series of events is *out of all proportion* to the actual threat offered, when "experts," in the form of police chiefs, the judiciary, politicians and editors *perceive* the threat in all but identical terms ... above and beyond that which a sober, realistic appraisal could sustain, then ... it is appropriate to speak of the beginnings of a *moral panic*.'[11] Sociologist Stan Cohen says that, in postwar Britain, the most recurring moral panics have been associated with delinquency and youth culture. He writes that various types of youth 'have symbolized – both in what they were and how they were reacted to – much of the social change which has taken place in Britain over the last twenty years [during the 1950s and 1960s].'[12] That argument could also be made about Canadian responses to the alleged postwar youth problem.

It almost goes without saying that commentary on juvenile delinquency was produced and circulated within the middle class, while the majority (though certainly not all) of those so labelled were the children of working-class parents. The fact that postwar experts increasingly adopted environmental rather than eugenic explanations for delinquency meant that professional views on the subject tended to avoid the notion – prevalent in earlier decades – that delinquents were inherently bad or immoral. But this emerging environmental perspective did not preclude discussion of psychological, individually based causes. While a typical argument might conclude that it was the social conditions of delinquency rather than delinquents themselves that were inherently immoral, a relatively pronounced determinism meant that, in practical terms, this distinction was often useless. Psychology was so often posited as directly shaped by the environment that there was no question of someone in a 'bad neighbourhood' not turning out badly herself; it was a tightly wrought and circular equation that kept the focus of concern squarely on individuals.[13]

Bad home life was the most often-cited cause of delinquency. Charles Goldring, superintendent of the Toronto Board of Education from 1933 through the 1950s, tended to use this explanation to absolve the school board of responsibility for the problem or its solution.[14] The phrase 'bad home life' was a marker of social difference that set off those who didn't fit postwar images of acceptability. 'Bad home life' was a catchall that could refer to the moral atmosphere of the home, to its physical conditions, or to the structure of a particular family unit. The phrase could point to poverty, a lack of religious education, a single-parent family, 'foreignness,' alcoholism, cramped quarters, or any other deviations from normative, upstanding, white, Anglo-Saxon, middle-class family life.[15] Thus, according to *Chatelaine*, a girl living in a crowded home 'is more likely to wander into trouble than her classmate who belongs to the local tennis club and can entertain her classmates in a nice home.'[16] The 'bad home life' formulation made working-class kids the default category of delinquents.

Next in line as most frequently cited cause of delinquency was the bad social environment, or the 'bad neighbourhood' – another means of rooting delinquency in working-class and immigrant communities. According to the United Welfare Chest's Youth Services Department, delinquency tended to concentrate in areas that already had 'other major social problems such as higher T.B. rates, extensive overcrowding as regards living arrangements, more frequent police and fire calls, greater concentration of bad social and moral influences, increasingly lower tax potential on buildings and houses, and a general lack of wholesome outlets for many of the basic needs of young people.'[17] In 1945 a worker for the volunteer youth service agency Big Brothers wrote of the downtown neighbourhood bordered by Bloor Street, Carlton Street, Yonge Street, and Sumach Street:

There are many connecting lanes running at the back of [the] side streets and parallel to them. These lanes are excellent warrens of refuge for activities which shun the light of day. The eastern half of the area is a congested area teeming with Anglo-Saxon children.

The people of this area make a very interesting study. It abounds with 'people of the shadows.' In an area of this kind the comedy and tragedy of life rub elbows every day: all the excesses and weaknesses of the flesh are exhibited ... In the eastern half of the area the people are mainly English, Irish and Scotch. These people are sturdy working class people, inclined to be suspicious, many of them decent and clean, others, physically dirty and morally corrupt. Children growing up in an area of this kind are exposed to influences which exaggerate the evils of life. Bad language, gambling, drunkenness, prostitution, are all too familiar.[18]

The Big Brothers worker had described an area that included part of Toronto's Cabbagetown. Only a few years after his report was made, another section of Cabbagetown was levelled, its crowded houses and back lanes obliterated by the construction of Regent Park, an early experiment in low-cost, easy-to-control, public housing.[19] The 'warrens' of the old working-class neighbourhood were replaced with large expanses of grass in an effort to limit shady activities while providing the healthful benefits of parkland. The rundown housing was replaced by low-rise apartment blocks where young people's access to the outdoors was restricted. Regent Park was an effort to use planning and structural design elements to control both the behaviour and the moral character of people and their neighbourhood. Forty-five years later, the project remains a testament to a regulatory approach that failed.

By linking delinquency to the characteristics of neighbourhoods, rather than the specific kinds of people who lived in them (the above ethnic references notwithstanding), social workers were trying to get at the structural causes of the youth problem. But their reluctance to cite poverty as the root of poor neighbourhood conditions led them to a deterministic argument of a different kind. For example, a 1943 report on delinquency prepared by the Toronto Welfare Council attempted to refute arguments that delinquency was a result of increasing numbers of immigrants in the city: 'The new residents, frequently of a different origin, with different religions and cultural backgrounds, may be said to have inherited the evil conditions of the area into which they moved. It seems proper to assume that, in such a case, delinquency is primarily a problem of neighbourhood relationships, standards and traditions, as well as one of conditions in individual families.'[20] The report claimed that delinquency was not a function of immigrant communities *per se* but of where immigrants ended up living in Toronto. But in failing to question the basis of the differences between various neighbourhoods, this geographic argument could not counter the prevailing popular assumption that immigrants were responsible for delinquency.

In the end, whether delinquency was blamed on neighbourhood and social conditions or on particular groups of people, the effect was the same. Both these perspectives meant that Anglo-Saxon, middle-class youth were vastly underrepresented among those who were labelled delinquent. Both these perspectives helped to construct delinquency as a problem with roots outside the Anglo-Saxon middle class and helped to constitute and reinforce differences between middle-class and working-class people, between Anglo-Saxon and ethnic communities.

To say that middle-class young people were rarely charged as delinquents is not, however, to say that discourses about delinquency had no part in their lives. The criminal charges that middle-class teens avoided were the most obvious but not the only effect of the panic over delinquency. Popular and official discourses about delinquency shaped the meanings that could be ascribed to the behaviours of all young people. Social worry over the issue justified broad regulation of adolescent lives. Especially in the realm of sexuality, the labelling of any behaviour or activity or person as delinquent was an effective way of marking it as beyond the bounds of acceptability. Delinquency discourses were central to the regulation of postwar adolescent sexuality.

Sex Delinquency, Delinquency as Sex

In the pamphlet collection of the Canadian Youth Commission, an American booklet called 'Teen Trouble' devotes four pages to a description of wartime delinquency. Almost all of the discussion is about sexual conduct.[21] To the authors of 'Teen Trouble,' delinquency meant girls on the streets and in taverns, girls capturing soldiers or going to juke joints; it was boys spending their big wartime wages on girls, and making ribald remarks to passing women. It was also truancy and vandalism, but these behaviours received scant attention compared to those more obviously connected to sex.

In 1951, *Chatelaine* magazine ran a feature about a teen 'sex scandal' in Kitchener, Ontario. Written by Hugh Garner, the piece was surprisingly titled, 'Youth Trouble in Kitchener.'[22] The careful headline stands in marked contrast to the sensational tone of the story. In the early 1950s, daily papers were full of reports of youth trouble; surely what made this case special – what made it worthy of a *Chatelaine* feature – was the sexual part of the story.

On one level, the Kitchener case was special because it dealt with explicitly sexual and 'immoral' behaviour. But it was special in degree only and therefore, like 'Teen Trouble,' did not need a qualifying head-line. Terms like 'delinquency' and 'youth trouble,' whether they referred explicitly to sexual behaviour or not, inevitably carried some sexual meaning. It's not that the trouble young people were allegedly getting into was always of a sexual nature, but that the social category of youth itself was understood to be a sexual one. In popular discourse, the terms adolescent, youth, and teenager marked individuals who were passing from the supposedly non-sexual category of childhood to the sexual cat-egory of adulthood, individuals who were, among other things, in the process of becoming sexual.[23] So long as the term delinquency was applied in a specific way to young people, as it was in the 1940s and 1950s, it would not be free of sexual connotations.

In analysing delinquency, it is important not to conflate the categories of gender and sexuality. In general, historical work that has looked at the overlap between sexuality and delinquency has tended to look primarily at the experiences of girls who were labelled delinquents.[24] In such work, delinquency is understood to have been sexualized by way of gendered discourses – that is, because of the differing assumptions about the proper limits of masculine and feminine behaviours. While there is much evidence from the postwar period to support this position, it is a line of analysis that does not account for the range of sexual dis-courses that shaped popular understandings of delinquency, nor does it account for the interest shown in the sexuality of boys by those adults concerned with the issue.

In the late 1940s and the 1950s, ideas about what counted as normal sexual behaviour and normal adolescent sexual development helped to establish the boundaries between what was seen as delinquent and what was not, boundaries that shifted depending on the class, gender, race, and ethnicity of particular individuals. Conversely, discourses about delinquency – the threat of being labelled a delinquent – worked to con-trol expressions of sexuality and to justify the sexual regulation of all young people. There was a tremendous back and forth between these two sets of discourses; indeed, it is hard to untangle them. On the one hand, concerned adults worried about the sexualities of 'known delin-quents.' Was it possible to keep them under control? Would they lead to social havoc? On the other hand, many defined sexuality itself as a path to delinquency. For instance, the offence known as 'contributing to juve-nile delinquency' was generally seen to be synonymous with introduc-ing young people, especially girls, to sex. It was feared that girls and boys introduced prematurely to sex would be transformed into delinquents or 'problem youth.' As the attorney general of Ontario wrote to a Family Court judge in 1952, 'Practically all the cases that one could find in connection with the matter [contributing to juvenile delinquency] dealt with sexual immorality in the presence of children.'[25]

According to Garner, the Kitchener scandal was 'a sordid story ... which, summarized in the press, gave the impression of an organized gang dedicated to the holding of sexual orgies.' The *Telegram* did run a front-page story on the case, under a huge, bold headline: '6 MONTHS, 10 LASHES FOR 9 AT KITCHENER.' But despite the article's sensational appearance, its description of the 'sordid' event – the most lurid in any of the Toronto papers – hardly evokes images of organized orgies: 'During the several hearings, witnesses described, among other things, an all-night party, interludes in bedrooms at some of the accuseds' and the girls' homes, and an episode involving three youths, two juvenile boys and a 14-year-old girl, in a car parked behind a district church.'[26]

In the Kitchener case, six young men between the ages of sixteen and twenty-four were charged with carnal knowledge of 'a girl under 16'; three were charged with indecent assault and one with contributing to the delinquency of a minor. A juvenile male was given an indefinite term in a reformatory. Six girls were charged with being or about to become juvenile delinquents by reason of indulging in sexual intercourse. The connection made between the girls' sexual behaviour (which may well have been consensual) and the deviant/criminal identity of the delinquent hardly needs to be underlined here. Five of the girls were also charged with shoplifting. A story in the *Toronto Daily Star* quoted the Kitchener chief of police who claimed that the shoplifting allowed the girls 'to dress up and look older than their years when they frequented the poorly conducted dance halls and loosely run restaurants' that he blamed for the scandal.[27]

Local responses to the Kitchener case were mixed and show the easy slippage between categories of sexual immorality and delinquency. While some post-scandal proposals were clearly meant to address the sexual nature of the 'crimes,' others were intended to circumscribe the activities of young people in a more general way. The mayor of Kitchener suggested castration for male sex offenders, while organizers of Kitchener's youth programs planned to expand services in an attempt to diffuse excess adolescent energy. The local police hoped to start up a boys' pipe band and choir; they suggested a nine o'clock curfew for people under sixteen years of age; they recommended 'license cancellation for any restaurants which become hangouts for delinquents'; and they established a four-man morality department. In the police initiatives alone we can see competing analyses of the troubles. Was the Kitchener case a problem of sex or a problem of youth? Or was it, as Garner suggested, a consequence of the overlap between these two categories, of what he called 'the aberrations of puberty'?

Of course, not everyone read the series of events in Kitchener as a major scandal. The *Globe and Mail's* angle on the story was about court precautions to protect the anonymity of the juveniles.[28] And, in a letter to *Chatelaine*, a woman from Quebec wondered what all the fuss had been about:

There was no mention of rape, abduction, molestation, dope – nothing seemingly, more wicked than sexual promiscuity on the part of a few young men and very young girls who looked, and in the present day *are*, much older than their years. Such episodes occur every day in every city and town of any size in the world where males and females mingle freely. Naturally, right-thinking people do not condone such behaviour and authorities do their best to combat it, but not in the primitive way that Kitchener has gone about it.

There was nothing in the actions of these youngsters to suggest perversion or abnormality, but after the humiliating, shameful experience they have suffered, it will be a miracle if any of them are ever again to have any normal feelings about sex.[29]

This letter suggests the proximity of 'delinquency' to commonly practised, if not condoned, sexual activities. In labelling consensual activities as delinquent, officials were not simply protecting the teenagers in question, they were protecting sexual standards.

What makes Garner's story unique among discussions of delinquency is the fact that he explicitly links the delinquency of young men to their sexualities. Usually, the sexual aspects of boys' delinquency were downplayed. For example, a report on street gangs in Toronto, prepared by the Big Brothers, notes that the older boys in the study were 'abnormally sex conscious.' But despite finding evidence of 'filthy language, obscenity, relatively open immorality (heterosexual and homosexual) ...' the researchers chose not to use these incidents to illustrate their report. 'We can not see that doing this would serve our purpose any more than the selections used [which were mostly about idleness, petty thieving, and gambling].'[30]

One case that was an exception to this tendency to downplay boys' sexual transgressions is a 1958 study of 'Negro and partly-Negro wards of the Children's Aid Society' (in Toronto). This study, of both boys and girls, did not hesitate to identify 'masturbation and other sex problems' as the most frequently displayed behaviour problems of the twenty-one black adolescents who were studied.[31] Without the protection afforded by whiteness, the boys in this study were subjected to a scrutiny that racially unmarked boys avoided.

When boys were presented as an undifferentiated category, when their racial and ethnic differences were glossed over – which was almost always – their sexualities were rarely remarked upon. In general, it was the sexualities of girl delinquents that made it into public discourse. Moreover, almost all girl delinquents had been labelled as such because of their sexual or moral behaviour. Girls were far less likely than boys to be brought to court over offences like theft, vandalism, or trespassing. Instead, girls were charged with having committed vague, non–property-oriented crimes like vagrancy, incorrigibility, and immorality.[32] But to say that boys' sexualities were not the topic of public comment or that boys were charged with a wider range of offences than girls is not to say that their sexual and moral behaviour was not also called into question. In fact, court reports show that during some years, the numbers of boys charged with morals-related offences was higher than the number of girls.

While most boys in Toronto were charged with petty offences like theft, property damage, and trespassing, an average of slightly more than 10 per cent of all charges laid against boys were the non–property-related, victimless behaviour charges that we tend to associate with girls: vagrancy, incorrigibility, indecency, and immorality. In 1946, for instance, the total number of charges faced by boys was 700, of which 124 were morals charges (vagrancy, incorrigibility, indecency, and immorality). In the same year, the total number of charges faced by girls was 93, of which 68 were morals charges. In all but one of the categories I counted, more boys were charged than girls.[33] This trend was repeated for seven of the eight years for which I had figures. In 1952, the last year for which data were available, boys were charged with 71 behaviour and morals-related offences and girls with 74. Unlike girls, boys were also charged with contributing to juvenile delinquency and indecent assault, which, as Karen Dubinsky has shown for the period up to the 1930s, was a category that sometimes marked consensual heterosexual activity.[34] While it is unlikely that definitions of immorality, indecency, vagrancy, and incorrigibility were identical for boys and girls, these are the charges that would be likely to account for the kinds of sexual misbehaviour noted in documents like the Big Brothers' study, Garner's article, the CAS study, and other social-work research.[35] At the very least, these documents suggest that boys' sexual behaviour was of interest to those concerned about delinquency. Case-file research on the behaviour charges in the postwar period would show to what extent.[36]

Female Delinquency as Sexual Transgression

In the midst of the Second World War, the Ontario Training School for Girls in Galt was taken over by the navy. A brief protesting the transfer of the building details prevailing attitudes about girl delinquents:

The offences with which girls were most commonly charged in the Toronto court in 1941 were theft, vagrancy, incorrigibility and habitual truancy. Parents are deeply concerned about the behaviour of these girls. Most of the girls sent to Galt were keeping late hours, running away from home, staying out all night and many of them were being 'picked up' by soldiers. Many of the girls show a definite tendency toward delinquency. Because of this there is a grave danger that some of the older girls may become 'camp followers' if they are released from the protection of the Galt Training School ... The need of a training school for delinquents and incorrigible girls is even more necessary than it is for boys ... They are not acceptable in foster homes and would shortly become a menace to the community if they were returned to their own homes.[37]

And not because of their engagement in theft. Sexuality is, obviously, the primary concern in this passage. Historically, it has been the primary basis for definitions of female delinquency, and in this respect the 1940s and 1950s were not a lot different from, say, the turn of the century. Phrases like 'keeping late hours,' as indicators of criminality, marked girls as being outside parental control and implied that once outside that control girls would express their sexuality in a manner dangerous to themselves and to their communities. In contrast, boys outside parental control were not necessarily assumed to be 'in trouble.' And when boys did get into trouble, as we have seen, there were more ways for them to do it. In 1946, boys faced 700 charges, for 36 different kinds of offences, at the Toronto Juvenile and Family Court. Girls appeared before the court on 93 charges for 7 different offences. While some of the discrepancy between boys' and girls' experiences of the justice system stemmed from the exigencies of their gender roles and from girls' unequal opportunities – to have the freedom to roam the streets where theft might be committed, for instance – it was also related to the moral and sexual attitudes of law-enforcement and court officials. As Steven Schlossman and Stephanie Wallach write in their study of female delinquents during the progressive era in the United States, girls were institutionalized for behaviour that, if done by adults, would not have been criminalized, and if done by boys would have been treated far less harshly.[38]

We can see this concern about 'immoral conduct' in a series of 1944 reports on individual delinquent girls at the Ontario Training School, which relocated to Cobourg when the navy took over the facilities at Galt. Prepared by Dr F.L. Nichols of the provincial Department of Health, the reports are especially concerned with the girls' family and economic backgrounds – almost all of them seem to be working class. Nichols is also concerned with the girls' sexual histories and the ways in which these are related to the girls' institutionalization. For instance, a fourteen-year-old Toronto girl was referred to the Children's Aid Society at the age of ten for accepting money from an older man for 'sexual interference' (which, the report makes clear, did not include intercourse). She was taken from her home for two years. While she was charged with theft a year after being returned to her parents, she wasn't sent to the OTS until two months after that incident, when her parents complained of 'her disobedience, truancy, late hours and male companions.' Another girl, a sixteen-year-old from Toronto, was warned by the Big Sisters 'not to be out on the streets at night. She continued to be out all night with men, at hotels, necessitating her commitment [to the OTS].' She was eventually allowed to leave on a work placement 'but continued her sexual activities, necessitating her return to O.T.S.' A fifteen-year-old girl from a small town near Guelph was sent to Guelph to work, 'where she had sex relations with numerous men, staying all night at hotels, and frequenting beer parlours. She was committed ...' In one particular report, we see the extent to which one girl understood adult concern about her sexuality to have been important to her incarceration. Nichols writes:

Her former mistakes she believes were:
1. Attending dances alone or with another girl.
2. Being picked up and allowing herself to be taken out during intermissions.
3. Allowing boys she didn't know to bring her home.[39]

These four examples are representative of Nichols's reports in general. Indeed they are representative of a whole variety of written sources for the fifteen-year period under study. Discussions about girl delinquents that do not mention sexuality are exceedingly rare. That female sexual transgression was criminalized was certainly a product of gender ideology, but it was also more than this. Girls who were labelled delinquent were not just violating the expectations that were attached to their gender, they were also threatening notions of the adolescent as not yet sexually mature, notions of sex as something to be experienced only by adults. Hence, the so-called immoral behaviours of delinquent girls left the girls' own claims on sexual 'normality' open to question. According to postwar experts, the development of sexual maturity was understood to be a fragile process for both boys and girls. Once off the path to a 'normal' heterosexual identity – a path that took different routes for boys and girls – one might be lost in abnormality forever. The importance of 'normalness' – itself a heavily gendered category – to postwar social organization and to the social organization of the latter twentieth-century 'self' made sexual transgression an issue with grave consequences.

In a 1959 research project, undertaken by a social-work student at the University of Toronto, the imperative of normalness was the guiding principle behind the research. This follow-up study of delinquent girls was based entirely on the heterosexual conduct they exhibited after being released from Warrendale, a residential 'treatment' centre in Newmarket. Most of the girls had been convicted of vague, behaviour-related misdemeanours like keeping 'late hours, questionable involvement with boys, truancy, disobedience and defiance.'[40] The conclusions of the study were generally positive:

Six girls [out of the twenty in the study] were married and most of the rest were dating regularly ... the nature and extent of dating seemed generally quite socially acceptable. With two exceptions the girls who were going steadily with one boy were those doing most of the dating. Both of the 'exceptions' were going out almost every night. This might indicate a kind of personal and hetero-sexual dissatisfaction and in these two cases it did seem to do so ... There have been two illegitimate pregnancies but both girls involved seemed to have faced the situation fairly realistically and to have matured from the total experience.[41]

Surprisingly, the passage gives quick treatment to the issue of unwed motherhood. In discussions of girls and delinquency, the spectre of the young, unwed mother was, at times, held up to demonstrate the fundamental gravity of the 'youth problem.'[42] The fear of girls' becoming pregnant was, in part, responsible for the longer sentences meted out to girls as compared to boys. If a girl could be kept under official surveillance until she was old enough to marry, the consequences of her sexual activity might be minimized.

Unlike a delinquent boy, the pregnant girl could never fully receive a second chance.[43] Her virginity, the sign of her compliance with social standards, was undeniably gone and couldn't be brought back. In some instances, marriage changed delinquent situations to respectable ones, a fact which suggests that the problem with teenage mothers wasn't their age or that they had engaged in sex as much as it was their having had sex outside of a legally sanctioned relationship. But so-called shotgun weddings weren't always proposed for the redemptive sake of the girl, or even of her child. Weddings were also proposed to redeem the standing of the bridegroom. In one case, a man charged with carnal knowledge of a fourteen-year-old girl produced a marriage certificate in court and his case was dropped.[44] In another instance, an eighteen-year-old youth spent three days in a Newmarket jail awaiting a hearing on a charge of having contributed to the delinquency of a pregnant fourteen-year-old girl. But, in an altruistic move that was widely reported in the press, a 'kind-hearted neighbour' put up a thousand dollars for the young man's bail and he was released to marry the girl.[45] After seeing them pictured in a Kitchener newspaper – smiling in dress-up clothes, admiring her ring – a family court judge from that city wrote to the provincial government complaining about the hasty and perhaps poorly thought out conclusion to the case. The deputy attorney general dismissed the judge's concerns about the brevity of teen marriages and the fate of their progeny, saying that 'the Marriage Act ... considers it more important that children should be born in wedlock than that the husband and wife should continue to live together.'[46] This legal ranking of illegitimacy above divorce and single parenthood, on the scale of social evils, suggests the severity of the climate faced by unwed mothers.

While there was considerable overlap between discourses about the girl delinquent and discourses about the unwed mum, these two categories were not synonymous. In the popular press, the unmarried, adolescent mother was as likely to be from a 'good' home and a good part of town as a 'bad' one. On the surface, at least, psychological theories were far more widely used than social ones to explain the causes of a middle-class girl's fall from grace. The most commonly cited theory was some version of: 'the birth of a child out of wedlock [is] a means of meeting unmet emotional and personality needs.'[47] By the mid-1950s, social-work students at the University of Toronto were referring frequently to

Leontine Young as the authority on this perspective.[48] Young argued against the position that the unmarried mother was a sex delinquent. Young women, she wrote, do not get pregnant by accident; the evidence on the subject 'points to the purposeful nature of the act.'[49] Though not a Freudian herself, Young's clinical work was taken up by Freudians as validation for psychoanalytic theories of female development.[50]

In psychologically informed discourses, the unmarried mother was less a marker for the moral and social disintegration of postwar society, or of youthful sexuality out of control, than she was a sign of female distress and emotional disturbance. In part, this had to do with the disproportionate attention paid to unwed mothers from 'good,' middle-class homes. As the products of postwar prosperity, their downfall was less easily attributed to the inevitable list of 'character weaknesses' that were applied to working-class girls. Far easier to attribute it to some kind of personal, psychological maladjustment. Indeed, Rickie Solinger, in her study of unwed motherhood in the United States, found that psychological explanations of pregnancy tended to be applied solely to white girls, who were almost without question assumed to be middle class. In contrast, the pregnancies of black girls, who were without question assumed to be working class and poor, were said to be the result of their lack of restraint and their tendency to engage in 'wanton breeding.' According to Solinger, the class and race positions of teenage mothers set the boundaries of the explanations applied to their situations.[51]

While in Canada psychological explanations of teen pregnancy were the most widely circulated, some experts did try to situate the problem in a changing social and cultural milieu. In 1957 and 1958, the Social Planning Council of Metro Toronto conducted research on five of the city's six maternity homes.[52] What they found was that while the number of 'illegitimate' births in Ontario had dropped since the war, from forty-eight per thousand to thirty-two per thousand in 1957, the mothers themselves were getting younger. Between 1936 and 1950, young women under twenty had accounted for 33 per cent of illegitimate births in the province. In 1957, that figure had increased to 40 per cent. Of the 585 mothers studied by the Social Planning Council, 45 per cent were under eighteen years of age. Ninety-nine per cent of them were white, and 32 per cent of them resided in Metro. Nineteen per cent came from other provinces.

Chatelaine picked up on the findings of the Social Planning Council's study, wanting to know who or what was to blame for the 'startling' statistics. Reporter Shirley Mair began her discussion by looking at the broad social factors that might have contributed to the increase in teenage pregnancies. Were 1950s teenagers too sheltered? Were parents denying their children guidance? Mair quoted an American expert who claimed that teenagers were too frequently unsupervised, their parents too lax. Major Mary Webb of the Salvation Army maternity home in Toronto was recruited to point the finger at modern social practices: going steady; mothers working outside the home; and the easy access teens had to cars and transportation. But after piecing together this list of what were becoming increasingly widespread, 'normal' activities, Mair cited a 1956 survey done by the Ontario Department of Public Welfare which claimed that 55 per cent of teenage mothers came from 'broken homes' or 'homes troubled by marital discord.'[53] Was a teen pregnancy a product of changing times or of a difficult family background (read: working-class or divorced parents) that had led to emotional instability? Were teenage mums just regular girls suffering the consequences of cultural change or were they special, tragic cases?

Obviously there was no single take on the issue of unwed motherhood among teenagers. But the pregnant girl served much less than other wayward teens as an example of social breakdown, as evidence of the 'youth problem,' in part because she was as likely to be from an affluent home as a poor one. Delinquents, generally, were working-class kids. While the pregnant teen was obviously a target of pronouncements about the so-called immoral behaviour of adolescents, she was rarely paraded publicly as evidence for this. This reticence may have stemmed from the extent and nature of her transgression – even to discuss her situation was to cross some boundary of social propriety. But it also has to do with the fact that the pregnancy of an unmarried girl moved that girl outside the bounds of 'youth.' A girl with a baby had crossed the line that marked adolescence as a time before the attainment of 'maturity.' Once pregnant, a girl could no longer be accommodated by popular discourses about adolescence.

It was, in part, this ability of pregnancy to pull a girl out of the youth category that led to understandings of unwed motherhood as an individual emotional problem. Delinquency was a social problem; pregnancy was a personal tragedy. Delinquent girls were seen as threatening, as having transgressed gender boundaries. They were wilful and assertive, more like boys. But pregnancy could put an end to that, rendering even the most independent girl more vulnerable, more feminine, easier to assimilate into the prevailing social order.

Girls and Gangs in Toronto

Much more likely to be offered up as an explicit example of the female delinquent was the 'gang girl.' How many such girls wandered the streets, it is impossible to know. Girls were not addressed by the majority of organized youth programs in the city. They were not mentioned in the numerous reports on gangs produced by both the public and private sector in the postwar period. In May 1949, a Miss Greene, of Central Neighbourhood House – a downtown social service agency – addressed a workshop about street gangs held by the Toronto Welfare Council. Apparently she described 'some of the peculiar problems which arise with regard to the girls in the gangs,'[54] but this reference is unique among the many that deal with the 'gang problem.'

Gangs (that is, groups of boys and young men, usually based on neighbourhood or ethnic associations) were the stereotypical image of urban, working-class delinquency at its most frightening (hence the response to the movie *The Wild Ones*). Any girl who would choose to share the company of boys who, by definition, were antisocial hoodlums, must herself have been deviant in some way. In a successfully prosecuted rape case, tried in Toronto in 1952, defence counsel explained to the judge their own particular definition of a 'gang girl':

Judge: What is a 'gang girl'? – so that I may understand it?
Defence counsel #1: A girl who has submitted to sexual intercourse ten times or
   more becomes a member of the gang. That is what a gang girl is known as.
Judge: Is that what you mean?
Defence counsel #1: At one sitting.
Defence counsel #2: A girl who takes part in multiple acts of intercourse and
   who will become a member of a gang and submit to acts of intercourse with
   other members of the gang without any palaver at all.[55]

If the defence lawyers could prove the witness was a gang girl, her credibility as a victim of gang rape would suffer. In this vein the defence lawyers were sure to point out that the witness had lived in Stanley Gardens for three years. This temporary housing project near the Canadian National Exhibition grounds had been set up to alleviate Toronto's severe postwar housing shortage. Services to the area were inadequate and living conditions were poor. Residents, not surprisingly, were mostly working class, the type of people whose children, defence counsel implied, would end up in gangs.

As they cross-examined the girl, the defence lawyers relied on the usual strategies to impugn her character: Did she wear make-up? Did she swear? How did she come to know sexual slang words? They also focused on the fact that her mother's father was 'Indian.' These were all efforts, deeply embedded in sexist and racist discourses, to construct the girl's character as an immoral one. But the team of five lawyers defending five young men needed to push beyond these fairly routine tactics. They needed to convince the judge that the sixteen-year-old witness consorted with gangs, 'that she has been accustomed to being in the company of a number of youths at one time.' As part of this strategy, they tried to present inadmissible evidence that the girl had allowed herself to be 'picked up' by seven boys at the corner of Queen Street and Woodbine Avenue and had accompanied them to Cherry Beach where sexual activity occurred.[56] Much time was spent discussing her clothes, her pants in particular, which she referred to as 'strides.' They were trying to establish that she consciously adopted a style of deviant, gang-related dress.

In the middle of the girl's testimony, one of the defence lawyers objected to the Crown's use of the word 'pants' to refer to the strides. 'Strides,' he said, 'are not slacks at all.' They were, apparently, a trouser-like thing, but with tapered ankles. The distinction was important.

Defence counsel #3: Now, these strides – what are they? Are they not sort of the girls' equivalent to the zoot-suiters pants?
Witness: I don't know what they are.
Defence counsel #3: You don't know what zoot-suiters pants are?
Witness: No, I don't.
Defence counsel #3: Never heard of that expression before?
Witness: I have heard of the boys being called zoot-suiters, but that is all ...

At this point the judge also confessed to ignorance on the subject.

Judge: Do you know why they are called zoot-suits?
Defence counsel #3: A suit that 'zoots,' my lord.
Defence counsel #4: Apparently they are suits for a certain group of people in Harlem where these zoot-suits first originated in New York ... [to the witness] Do you know this: Are the cuffs on the bottom of the men's trousers – what I called 'zoot-suit pants' – are they as narrow as those on the girls' pants that you called strides?
Witness: I don't know anything like that at all.[57]

As the lawyer said, zoot-suits were a style borrowed from black and Hispanic neighbourhoods of New York and Los Angeles. The jackets had broad shoulders, and the loose, 'draped' pants, known as strides, tapered down to very narrow cuffs. According to one American observer there was no singular category of zoot-suiter, in spite of newspaper reports to the contrary. Some wore the suits to mark their commitment to jitterbugging (a dance style that was frowned upon because of its suggestive movements). For others, the suits flagged their resistance to the mainstream; they were a sign of class and ethnic solidarity.[58] In both the States and Canada, zoot-suits were the symbolic opposite of service uniforms and tended to brand those who wore them as not only delinquent but as unpatriotic.[59]

Mariana Valverde has looked at press coverage of so-called zoot-suit gangs in Toronto papers in 1949.[60] Six years after zoot-suits were blamed for what were primarily race riots in Los Angeles and New York, Toronto officials began to treat youth in 'flashy clothes' as dangerous to the social order. Valverde cites a number of news stories where minor crimes and misdemeanours were transformed into serious infractions because of the clothes worn by the perpetrators. A number of these articles mentioned that girls were involved with the gangs, as active participants, as supportive bystanders, and as the provocateurs in intergang hostilities. Valverde says that no matter how young women participated in gangs, or to what extent, they were routinely painted as the bearers of a deviant femininity and as girls who were bound to engage in sexual misbehaviour.[61] Because of their assumed assertiveness and the fact that their actions were collective ones, gang girls were perceived as far more of a social threat than the isolated girls in maternity homes.

The local focus on the zoot-suit gang probably had more to do with media sensationalism than with the actual numbers of zoot-suiters in Toronto. Although public discussions of the 'gang problem' among less excitable commentators, such as social workers and youth leaders, frequently asserted the seriousness of the problem, zoot–suits were rarely mentioned. In 1949, the Welfare Council Youth Services subcommittee on gangs claimed the gang problem was bad and might get worse.[62] They guessed that there were nineteen or twenty 'identifiable gangs' of fifteen- to twenty-four-year-olds in the Toronto area, with a total of about 2500 members. While subcommittee members claimed that most of these young people were unemployed, with no more than grade 8 education, they also made a point, unlike the media, of saying that they didn't necessarily come from 'low-economic homes.' Rather, gang youth came from homes 'in which there is some difficulty.' There was no mention, alongside this attempt to decentre class, of whether race or ethnicity was important in these groups, or whether they were made up of boys or girls.

In their work on girls and 'youth sub-cultures' in Britain, Angela McRobbie and Jenny Garber suggest that girls were far less likely than boys to join gangs because they were kept closer to home by their families. In part, girls were (and are) kept under tight rein because they tended to have more household responsibilities than their brothers. Moreover, parents were concerned about the sexual opportunities (pleasurable and coercive) of the outside world and about protecting their daughters' virginity. In general, girls were less likely than boys to 'hang around' in public places.[63] British oral historian Steve Humphries writes that girls who did get involved with gangs were looking for excitement that couldn't be found with their families.[64] Gang boys had access to money and provided girls with entertainment; they were snappy dressers and protected girls from harassment by other men. Boys, says Humphries, claimed girls as status symbols and markers of their virility.[65]

Solving the Youth Problem: Recreation as Moral and Sexual Regulation

One cannot overestimate the magnitude of the response to the issue of juvenile delinquency in the postwar period. Apart from frequent coverage in Toronto's three daily newspapers, delinquency was the subject of feature stories in magazines, of educational films, and of mass-market fiction.[66] Certainly, the popularity of delinquency as a compelling social issue waxed and waned between the end of the war and 1960, but it was never absent. And as a discursive construct, delinquency produced a multitude of organizational practices and relationships.

Concepts of delinquency organized the work of the Juvenile Court. They informed the activities of the city Parks Department, and of the Toronto Recreation Council's Sub-committee on Recreation and Housing. The Committee on Public Welfare set up a Special Committee on Juvenile Delinquency in 1944, and the same year it set aside $1000 to do a survey of delinquency across the city. In March 1945, the Committee on Public Welfare organized a meeting of more than 100 social agencies to talk about setting up a coordinated civic body to deal with the issue. In 1949, the Welfare Council held a two-day institute on 'Community Planning for Dealing with Gangs' that was attended and reported on by various municipal employees. A Mayor's Committee on Juvenile Delinquency presented a report to City Council in January of 1950. The 1954 provincial Select Committee on Reform Institutions entertained briefs from Toronto officials when it looked at juvenile delinquency. The Ontario attorney general set up a survey on gangs across the province in November 1958. The federal minister of justice established a Committee on Juvenile Delinquency in 1962.

Such state initiatives, of which this is but a partial list, received considerable extra-state support. Ideas, money, personnel, and resources moved back and forth among various departments of the local government and voluntary organizations. Private citizens wrote to the mayor offering their services to fight the youth problem. Organizations like the Board of Trade, the Toronto Home and School Council, the Woman's Christian Temperance Union, and the Women's Law Association actively studied the issue and sent briefs and letters of advice and encouragement to municipal politicians and bureaucrats. The Toronto Welfare Council (later the Social Planning Council) provided city departments with the results of its research, as did the Big Brothers. The United Welfare Chest established a Youth Services Department with the involvement of some forty-nine social service organizations and several city officials. From this list we get a sense of the magnitude and diversity of the concern generated by discourses about delinquency. The voices of the 'concerned' were not isolated; rather they represented a broad range of middle-class social comment.

While there was no single approach to delinquency in Toronto in the 1940s and 1950s, there were some strategies which were more popular than others. Many thought that the provision of wholesome recreational opportunities was critical in the struggle to keep youth – mostly boys – off the streets and out of trouble. Supervised activities would keep young people under the watchful eye of a responsible and respectable adult. And, if they were busy they wouldn't have to resort to questionable means of dissipating all that youthful energy, sexual or otherwise. Calls for recreational facilities and services as a means to curb delinquency and to sublimate adolescent sexuality were not unique to the postwar era. Even G.S. Hall, a staunch proponent of adolescent freedom, drew the line at free expression of sexuality, worrying about the consequences it might entail. Hall recommended that young people channel their sexual energies into a variety of strenuous activities, from dancing to sports: 'Activity may exalt the spirit almost to the point of ecstasy, and the physical pleasure of it diffuse, irradiate, and mitigate the sexual stress just at the age when its premature localization is most deleterious. Just enough at the proper time and rate contributes to permanent elasticity of mood and disposition, gives moral self-control, rouses a love of freedom with all that that great word means, and favors all higher human aspiration.'[67]

Carolyn Strange notes that similar strategies were proposed to control delinquency during the First World War: 'the TLCW [Toronto Local Council of Women], the Toronto Playground Association and the civic administration were already convinced that regulated pleasure was a moral prophylactic against crime and immorality.'[68] Post–Second World War social workers and civic bureaucrats wouldn't have used such language, though their approach to the problem was similar. Recreational activities were thought to be both preventive and corrective. In organized youth groups, those who were already delinquent could be shown options and alternatives to their previous behaviours. Those who had not yet been accused of delinquency would be kept busy. Both categories of youth would be supervised by youth workers. As prominent Toronto psychologist W.E. Blatz, director of the Institute for Child Study at the University of Toronto, wrote in an article in *Maclean's*, 'There should be many more teen-age clubs where boys and girls can mingle and make adjustments which will be enormously important to them in later adult life; where they can sublimate their sex appetite into directions which will aid them to maintain the ideals of chastity and faithfulness which our social culture considers to be essential.'[69]

The difference between this position and Hall's was Blatz's concern not simply with sublimation but with the construction of well-adjusted adults. Blatz – whose well-known theories on child development had been worked out on the Dionne quintuplets as well as on the upper-middle-class children who attended St George's nursery school in downtown Toronto[70] – was mainly concerned with 'normal,' non-delinquent children and their parents who were worried about the consequences of teenage obsessions with idols like Frank Sinatra. Civic officials and social workers, on the other hand, worried about the unsublimated 'impulses' of working-class youth and how these impulses might manifest themselves in less innocuous forms than idol worship. For the most part, recreation organized through groups like the Big Brothers and the Boys' Brigade, or through community centres, was directed at working-class boys. It usually involved some kind of sports and was seen as a way of constructively channelling what might otherwise have been destructive adolescent energies.

As late as 1958, the Social Planning Council of Metropolitan Toronto acknowledged that girls were largely underserved by youth service organizations.[71] Obviously, little had changed since a 1943 study by the YWCA found that the needs of working-class girls in the Dovercourt-Lansdowne area were poorly served by both voluntary organizations and the city.[72] That study found that girls' parents wouldn't let them go to local parks because they were full of boys and were thought to be 'too tough.' The girls interviewed for the study said they liked skating at city rinks, but the times available for girls were limited. They said that groups like the Girl Guides were 'dull and tedious,' and that they were out-of-date and too 'young' for teenagers. When asked what they wanted, they suggested sports and dancing. They also wanted clubs where they could discuss boys and dating. And, mostly, they wanted to be involved in mixed (girls and boys together) social groups, the kinds of organizations that served teens in middle-class neighbourhoods. In the mid-1940s, 'teen canteens' and 'teen clubs' opened in collegiates and community halls to entertain high school kids on Friday and Saturday nights. While some were initiated by students themselves, others were organized by 'concerned parents.'

In various ethnic and racial communities, these teen social clubs took on meanings steeped in the inequities of the dominant culture. *Crestwood Heights* notes, for instance, the existence of Jewish youth groups in Forest Hill.[73] The study notes instances of discrimination faced by Jewish young people at school and the types of anti-Semitism expressed in the community at large. In the face of exclusionary practices in their high school, Jewish teens organized their own fraternities and sororities (although their parents were not always in favour of such moves).[74] The children of Italian immigrants also developed their own courtship structures within the bounds of their communities. Franca Iacovetta writes that religious festa and other family-centred celebrations provided opportunities – 'closely supervised by relatives' – for young men and women to meet and socialize in a familiar environment.[75] Similarly, a prominent member of Toronto's black community told members of the Social Planning Council that he had been organizing parties and small dances in his home for black teenagers.[76] A report from the Social Planning Council concluded that 'the problem[s] of Negro teen-agers and young adults in the area of social relationships were serious, and were not being adequately faced. As the Negro boy or girl approaches a marriageable age, contacts with whites become more restricted and they become more dependent on opportunities for establishing social relationships with members of their own race.'[77]

Of course, middle-class white gentiles were also organizing race-, religion-, and class-specific groups, although they didn't identify them as such. In 1945, *Chatelaine* ran an article on how to set up a teen canteen.[78] Admission might be 25 cents; separate rooms might accommodate congenial chatting, ping-pong, listening to records, and dancing; food might be served at cost. Chaperonage was to be minimal, or 'imperceptible,' as the *Telegram* put it. According to Mrs E.C. Trevor, organizer of one such Toronto club, 'I know from my own experience that these boys and girls don't want to be chaperoned by their parents. They want to play at being grown-up and to feel that nobody's bossing them.'[79] They wanted – and were given – a chance to express their (hetero)sexualities in coed groups. The approach was directly opposite to that most frequently taken by middle-class adults to children from poor families. Middle-class young people had regular, sanctioned opportunities to practise their heterosexual skills, to mingle with the opposite sex. They were provided with supervised activities where expressions of heterosexuality were not only permitted, they were expected and, indeed, hoped for. At mixed social clubs, chaperoned dances, and parties, adults and teens together constructed 'a wholesome setting for the boy-crazy girl or the girl-crazy boy.'[80] Middle-class sexual energies were perhaps perceived as less likely than working-class ones to erupt in an antisocial manner.

Solving the Youth Problem: Regulating Teens' Access to Urban Space

There were those who thought the emphasis on recreation was just one of many ways that modern teenagers were being molly-coddled by their elders. As W.R. Cockburn, chair of the Toronto Board of Education said in 1946, too much energy had been put into 'play' as a means of solving the delinquency problem.[81] But recreational efforts had never stood alone. Other less subtle forms of regulating teenage morality were always operating in the ongoing effort to conquer the youth problem.

What Cockburn seems to have missed is that 'play' was just one of the effects of recreation programs. Organized activities were also, perhaps primarily, designed to foster surveillance of youth by adults. For both boys and girls, a 'tendency toward delinquency' could mean little more than a tendency to hang out in unsupervised places. Street corners and any number of 'disreputable' commercial establishments were thought to lead boys and girls astray, the boys into gangs, the girls into immoral-ity.[82] A 1946 editorial in the *Globe and Mail* discussed efforts by the Police Commission to study poolrooms 'and other such places where youth congregate ... Indeed, there are some who feel that the pool rooms, as well as some hamburger restaurants, are a menace and should be closed altogether.'[83] In a surprising display of social awareness, the *Globe and Mail* countered these suggestions by inverting the relationship they constructed between the social and the environmental: 'Like dance halls, beverage rooms and some other places where people meet for entertainment, the conditions under which the places are run are the important factors.'

In recognizing that 'places' themselves were inherently neither 'good' nor 'bad,' the *Globe and Mail* cut short discussions of simple, blanket solutions for the various 'youth problems' that came under the headings of delinquency and immorality. More typical were arguments that a particular spot would inevitably lead to immorality and, hence, needed to be shut down. For instance, in 1945, a member of the Ontario Training School Advisory Committee wrote to the attorney general complaining about the Silver Slipper Roadhouse, also known as the Kingsway, in Swansea:

If you were to go down ... any Sunday night between 7 and 8 o'clock, you would see a long queue, four wide, largely of teen-age youngsters waiting to get into this roadhouse. Our information is that they sit around and drink 'coke' and what have you, until 12.01 A.M. when the dance starts.

It is quite obvious that the habit of these teenage young people, spending Sunday evening this way and not getting home until the wee small hours of the morning, is having a very detrimental effect not only on their health but on their future, and we feel that it would be advisable for your Department to investigate and see if something can be done to stop this, as juvenile delinquency is becoming a terrific problem and this place is only a feeder to further delinquency.

... in the opinion of the writer this dance hall (and I assume there are others like it) is doing more harm to the young people of the city than any gambling place ...[84]

In 1946, a writer for the Toronto tabloid *Justice Weekly* made similar connections between dance halls and problem youth in a story that read like something written in the early part of the century:

While Grand Juries, temperance cranks, jurists and social welfare folks are blaming beverage parlours, both men's and women's, as being responsible for much of the crime, immorality and drunkenness so prevalent these days, overlooked are the dance halls where just as much, if not more crime, immorality and drunkenness get their start. In most of these dance spots, no attention is paid to the ages of the patrons, many of whom come stag and 'pick up' members of the opposite sex for dancing purposes, and then, in many cases, almost anything can happen and does happen.[85]

This focus on dance halls emphasizes their primary difference from other 'bad' places (for instance, poolrooms and hamburger joints): dance halls catered to, indeed they depended on, the patronage of young women as well as that of young men. As places where young people of both sexes would gather, dance halls had the potential to foster not simply delinquency, but sexual immorality and sex delinquency. Surprisingly, dancing, in a general sense, was seen as a wholesome activity. School board trustees, ministers, and youth group leaders all encouraged dancing, as long as it was supervised, say in a high school gym or church basement.[86] In unsupervised dance halls, dancing could be dangerous and lead to who knows what forms of vice, as the tabloid writer suggested. But for teenagers who were working, who no longer had access to Friday-night dances at the high school gym, dance halls were an obvious source of entertainment. Public lament about dance-hall dangers were as much about the places themselves and what they stood for as they were about the people who frequented them.

In 1944, concerns about youth, where they congregated, and what they did in those places inspired City Council to propose a nightly curfew. Council made an official request to the police and the Juvenile Court to enforce the provisions of a seldom-used provincial statute, the Children's Protection Act. The act banned anyone under sixteen 'from places of entertainment after 9 pm, unless accompanied by his [sic] parent or guardian ...'[87] The idea behind the curfew was to keep young people off the streets (where they were outside of adult control) and out of commercial places of entertainment, like movie houses or dance spots, which might incite them to illicit activities.[88]

While council voted in favour of the idea, parents reacted negatively. The response of community groups was not quite so clear. Although participants at a conference of service organizations felt that a curfew was not necessary, 'at the same time, the conference recommended "wholesome and discretionary enforcement of the Children's Protection Act" to prevent children loitering on street corners, in refreshment

places and around places of entertainment after 9 p.m.'[89] The confer-
ence-goers were alluding to the worrisome beverage rooms, dance halls,
and hamburger 'joints' – all places most likely to be frequented by working-class youth, all places where sexual temptation was thought to exist.
As two fifteen-year-olds wrote to the *Toronto Daily Star*: 'Why don't they
clean out all the cheap dance halls where not only 'teen-age youngsters
but also the older crowd go. These dance halls represent one reason for
making the curfew and causing all this disturbance. We 'teen-agers go to
school five days a week and have two hours' homework each day. We
visit the library once a week and when the week-end comes we like to go
out for some good clean entertainment, such as movies, bowling, roller
skating, concerts or even school affairs.'[90] The writers did not need to
add that high school kids, in the 1940s, were mostly middle-class kids,
and that common-sense notions about 'middle classness' meant that
they were assumed to be self-regulating, that is, capable of staying out of
serious trouble. They were not the ones for whom the curfew was
intended.

Nothing ever really came of the curfew. The police enforced it for a
short while, but then they eased off. Calls for curfews in later years were
equally unsuccessful. But there remained other, less dramatic, more easily implemented strategies for regulating the use of, and access to, public
space in the fight against the immorality of youth. For instance, the
school board refused to permit mixed (boys and girls) swimming in the
pools under its jurisdiction,[91] and the city refused to turn on the lights at
public skating rinks on Sundays. As Frank Tumpane wrote in his column in the *Globe*, 'the principal argument [about the rinks] seems to be
that in some manner "moral standards" would be lowered.'[92] Amuse-
ment parks and resort areas were also subjected to Sunday closing laws.
Some people suggested that Sunday closing regulations, enacted to protect Christian 'moral standards,' were in fact encouraging delinquency.
Without proper recreation, kids would become idle, and that's when
they would end up in trouble. At one point in 1946, the City Recreation
Department brought together a group of young people to brainstorm
about the types of things teenagers might actually be permitted to do on
a Sunday.[93]

Like the curfew, Sunday closings were more likely to affect working-
class than middle-class youth. On Sundays, middle-class youth did not
need to rely on downtown commercial amusements; they could spend
the day in comfortable homes or in the neighbourhood parks that grew
increasingly spacious the farther they were from the city centre and

working-class neighbourhoods. It is also important to remember that in the 1940s, Sunday was the only day off in a six-day work week; and on that day teenage wage-earners were prevented access to the amusements that high school students without jobs were free to enjoy on Saturday. The point here is not that middle-class teenagers were not subject to moral regulation, but that they were thought to be adequately regulated in much of the recreation they pursued – in the family backyard, at piano lessons, at summer camp, at the homes of classmates, in extracurricular activities at school. Perhaps more important, they were also perceived to be more capable of regulating themselves (of having internalized social values), while working-class young people needed external controls.

The moral regulation of young people who worked did not just encompass their off hours. The Factory Act prohibited children under fourteen from working in certain types of places, while fourteen- to sixteen-year-olds could work only at the restricted places before 6:30 p.m. In 1944, the acting deputy minister of public welfare wrote to the minister to inform him that moves were afoot to strengthen the restrictions: 'I am advised by the Department of Labour that restaurants are listed as one of the places in which employment is so precluded or limited. Bowling alleys, theatres, and bingo halls, do not fall within the excluded places. I am further advised by the Department of Labour that there is presently under consideration an amendment to the Factory Act which will enable that Department to control the employment of children in any places not presently listed.'[94] In 1944, Bill 64 amended the Factory, Shop and Office Building Act, extending the definition of shop to include bowling alleys, poolrooms, and billiard parlours.

Curfew proposals, labour legislation, and Sunday closings were the most obvious efforts to regulate the use young people (and others) made of unsupervised public space. But these were supported by more subtle means of control, like 'morality lights.' Apart from their peculiar name, there was nothing special about these spotlights, which were affixed to school buildings and mounted in some parks. Although the lights were probably most useful in protecting properties from vandalism, this was not always the main motivation for their installation. In 1947, school board chair Isabel Ross claimed that 'Evening patrolmen are no substitute for "morality lights" in preventing school yards from becoming lovers' lanes.'[95] At a cost of $900 per school per year, the decision to mount the lights was not made lightly. In 1950, Parent–Teacher Associations at Jarvis and Humberside collegiates requested lights because 'darkness' on school grounds was 'conducive to immorality.' Opponents of the lights claimed 'that what goes on in the shadows of school grounds at night is certainly not educational and therefore public school supporters should not be required to pay for guarding the morals of the public at large.' But Mrs Ross, who by this time had finished her term as chair, represented majority opinion by reminding the dissenters that, 'I am my brother's keeper.'[96] The lights went up.

It's in the various proposals for solving the delinquency problem that we see most clearly the way notions of adolescence as a sexual category came to define delinquency in a similar light. That both boys and girls were subjected to forms of sexual regulation, as part of delinquency prevention, suggests that an analysis of gender alone is not enough to explain the sexualization of the category. Discourses about youth, class, race, and ethnicity all contributed to this process as well.

The relationship between discourses about sexuality and discourses about adolescence helped to establish the boundaries between what was seen as delinquent in the postwar period and what was not, what was 'normal,' approved sexuality for young people and what was not. The fear of being labelled delinquent was an effective form of self-regulation, a threat to those who might transgress sexual or moral standards. Discursively, delinquency worked to control expressions of sexuality and to justify the sexual regulation of all young people, not just those who were labelled as delinquents themselves.

5

'Why Can't I Be Normal?': Sex Advice for Teens

In the years after the Second World War, 'normality' was a primary marker of difference between individuals and between groups of people. As defined by increasingly popular psychological and psychoanalytic theories, normality was the desired result of an individual's emotional and psychic evolution, a product of social and environmental factors.[1] Such had not been the case as recently as the 1920s when normality and abnormality were seen, primarily, as bodily and not psychic conditions.[2] While biological explanations have never been completely overturned, the relationship between biological and psychological theories has undergone substantial transformation over the course of this century.

A few years ago, I stumbled upon a 1951 paperback edition of Radclyffe Hall's lesbian novel, *The Well of Loneliness*, first published in 1928. The front cover of the paperback has the usual 1950s lesbian pulp imagery: two white women; one blond, one brunette; one staring directly at the viewer, the other, in profile, looking away. And while the front cover, promising 'the strange love story of a girl who stood midway between the sexes,'[3] shows indisputable signs of 1950s mass-market publishing, it's the back cover that most clearly defines the distance between the novel's original 1928 edition and its reissue twenty-three years later. Turning the book over, one reads, in an anguished blue type, 'Why can't I be normal?' It's an anachronistic question that would have held little meaning for Stephen Gordon, female invert and heroine of Hall's novel. In the 1920s, Stephen Gordon's inversion was not portrayed as a case of arrested development nor as the result of inadequate parenting. As Hall wrote of it, inversion was congenital, and born inverts, like Stephen, spent little time wondering about cures or routes to normality – in her day, you were either normal or you weren't. Normality was a state of being, not a psychological and developmental triumph. Consequently, Stephen was much less interested in changing herself than in changing the level of social tolerance for inversion in general.[4]

The increasing influence of psychology in the post-Second World War era meant that, by the 1950s, Stephen's take-me-as-I-am attitude would have been seen as a failure in her character. A teenager following her example would have been seen as unrealistic at best or, more likely, as immature or lazy. For post-Second World War teens and those who advised them, adolescence was a time of learning about and being measured by prevailing social standards. As adults in process, adolescents were in training for a 'maturity,' which was equated with nothing if not normality.[5] Failing to measure up, for any number of reasons, could have significant consequences.

What counted as normal and what did not were both discursively organized categories, articulated by and to a variety of institutions and practices. Science, the school, the family, medicine, and the field of mental health all contributed in significant ways to the production and circulation of the various discourses about normality that were available in mainstream, popular culture. While 'normal' was a term used to assess many aspects of postwar life, from cleaning habits to parenting styles, it was more often than not brought to bear on matters of sexuality and gender, perhaps because these, especially, were assumed to be fragile. They were understood to be the culmination of a delicate process of emotional development, one that might easily be corrupted – a perspective rooted in the increasing popularity of Freudian ideas. Sexuality, more than almost anything else, was understood as having the potential for abnormality in its expression.

Of course, concerns about sexuality were not unique to the postwar era. In western cultures, the hierarchical opposition between appropriate and inappropriate sexualities has proved, historically, to be a common means of organizing the distribution of power. Those on the sanctioned side of the opposition – the normal, in the postwar case – benefit from the privileges of inclusion in the social order. Those on the undesirable side experience marginalization and exclusion. But as deconstructionists will tell us, the separation between the terms of any binary opposition is not complete. To some extent, the definition of each is located within the other. The one is what the other is not. The terms themselves are relative, making sense to us only as a dyad. If there was no abnormality, the concept of normality would not make sense. Nor would there be such a fuss about continually shoring it up.

With the widespread circulation of some aspects of Freudian theory, the line between normal and abnormal grew less distinct, and so more threatening. Freudian suggestions that even the most 'natural' and 'normal' sexual instincts were open to perversion meant that sexual development came to be perceived as a process of potential peril. With the wrong influences, anyone's sexuality could veer hazardously towards abnormality. Kinsey, claimed nervous commentators, had made that abundantly clear.

With the publication of his reports on male (1948) and female (1953) sexual behaviour, Alfred Kinsey and his team of researchers had shaken North Americans with carefully documented evidence of widespread variation in sexual practices.[6] As Eleanor Rumming wrote in *Saturday Night*, Kinsey's book called into question popularly accepted bounds of normality. 'Normality,' she concluded, 'is what most people do. Dr. Kinsey's book on the Human Male showed that what most people do is far more varied than public morality is prepared to admit.'[7] Rumming's definition of normality, based on statistical evidence and a liberal ethic, was not shared by everyone who wrote on Kinsey's work. And while Kinsey's own perspective was, in some senses, a liberal one, he didn't necessarily share Rumming's point of view.

Kinsey tried not to speak of either normality or abnormality, terms that he said had no place in a scientific vocabulary.[8] Instead Kinsey talked about biological possibilities and variations in human behaviour: 'Whatever the moral interpretation, there is no scientific reason for considering particular types of sexual activity as intrinsically, in their biologic origins, normal or abnormal ... Present-day legal determinations of sexual acts which are acceptable, or 'natural,' and those which are 'contrary to nature' are not based on data obtained from biologists, nor from nature herself.'[9]

It was 'nature' that provided the single most important yardstick in Kinsey's work. He evaluated human behaviour not in terms of normality, which he considered to be a subjective quality, but in terms of its correspondence to the behaviour of other mammals. 'Interpretations of human behavior would benefit,' he said, 'if there were a more general understanding of basic mammalian behavior.'[10] In this particular case, Kinsey was talking about the amount of time it takes for human males to ejaculate, the point being the unfairness of labelling men who ejaculate quickly as somehow sexually deficient. Chimpanzees, he said, can effect ejaculation in less than twenty seconds: 'It would be difficult to find another situation in which an individual who was quick and intense in his responses was labelled anything but superior.' While the word 'normal' was not used, it seems Kinsey did have an 'ideal' in mind. From this ideal there may be deviations – a markedly different concept from abnormality – but the ideal itself is the way 'nature' intended things to be.

Kinsey's frequent references to the animal kingdom contributed to his understanding of his own work as free from the social and moral biases that he found so distasteful in other studies of sexuality. He presented his project as science, plain and simple. And while he made many derisive comments about contemporary moral standards, he disdainfully claimed these were outside the scope of his study. In the end, it was Kinsey's attempt, successful or not, to divorce his discussion of sexual behaviour from both morality and value-laden concepts like normality that gave his work its tremendous impact on the whole system of sexual meanings.

Not surprisingly, Kinsey's rejection of a moral line of argument provided plenty of fodder for reviewers of all persuasions. Some, like Eleanor Rumming, translated the reports' findings into a call for the realignment of moral standards to reflect people's actual experiences.[11] Others worked feverishly to insert Kinsey into the very discourses he'd tried to decentre, asking, for instance, what the sex studies meant in terms of working definitions of normality. A piece in *Saturday Night* cited Yale psychiatrist Robert P. Knight, who used Kinsey to argue his own position that normality was definitely not a question of biological possibility. It was, instead, a product of well-kept moral standards: 'The common cold, says Dr. Knight, has about the same incidence as homosexuality (that 37 per cent of all U.S. males have some homosexual experience) in the Kinsey figures. But the prevalence of colds, says Knight, does not make them normal.'[12] That Kinsey had distinguished between medical normality (lack of any type of harmful or injurious physical condition) and sexual normality (a non-scientific, moral standard), was a point lost on Knight.[13] In Knight's construction, there was a very fine line between normal and moral, a semantic turn that would become perhaps too familiar to the teenagers who negotiated the sexual terrain of the post-Kinsey years.

Advice for Teens

In popular magazines and in prescriptive literature and films, young people were offered tools and strategies to use in the construction of themselves as normal sexual beings. They were offered the promise of normality – a position on the inside of the social body – in exchange for conformity to rules and standards of behaviour that, in many cases, had implications beyond the sexual realm. Normal was about being middle class, normal was about whiteness and not being 'ethnic,' normal was about proper expressions of gender.

As we have seen, North American postwar sexual discourses were a conduit for fears and apprehensions about changes in the global balance of power, about the changing shape of the family, about the effects of the new prosperity. In this chapter, I argue that the symbolic positioning of teenagers as 'the future,' as those who would carry the 1950s forward, made them a likely target of interventions meant to maximize normality and therefore maximize stability and social order against the uncertainties of modern life. Sex, as the basis of family life – that 'psychological fortress ... [that] might ward off hazards of the age'[14] – was too important to be left to nature or circumstance. In their attempts to 'shape' teenagers, adults tried to assuage their own insecurities.

Attempts to shape teenagers into proper adults were certainly not unique to the post-Second World War era. What is significant, however, is the way postwar efforts focused on sexuality as a requirement for the production of marriageable adults. In the 1940s and 1950s, adolescents were assumed by many to need sexual guidance before assuming their 'inevitable' marital roles. Around the turn of the century, by contrast, one prepared for marriage by learning gender-specific domestic and economic skills. Certainly, as Karen Dubinsky has pointed out, adolescents in earlier decades were warned about the dangers of sexual transgression,[15] but these warnings were not necessarily part of broader 'positive' and productive attempts to regulate the development of 'normal' sexual individuals. The latter did not begin until the 1920s and 1930s, when sexuality was increasingly being portrayed, via medical and popular instructional discourses, as important to heterosexual marriages.[16] The 'new' companionate marriages of the post-First World War era were to be held together by friendship and the sexual satisfaction of both husband and wife. Promoters of this 'new' form of heterosexual partnership advocated education about sex for those on the verge of marriage, warning of the danger to marriage of sexual 'deviations.' By the postwar years, companionate marriage was no longer new or unusual. Still, it was assumed that young people, at ever-decreasing ages, needed to be prepared for it. The growing prominence of psychological notions about the fragility of the process of attaining sexual maturity meant that one could rarely be too careful or too concerned about the brides and grooms of the future.

Sex advice for teens appeared in inexpensive pocketbooks, in pamphlets, in magazine articles, and in educational films on love, dating, and sex.[17] There are limits to using this type of prescriptive material for research purposes. Certainly it was not used by all young people, and it is difficult to determine who, in fact, did engage with it. One might also raise questions about the extent to which different groups of young people supported the ideas contained in the books, articles, and films, about the distance between 'advice' and 'reality.' But the possibility that young people did not subscribe to the information about sexuality and sexual behaviour they received from adults does not negate the role of that 'advice' in constructing the normative standards by which teens were judged. Lesbian and gay literature is full of examples of individuals who have 'acted' against normative standards while at the same time suffering emotionally because of them. Martin Duberman makes this point splendidly in his book *Cures*, where he describes the disjunctures he felt while visiting a psychiatrist by day – whose goal was to cure his homosexuality – and gay liberation meetings at night.[18] Discursive constructions of good teenagers and bad teenagers, of healthy sexuality and immoral sexuality, may not have been the immediate determinants of teen behaviour, but they did influence the context of that behaviour and the meanings that would eventually be ascribed to it.

There was no explicitly Canadian popular discourse of teen advice. Canadians, expert and lay person alike, borrowed heavily from American work in this area. Canadian magazines published American authors and suggested the titles of American books to their readers. There was very little difference between what appeared in *Chatelaine*, for instance, and what was published in U.S. pocketbooks. Marion Hilliard, who to my knowledge was the only Canadian to have published sex advice books in this period, used British and American publishers.

Magazine advice columns and features directed at teens – primarily girls – were generally related to the etiquette of dating. They discussed the ways a young woman might go about attracting a young man, or, if she had one, how to keep him. Books covered a broader range of material and tended to address a mixed audience. Most spent some time on the physical basics of sex education – the workings of genitals and reproductive organs, where babies come from, personal hygiene. This information was generally contextualized by lengthy discussions on the 'joys'

It was widely assumed that, without proper supervision, children and youth would inevitably run into trouble. These boys have had their ball confiscated by a neighbour on King Edward Avenue in Toronto (28 May 1946).

The combination of boys and alley-ways was especially suspect. This alley is located near Woodgreen Community Centre in Toronto (31 May 1946).

Boys outside a luncheonette. Still from the film *The Meaning of Adolescence*.

Organized, supervised activities were thought to keep young people out of trouble. Sports were particularly prized as a means of channelling excess energies, sexual or otherwise, in socially desirable directions. Playground at Norway School, Toronto (20 May 1946).

Toronto high school students performing in a physical-education display called Gym Window held at Maple Leaf Gardens, 1952.

Dance halls, 'hamburger restaurants,' and other unchaperoned and 'disreputable' commercial establishments were thought to provide the type of unsavoury moral climate that would lead to sexual delinquency. Social critics argued for the closure of such meeting places and for curfews for youth under the age of sixteen. Still from the film *The Meaning of Adolescence*.

With proper adult supervision, school dances were said to provide an excellent opportunity for girls and boys to practise their heterosexual skills. Sock hop at Glebe Collegiate, Ottawa (3 March 1954).

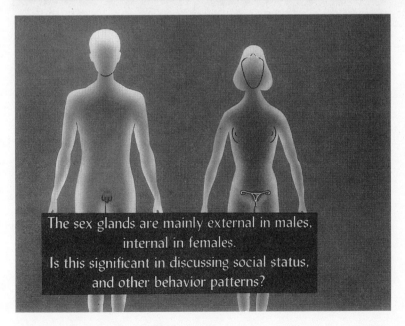

Growth of hair in different areas of the body,
voice change, and various other body changes
are among the secondary sex characteristics.

The sex glands are mainly external in males,
internal in females.
Is this significant in discussing social status,
and other behavior patterns?

Diagrams from the film *Physical Aspects of Puberty.*

Learning about menstruation. Still from the film *Physical Aspects of Puberty.*

NORMAL GROWTH
CHART

9 MONTHS   2 YEARS   5 YEARS   10 YEARS   15 YEARS

When applied to the physical and emotional changes of puberty, concepts of normality operated as a standard against which young people were judged, by others as well as themselves. The space between normality and its abnormal opposite was a powerful regulator of postwar life. Still from the film *The Meaning of Adolescence*.

Advice literature (*left, below, and opposite*) attempted to offer young people tools and strategies to use in constructing themselves as normal beings.

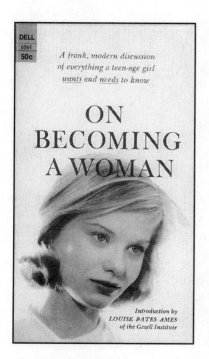

DELL
6564
50c

*A frank, modern discussion
of everything a teen-age girl
wants and needs to know*

ON
BECOMING
A WOMAN

*Introduction by
LOUISE BATES AMES
of the Gesell Institute*

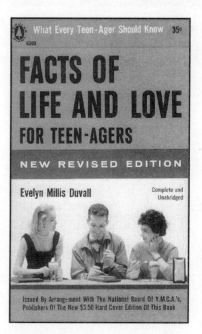

What Every Teen-Ager Should Know   35¢

6203

FACTS OF
LIFE AND LOVE
FOR TEEN-AGERS

NEW REVISED EDITION

Evelyn Millis Duvall   Complete and
Unabridged

Issued By Arrangement With The National Board Of Y.M.C.A.'s,
Publishers Of The New $3.50 Hard Cover Edition Of This Book

'As the time for Mary's first menstrual period approached, her mother explained about the changes that would take place, instead of leaving her [Mary] to pick up startling and inaccurate information from her schoolmates.' Quotation and still from the film *Social-Sex Attitudes in Adolescence*.

'About this time, Mary developed a strong sudden friendship with Lucille Williams. It seemed that Mary could talk better with Lucille than anyone else. They had no secrets from each other; they were inseparable. To Mary's mother it seemed unnatural, this continual intimacy, this concentration of affection on one not very unusual girl.' Quotation and still from the film *Social-Sex Attitudes in Adolescence*.

'But after a few weeks [of going out together], both knew it was different. Petting wasn't just a form of entertainment or an experiment. It was a real affection and mutual respect.' Quotation and still from the film *Social-Sex Attitudes in Adolescence*.

Not only did good posture represent good character, it was also said to benefit the health of a girl's reproductive organs. These girls are the winners and runners-up of the posture contest at the High School of Commerce in Ottawa (18 November 1954).

Although adult detractors called the music of Elvis Presley disgusting, immoral, and a catalyst for delinquency, eight thousand fans showed up at a 1957 concert in Ottawa to see him perform. An Ottawa convent school expelled eight students for having attended the concert.

Giving children an image of American womanhood.

An invitation to learning.

These comic book images and their captions (*above and opposite*) were used in Fredric Wertham's book, *Seduction of the Innocent*, to demonstrate the adverse influence of comic books on the normal sexual and moral development of children.

In ordinary comic books,
there are pictures within
pictures for children who
know how to look.

Children call these "headlights" comics.

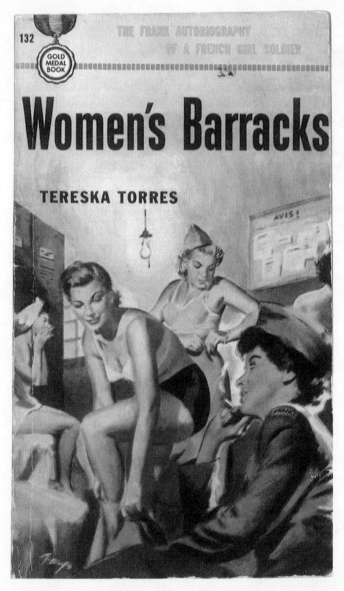

Women's Barracks

TERESKA TORRES

A single scene of lesbian seduction in this pulp novel generated two days of discussion in an Ottawa courtroom in 1952, as witnesses for both the defence and the prosecution argued about the impact the scene would have on the 'normal' teenage girl reader.

of both masculinity and femininity (so long as they were expressed by the proper sorts of people in the proper sorts of ways). Thus established, the heterosexual framework was pursued through the stages of pre-dating, dating, engagement, and marriage, with related discussions about good grooming, how to hostess a party, how to meet your date's parents, and other essential skills of the successful girl or boy. The tone in both books and magazines was enthusiastic and upbeat. Being a modern boy or girl was a swell thing.

The books I refer to here are not to be confused with the marriage manuals that were popular in earlier decades and which continued to be published after the war. The 'frankness' of the earlier volumes had no place in the primers for adulthood directed at postwar teens. For instance, the prime Canadian example of the marriage manual, Rev. Alfred Henry Tyrer's *Sex, Marriage and Birth Control*, originally published in 1936, contained chapters on 'Conception Control,' 'Different Positions for Intercourse,' 'Temporary Impotence,' and 'Venereal Diseases.'[19] Teen books, on the other hand, had chapter headings like 'How to Get – and Keep – Boys Interested,' 'All about Dating,' 'Shy Today and Popular Tomorrow.' The new advice genre grew, in part, from changing social mores and the rise of self-regulatory discourses of personal development. It may also have reflected changes in marriage and dating patterns. In the 1950s, children were 'dating' by the age of twelve or thirteen and marrying around the age of twenty, which gave them only five or six years to prepare – especially sexually – for what was assumed to be the eventuality of matrimony. Interwar marriage manuals had been written for young men and women. The 1950s advice books about sex were written for boys and girls who, despite impending marriages, were barely past childhood.

As with the advice books, postwar teens were also the target audience of growing numbers of educational films. While educational films were not new in and of themselves, the style and content of these 'how-to-grow-up' teenage-guidance films were unique to the postwar period. The films were more serious than the advice books, their tone set by the ever-present voice of a male narrator. Produced in Canada by the National Film Board and by private production houses, such as Crawley films in Ottawa, for distribution by American textbook publishers, the films played before 'captive' audiences in school classrooms, at youth groups, and, sometimes, on television. Perhaps because of this, their approach to content was more cautious than that followed by the advice authors. Whereas advice books were consumed privately, perhaps even secretly, films were viewed in public, sometimes in mixed groups of boys and girls. To some, who thought sex education the responsibility of parents and not the state, such materials were both ill-advised and dangerous. Boards of education could face protest by offended parents and embarrassed teachers for using them. Hence, the restrained tone of the films was not surprising. It probably helped facilitate the securing of an audience.

It's in the films that one sees most easily the way teen advice was implicated in the construction of postwar middle classness. These films flagged class in any number of ways, from simple matters like the predominance of spotless and well-furnished two-storey houses, where children did not share bedrooms and where mothers were full-time homemakers (even if widowed), to the homogeneity of students in a classroom, to assumptions about dating, marriage, and future careers. *Joe and Roxy*, produced by the NFB, was the only one of the thirty-seven films I considered that featured working-class teenagers: a girl living in an apartment with her mother who had been deserted by her husband; a boy whose father was a tradesman who tried to discourage his son from pursuing engineering. Among the sweater-set crowd, in the American-style soda shops that furnished many of the other films, Joe and Roxy would have been uncomfortably out of place.

More typical was an American film called *Are You Popular?*, first produced in 1947 and updated in 1958. In both versions of this film, postwar class differences are central to the story line. To make its point the film contrasts Ginny and Caroline. Ginny is the unpopular girl, packaged in multiple working-class signifiers. Her jewellery is big and gaudy, her clothes are fussy, her hair is too old for her age, she 'yoo-hoos' the other kids in the cafeteria. And, we find out from the solemn-toned male narrator, she goes parking with boys at night. Caroline, on the other hand, is very popular, in an easy kind of way (which is, of course, the right way). She is dressed simply. She greets her friends calmly and pleasantly. She is 'interested in girls rather than boys.' She offers to help with the school play. She does not 'park' with boys in their cars.[20] She will, however, go on a date with a boy if it is okay with her mother. She will be home before an agreed-upon curfew. And, when she and her date arrive home, mother will greet them with a tray of fresh brownies. For both Caroline and Ginny, class, moral character, and popularity are indivisible.

In all of the films, all of the characters are white. None speak with accents or have 'foreign'-sounding names. There is no mention of the way religious or cultural differences might affect one's popularity or one's ability to date or how one approaches marriage. Several films do suggest, however, the importance of marrying someone from a similar background. Overall, nothing disrupts the seamless representation of middle-class dominant culture. Certainly nothing suggests that the advice on growing up given in both the books and the films might not be useful to everyone.

The Straightness of Normality

There was a remarkable conformity among the different advice books and films about what constituted normality. While it was talked about as a unitary category, normality, in these texts, differed for boys and girls, teens and adults. And while it was presented as a self-evident descriptive, normality was constructed through a complex formation of professional and popular discourses, all of which were easily bent to serve moral ends. Biological and psychological discourses, which at times contradicted each other, were tucked comfortably alongside the most 'unscientific' common sense. The end result of this eclectic approach was a peculiar mix of essentialist theory, moral coercion, and behaviouralist strategy that was all meant to inspire teens to 'do the right thing.'

At its most basic level, normality was grounded in notions of the supposedly biologically rooted mutual attraction of males and females. Addressing young women, Ann Landers wrote in her 1963 book, 'Of course you would not be normal if you were able to keep your mind off the boys, completely. And no normal boy is able to keep his mind off girls *completely* either.'[21] While heterosexual desire, on its own, wasn't enough to guarantee one's status as normal, it was essential. In the limited world of the teen manual, homosexuality marked the extreme outer edge of the abnormal. Homosexuality existed as that place in the books where discussions of abnormality were up front and explicit. It was a subject the more reticent films rarely touched.

In her 1960 book, *Sex and the Adolescent*, journalist Maxine Davis wrote, 'Human beings have always been frightened by phenomena which seem to be unnatural. For example, before they learned something about astronomy they were terrified by the eclipse of the sun by the moon; they thought it was the end of the world. Today, the average healthy adult has a *comparable* aversion to homosexuality; he thinks it a dreadful incurable disease or an unnatural emotional deformity' (emphasis mine).[22] And while Davis claimed she wanted to allay these types of fears, homosexuality remained, in her text, something vastly remote from everyday life. Indeed homosexuality was constructed as so outside the range of normal teen experience that it was presented in all of the books as an external threat. Homosexuals were other people – not, certainly, teens themselves. Thus, most of the information about homosexuality that found its way into these books was intended to help boys and girls to protect themselves from deviants.

In her often-cited book *Teen Days*, Frances Bruce Strain, a proponent of sex education in American schools, wrote: 'Adults call these persons homosexuals. High-school students have their own names for them. One must know of them in order that they may be recognized and avoided.'[23] Lester Kirkendall, another well-known American sex-education expert, warned teens that they needed to know about homosexuals because young people were likely to encounter them as they began to venture afield from their homes. He claimed that homosexuals were most likely to be found in large cities and 'around places where it is common for only men and boys, or girls and women, to gather.'[24] He went on to explain how the careful teenager would be able to turn away the homosexual's advances. While Kirkendall and the other writers never explicitly explain how to tell the homosexual from someone who was normal, they did provide clues. First, homosexuals are male (lesbians are barely mentioned in the six books I'm referring to). Second, homosexuals are adults.

'True homosexuality,' according to Davis, is 'an unfortunate adult maladjustment.'[25] As a product of failed, slowed, or reversed sexual and emotional development, homosexuality is a condition that couldn't possibly be determined (or diagnosed) until the 'transitional phase' of adolescence was completed. Of course the irony in this is that homosexuals were then considered by psychologists to be in an arrested state of adolescent development – they were seen as immature.[26]

Different writers had different explanations for the cause of a sexual aberration like same-sex desire. Strain said it might be due to the unavailability of the opposite sex at a crucial time of development – for instance, in the case of boarding schools. She also suggested other reasons related to poor family conditions or unpleasant early experiences.[27] Lester Kirkendall looked primarily to the home to find the cause of homosexuality: 'Some [people] ... are so unfortunate as to be blocked in their normal development by conflicts with their parents, unhappy home conditions, lack of opportunity to build friendships, timidity, poor social adjustment, and possibly poor physical conditions. A combination of factors thus produces the homosexual, an individual who might with better fortune have followed the normal processes of maturing and growing up.'[28]

The developmental focus on the causes of homosexuality made it possible for the broad range and occurrence of same-sex affections in teenagers' own lives to be corralled and put to good ideological use. In typical models of heterosexual development, there existed a secure place for same-sex attractions, or crushes. Homosexual feelings or intimacies experienced by young people themselves were recuperated by advice writers as essential steps on the road to heterosexual normality. Most people, the writers claimed, go through some sort of homosexual 'phase' at some point in their lives. Evelyn Duvall, who was recommended to Canadians in *Chatelaine* magazine, constructed a continuum of affectional and sexual ties that began with 'same sex, same age' interests, passing through 'same sex, older age' crushes on the way to 'other sex, older age,' before finally reaching the real thing, the 'other sex, same age' stage of 'love development.'[29] In this model, homosexual ties are seen as preparation or practice for heterosexual relationships. In their book *On Becoming a Woman*, Mary McGee Williams and Irene Kane discussed same-sex crushes as good training not only in sexuality, but also in terms of gender roles. 'There's nothing wrong with idolizing a woman – if it's kept under control *and* if she's a person worthy of your respect. As a matter of fact, it helps to have a model on whom you can pattern your behavior, and it's a step in learning to be a woman, to learn to admire a good and admirable one.'[30]

Homoerotic desire in this sense was not only normal but desirable. Nevertheless, it was important that this 'not unusual part of growing up' did not expand into an active desire for physical contact – it was important to keep clear the boundaries between normal and abnormal. Should such transgressive feelings arise, the young person was advised to seek counselling to find out why his or her 'emotional development [was] being delayed beyond what [was] considered normal.'[31] The assumption was always that any same-sex sexual behaviour indicated a developmental stage that had been taken too far. Moreover, it was nothing a few new friends and some vigorous sports activity wouldn't put back on track.

Little attention was paid by these authors to concerns young people might have had about their own sexual identities, worries that they themselves might have been 'a little queer.' Ann Landers was the only writer to approach homosexuality from this angle, and she only talked about boys, claiming that they accounted for 70 per cent of her mail on the subject. They are the ones, she wrote, who were 'tortured with guilt and self-hatred ... terrified that someone may learn they aren't "like everyone else."'[32] They were the ones who, 'yearn to be normal.'

Perhaps because of the letters she received, Landers was more willing than her colleagues to make a distinction (albeit an unhappy one) between homosexuality as a phase and homosexuality as a tragic future. While she believed sexual identities to be the result of a process of emotional development, she saw that process as relatively quick and finite. Thus Landers, unlike the other writers, thought that one could be an adolescent and a homosexual at the same time; homosexuality was not necessarily a phase. However, she also claimed that cures were possible, although their chances of success were greater if 'the homosexual seeks professional help in his early teens.' But one wonders whether the young homosexual would have pursued such a course of action while everyone around him (or her, invisible though she was) was saying that homosexual feelings were a normal part of growing up. How was one to know the difference between homosexual desires that were 'twisted and sick' and those that were preparing one for heterosexual matrimony? The negotiation of the normal/abnormal boundary could be very complicated.

Never one to cut off hope, Landers stressed that much could be done in terms of 'adjustment' to homosexuality. She claimed that, 'Psychiatric therapy can, in most cases, give the homosexual some understanding and insight into his problem. It can help him adjust to his condition and accept himself as he is.'[33] What that acceptance might look like in a society where homosexuality was rarely acknowledged, let alone tolerated, Landers didn't say. And if the young homosexual didn't already feel the extent of the distance between 'himself' and those laying claim to normality, Landers helped him along by suggesting to her non-homosexual readers: 'Be thankful you have been blessed with healthy, normal sex drives, and remember that not all boys and girls are so fortunate. When you encounter people who are 'different,' remember that their lives are probably unbelievably difficult and that they are faced with the enormous problem of adjustment. You can help by understanding.'[34]

Most of the advice writers claimed that they wanted to reduce people's fear of homosexuality although, clearly, they weren't interested in calming young people's personal fears about living homosexual lives. Instead they focused on widespread social fears of homosexuals in the culture at large. It was widely believed in the 1950s, as it is by many today, that young people could be inducted into homosexuality by older homosexuals. In developmental theories of homosexuality, contact with

an adult homosexual was one event that might send normal development astray. A particularly vitriolic version of this theory appeared in
the American digest magazine *Coronet*:

All too often, we lose sight of the fact that the homosexual is an inveterate
seducer of the young of both sexes [sic], and that he presents a social problem
because he is not content with being degenerate himself; *he must have degenerate
companions, and is ever seeking younger victims* ...
    ... He demands a partner. And the partner, more often than not, must come
from the ranks of the young and innocent. (Emphasis in the original.)[35]

Davis wrote that if a young boy is seduced by an older man and 'has
repeated relationships with adult homosexuals, there is a serious risk
that his originally normal instincts may eventually become permanently
perverted.'[36] Homosexuality, in this instance, is not something you perform or do, or something you are, it is something that might happen to
you. This meant that, despite the 'naturalness' of heterosexuality and the
abnormality of homosexuality, young people were vulnerable to derailment from the straight path. As long as homosexuality was understood
to be an external threat, notions of the 'naturalness' and inevitability of
heterosexuality were left unchallenged.

Normal Gender Makes Normal Sexuality

In teen advice books and films, the relationship between sexuality and
gender was a fluctuating one. While postwar theories of homosexuality
relied less on notions of gender inversion than earlier theories had,[37] theories of heterosexuality, by contrast, were heavily steeped in ideas about
the proper fit between gender and sexuality. Whereas one could be a
homosexual without feeling the inversion of gender, one could not be a
successful heterosexual if one's gender was out of line.
    Girls and boys who did not match prevailing images of masculinity
and femininity – sissies and tomboys – were a challenge to the firmness
of the boundary that split off abnormal from normal. But, surprisingly,
not a single writer mentioned the possibility that these children might
turn into homosexuals. Doing so might have given too much credence to
theories that homosexuality was a biological condition, as Kinsey had
tried to show, and not a perversion of normal instincts or evidence of
relaxed moral standards. To succumb to biological arguments about the
basis of 'abnormalities' would have necessitated an admission of the

futility of sex education and other regulatory measures as a prophylaxis against deviations from social norms. Such arguments would have put these writers out of business. So in the few discussions of tomboys and sissies that appear in these texts, there is no mention that the improper alignment of gender might have non-heterosexual consequences. Instead we read merely of the difficulties that femmy boys and butch girls faced in the schoolyard. The hope was always that the "minuses" of their sex'[38] could be rehabilitated. While homosexuality was thought to be the result of (failed) adolescent development, sissyness and tomboy-ness were presented as conditions that (successful) adolescent develop-ment could cure.

In the late 1940s, Kellogg's cereal company ran a regular ad in *Chate-laine* magazine that was formatted to look like a column by 'psychologist Janet Power.' A 1948 instalment was entitled 'Barbara Is a Tomboy.'[39] Psychologist Power (!) responded to a letter from Barbara's mother describing her daughter's habits and asking 'How can I make Barbara more feminine, yet not curb her high spirits?' Power suggested that Bar-bara's mother ignore 'her tomboy antics' and instead praise Barbara 'for everything feminine she happens to do.' Barbara's mother was to encourage a closer relationship between Barbara and her sister, to take Barbara shopping, and to give both daughters more responsibility in the home. Eventually, Barbara would calm down when she learned how proud it makes her mother: 'Remember, stress CONSIDERATION OF OTHERS and GOOD MANNERS. At first Barbara will obey just to please you, but quiet, normal gentleness will soon become a habit with her. Show Barbara it's fun to be a DAUGHTER to you and FATHER – not a tomboy!' (emphasis in original).[40]

Femininity in this case is a matter of behaviour modification; it is not something one feels, but something one learns. Several versions of this approach were expressed in teen advice books and guidance films. The writers made clear that while young women have an inherent capacity for femininity – it is, after all, a 'natural' product of their biological femaleness – they need instruction so their femininity will attain the proper shape. 'Most of what goes into making a woman act and behave and feel like a woman is learned as she grows up ... Learning to enjoy boys as persons, to like men without being afraid of them on the one hand or being too overwhelmed by them on the other, learning to enjoy the fine arts and skills of being a real woman, with all the satisfactions and challenges that lie before women today – these are important, and they are for you to learn.'[41]

But with questions around gender identity, as with other topics, there is a continual tension in these texts between 'modern' psychological theories and 'old-fashioned' explanations that draw on biology. Either set of theories could be easily adapted to meet the exigencies of moral discourses. That these two positions could, at times, be contradictory was a theoretical and narrative puzzle the advice writers left unsolved. In a 1942 book directed at parents and teachers, Frances Strain suggested that tomboys and sissies be referred to the family doctor to determine 'the underlying physical basis' of 'the problem.' She also said that when such children enter adolescence and their hormones start up 'either naturally or through medication, the minuses may both become pluses, delicate boys become virile and strong, stalwart girls become graceful and more feminine, ready to be to each other not pals but "dates" and sweethearts.'[42] Here, her advice differs from the behaviour-training approach of the Kellogg's ad. But, four years later, in a book directed at young adolescents, Strain was caught between biological and psychological perspectives when she said that femininity in boys 'is just on the surface. Given a chance, these boys swing back to normal.' Should that not happen, or if it could not 'because of individual make-up,' they would just have to 'live within the scope of their tastes and skills ...'[43] They would have to 'adjust.' No need for hormonal remedies here. Whether the different exercise of biology in Strain's two books represents an updating of her theory or her attempts to be more upbeat with children than with adults, it is hard to say.

In most of the books and films, biology was presented as the source of things good, while environmental and psychological/emotional factors were what turned good things into bad ones. This is very clear in Strain's later book where she based her discussion of ideal genders on 'nature':

Boys are to be fathers and providers. They become broad of shoulder, long of limb, fleet of foot, stronger, tougher and more combative. The animal world gives plenty of evidence of male equipment for this task of winning a wife, protecting and caring for a family. The magnificent antlers of the bull moose and his roaring mating call up in the north woods has inspired many a dainty little doe and won her to him. The bull seal with his mighty tusks, the lion with his massive head and mane, the game cock and his spurs, all of these are Life's provisions for the male of the species.[44]

Unnatural gender types, like sissies and tomboys, were frequently said to be the fault of parents; a bad home life could turn one's 'natural,' normal constitution inside out. Learning to maintain gender boundaries, to express the right kind of masculinity or the right kind of femininity, was partially a matter of giving shape to the kind of biological urges evident in the 'animal world.' As Evelyn Duvall wrote, 'most young people have a strong urge to be normal ...'[45] To do so, adolescents were to become the opposite halves of a heterosexual whole. Learning to date, then, was a means of building on biology, trying on heterosexuality and fulfilling gender requirements. The reader of *On Becoming a Woman* learns that womanliness, for instance, is not something complete unto itself; it is something to be 'practised' on men. To be a 'truly feminine woman,' according to Williams and Kane, a woman had to 'really *like* men.'[46] This didn't mean, however, that she joined them for games on the ball field. Girls needed to like boys in ways that would make them into dates, not into pals. Although there were many ways for boys and girls to be together, only one was evidence that nature was unfolding as it should.

Dating as Heterosexual Practice

If anything marks postwar ideologies about gender and sexuality and the relationship between the two categories, it's dating. Much has been written about dating as a fairly recent, North American institution. Beth Bailey, Ellen Rothman, and others have discussed the various historical factors that shaped the adoption of the 'dating system' by young Americans.[47] In most of this writing, dating appears as a series of events or customs that change with the economic and social climate. But, as Karen Dubinsky has pointed out, these histories of courtship fail to look at dating as a key aspect of the institutionalization of heterosexuality.[48] Neither have they looked at the ways that dating contributed to the construction of the teenager as a particular kind of sexual being, or at the ways that dating was as important for those who did not participate in it as it was for those who did.

In her study of young, working-class women in turn-of-the-century New York, Kathy Peiss talks about the opening up of opportunities for heterosexual sociability for working-class women.[49] This mixing of the genders didn't become the norm for middle-class youth until somewhat later. Paula Fass suggests that it came about with the increasing numbers of coed colleges in the 1920s, and with the increasing enrolment in mixed-sex high schools.[50] It was in these institutions that youth began to be perceived as a distinct sector of society, a cohesive group with its own tastes, traditions, and norms. High schools also brought adolescents together in a way that made them targets of adult/expert observation and intervention. For instance, post-Second World War high schools provided the audience for the how-to-grow-up-properly films I've mentioned in this chapter. Without the large numbers of young people collected in state school systems, it is unlikely such films would have been profitable.

As Peiss makes clear, 'dates' outside the home were not an invention of the middle class nor of the twentieth century. What was different about middle-class dates as they evolved in the 1920s and the decades that followed was that middle-class dating became *the* socially approved system of boy-girl interaction, with its own rituals and peer-enforced norms. Other situations in which boys and girls found themselves together in the service of their sexuality came to be censured. This transformation had a lot to do with changing economic conditions after the First World War, the growing proliferation of cars, and the availability of commercial amusements.[51] In order to date, one had to have money, somewhere to go, and a means of getting there.

By the interwar period, claims American historian Beth Bailey, dating had come to be organized along competitive 'economic' lines. In the 1930s, young men and women were keen to have as many dates as possible. Popularity was both an outcome of and a contributor to dating success. Bailey cites American sociologist Willard Waller who described the 'dating and rating system' as he saw it in the late 1930s.[52] To be popular and successful, Waller said, men had to have material advantages – access to disposable income, cars, the proper clothes, and so on. Women, of course, didn't compete on this same level. For a woman to be popular she herself had to be seen as valuable and in great demand. Thus, she tried to be seen with men who rated, turning down those who didn't or those who insulted her worth in the marketplace by asking her out at the last minute. As Bailey understands it, the rating and dating system was based on the conformity that was central to middle-class youth culture as well as on the competition that was a product of a nascent consumer society.[53]

By the 1950s, this constant changing of partners was all but lost as teenagers began to invest themselves in serial monogamy via the institution of 'going steady.' Again historians locate the source of this shift in the economic and social conditions of the larger society. After the war, says Bailey, teens used the dating system as a means of escaping the intense competition of the burgeoning consumer culture.[54] Elaine May says that dating habits were part of a larger search for security and stability during the cold war.[55] But dating was not merely a reflection of the larger economic and political circumstances. Dating was also a means of organizing social relations among youth. Peer-enforced standards of behaviour, encouraged by adults, brought the regulation of what was normal down to the level of young people themselves. As a public display of one's ability to fit in or not, 'going steady' was a requirement of popularity that made those who were not participating in its rituals obvious. Serial monogamy, with its lack of spontaneity – its stability – made the unattached especially visible. The problem is summed up by a young woman in Sylvia Fraser's autobiographical book about Hamilton, Ontario, in the 1950s: '"It's better to stay home than to go with someone you don't like," I assure her, knowing that I'm lying. All social life at Hamilton High is strictly two-by-two, as in Noah's Ark. Not to date is to be an object of scorn or pity.'[56] Once on the outside of the coupled world, the chances of getting in were fewer than they might have been in the constantly changing social scene of the thirties.

For all its significance as a teenage institution, going steady was not, by any means, free of adult influence. Teachers, journalists, filmmakers, advice-book writers, and parents all did their best to keep this form of dating consistent with larger social norms. While boys and girls could mark the boundaries of their social worlds in terms of who was with whom and who was alone, adults attempted to keep limits on the entire dating system, especially in terms of sexual expression and how interactions between boys and girls reflected contemporary ideologies about gender.

Adults in the postwar period, who would have been more familiar with the 1930s version of dating, were torn over whether or not teenagers should be encouraged to go steady. American marriage counsellor Clifford R. Adams, writing in *Chatelaine* in 1948, claimed that 'courtship is much more wholesome and sincere than it was a few dozen years ago.'[57] For him the trend towards serial monogamy was a sign of maturity and a stabilizing of moral standards that had been shaken by the war. Ten years later, Dr Marion Hilliard, a frequent contributor to *Chatelaine* on issues of sexuality, claimed, disdainfully, that going steady was little more than insurance for teens: 'Both boys and girls drift into these comfortable arrangements. They never have to make any effort to learn to handle a new situation or adapt to different personalities. They settle down into this teen-age pattern so completely sometimes that they find they can't even dance with other partners. They know one another's minds and opinions as well as the lyrics of their favorite hit tune. They become fixtures in each other's homes. When they can support each other, they get married.'[58] In going steady, Hilliard saw a way for teens to express their conformity and to keep themselves ensconced in over-protected lives.

Writing for *Maclean's* in 1959, Sidney Katz showed a comparable lack of enthusiasm in an article called, 'Going Steady: Is It Ruining Our Teen-agers?' Katz likened the practice to a social disease, claiming it had reached 'epidemic proportions.'[59] For him monogamous dating was a disturbing sign of the impact of postwar social-welfare measures: 'Chil-dren, evidently, have absorbed in concentrated form, the adult emphasis on security as evidenced by our own advocacy of health insurance, pen-sions and guaranteed annual wages. The teen-agers' premature conser-vatism and excessive desire to conform are also symptomatic of their search for security.'[60] Katz saw teens as the inevitable product of too much prosperity. They were passive and lacked initiative. Why else would they be content to settle so early into staid and routine patterns of coupling? He also claimed that top kids in the social system didn't suc-cumb to social pressure to go steady. Nor did immigrants. According to Katz, these two groups (which he constructs as internally cohesive and mutually exclusive) were more enterprising. Like other writers, it was Katz's contention that going steady was a 'female device,' developed by girls to achieve their own ends. Boys who participated in it willingly, he says, lacked masculinity.[61] They were not on the way to becoming nor-mal men.

Other writers saw monogamous dating in a different light. For Wil-liams and Kane it was good preparation for marriage.[62] And Frances Strain is enthusiastic about what she calls the 'dating pyramid,' the road to marriage itself and the culmination of normal heterosexual develop-ment. 'This wonderful social structure,' as she describes it, starts with group dating, then double dating, single dating, going steady, courtship, engagement, and marriage. The whole process begins around the age of thirteen or fourteen and ends with the nuptial event at the age of twenty-three or twenty-four.[63] (Her age limits reflect her immediate postwar publication date; later in the 1950s, they would have been lower in both cases.) In this model, dating was practice for marriage, a useful way of training sexuality into a desired mode of expression, of normaliz-ing it. Dating was the socially approved arena for young men and women to practise their masculinity and femininity on each other.

To the extent that it became institutionalized, with numerous ritual and structural intricacies, dating offered advice writers no end of opportunity to intervene in young lives. Dating, though the 'natural' expression of heterosexuality, was not something that just anyone could do properly – it had to be taught, and adults were more than happy to take on the job of teaching. As in the learning of masculinity and femininity, advice writers claimed no contradictions between their assertions that heterosexuality was 'natural' and the assumption that it was an identity and a practice that had to be achieved: 'Both girls and boys must learn how to be smooth in their dating. None of us is born with the attributes of being a good date ... Such learning can be fun, and it is important without question. On it hangs our feeling of being a successful member of one sex or another.'[64] In this passage, Evelyn Duvall is talking about grooming and being punctual and wearing the right clothes. But success as a dater, and as a young man or a young woman, was based on more weighty issues than these. Once one was in the dating system, one had to be able to stay there without 'getting into trouble.' Fears around the extent of sexual activity between daters was one topic on which the anti-going steady adults agreed with those who were for it. But while the latter thought going steady was a way to control sex between teenagers, the former believed it encouraged dangerous intimacies. Sidney Katz cited the results from a poll published in *Canadian High News* in which 82 per cent of parents were opposed to their daughters' going steady. They were afraid 'something might happen.'[65] No mention was made of their sons.

Ann Landers shared the parents' concerns: 'It is unrealistic to assume that healthy, red-blooded high school kids can be together day in and day out, month after month – sometimes year after year – and keep their physical urges under perfect control.'[66] Sex, she warned, was a 'dangerous by-product of going steady.' Marion Hilliard thought the same: 'As a doctor I don't believe there is such a thing as a platonic relationship between a man and woman who are alone together a great deal.'[67] A strong sex drive was seen to be normal (for boys and girls, according to Hilliard), but a teenager needed to and could learn how to control it, because 'Uncontrolled, this force can take over and direct you.'[68] For those who agreed with Hilliard, sex education, like that found in the advice books, would give teenagers the moral grounding to stem their physical inclinations.

Some sources downplayed discussion of sex, perhaps because of a fear that too much sexual knowledge was, itself, a dangerous thing. Reading *Chatelaine's* regular column 'Teen Tempo,' one could assume that the extent of teenage girls' concerns with sex stopped at whether or not to permit a goodnight kiss on the doorstep. Most dating how-to films, which were ostensibly presenting real teenage couples, managed to skip quickly over sex as an issue that might be of concern. In an American film called *Going Steady*, shown on a 1954 CBC talk show, *Youth Takes a Stand*, sex is introduced and dismissed in three short lines:

Marie: Going steady? Yes, I guess I have been going steady.
Mother: I hope Jeff doesn't feel he has the right to take liberties.
Marie: Oh mother.[69]

The film was shown as part of a special episode on going steady. The conversation between Marie and her mother contains the only reference to sex in the entire program. A 1957 film, *How Much Affection?*, produced by Crawley Films of Ottawa for McGraw-Hill Books in New York, is unusual in that it dances around sex without actually having to say the word:

Mary: Tonight the feeling between us kept getting stronger and stronger. And on the way home we stopped and parked. And then things seemed to happen, till we nearly —— [Mary glances down at her dressing table, Mother stands by looking concerned, there is a long pause] – It was so close. Suddenly I realized what we were about to do. I asked Jeff to take me home. I guess he felt ashamed too. He said he was sorry, that it was his fault.
Mother: Do you think it was his fault?
Mary: Oh mother, I don't know what to think, I'm so mixed up. I don't even know if I want to go out with Jeff again.[70]

Mary and her mother have a talk about feeling 'warm and affectionate' and about the times when 'your physical urges fight against your reason.' When Mary next runs into Jeff at school they apologize to each other. Later they see 'poor Eileen' and her baby on the street. Her baby was born five months after a hasty marriage to Fred. Her face looks haggard. We are to assume Mary and Jeff learn from her 'mistake.'

Joe and Roxy, produced by the NFB, is the one film that shows working-class teenagers. Also produced in 1957, it isn't quite as dramatic or explicit in its message as *How Much Affection?*, although it does include images of sexual behaviour.[71] We see a young couple hanging around the girl's house, unchaperoned, after school.[72] The boy fixes a broken toaster. They start to play tag. He chases her. He tackles her on the couch. They end up on the floor kissing. They stare into each other's eyes. He starts to feel uncomfortable and gets up to tidy up his repair job. When he comes back to the living-room the two are shy with each other and sit apart on the couch. They talk about getting engaged. They start to rough-house but then they grow quiet. The narrator intervenes: 'Moods change very swiftly at 17, gay and raucous and tender. An age of many moods and many doubts.' Sex is there and not there at the same time.

These reticent portrayals of teenage sexuality were at odds with advice-book discussions of sex as powerful and 'awe-inspiring.' Teenagers were supposed to learn about sex as a wonderful natural urge, but then they were to ignore or control that urge until they were legally sanctioned to express it. People like Marion Hilliard assumed it was impossible; she frankly told girls not to trust themselves and to keep out of any situation where sex might occur.[73] Other writers thought the right information presented in the 'right way' would prepare girls 'to deal with the power [their] "femaleness" places in [their] hands.'[74] While we all have urges, we are quite capable of keeping them under control. Heterosexual desires might have been normal, but only if expressed under certain conditions.

In her book *Young, White and Miserable*, Wini Breines talks about the crazy-making contradictions that faced young American women in the 1950s. In a consumer culture that celebrated youth and sexuality it appeared there was a new openness to sex. Certainly, postwar teenagers had plenty of opportunity to engage in sexual activity. The emphasis on coed activities at school and after, combined with the privacy that was inevitable for at least some part of almost every date, put heterosexual boys and girls in extremely close proximity to each other's sexuality. But, as Breines says, this openness and opportunity unfolded in the context of 'prudish families and narrow, even cruel, sexual norms.'[75] But unfold it did. In his 1953 study on women, Kinsey found that 'very nearly 50 per cent of the females who were married by the age of twenty had had pre-marital coitus.'[76] He also says that the rates of premarital coitus for women had remained relatively constant, with only minor increases since 1930.[77] What was similarly surprising to his 1950s readers was Kinsey's claim that 90 per cent of all the women in his sample had engaged in premarital petting, while the figure rose to 100 per cent for those who subsequently married.[78]

In the face of widespread sexual behaviour among adolescents, advice writers continued their attempts to construct normal heterosexuality as a relatively non-sexual practice until marriage. Despite timid discussions about goodnight kisses and popular articles by learned women and men on the dangers of petting, teenagers did continue to engage in a range of heterosexual sexual activity, although as Breines says, it wasn't always pleasant or fun:

I mention only in passing, despite its importance, the terror of pregnancy, shared by girls who considered or engaged in sexual intercourse. It mediated girls' appropriation of the pleasure-seeking ethos of sexualized consumerism and diminished their pleasure of heterosexual sex. The point ... is not that this fear was unique to white, middle-class adolescents in the postwar years, but that this juxtaposition of sexual opportunities and encouragement with ignorance, condemnation, humiliation, and the unavailability of birth control is unusual.[79]

When the social norm meant waiting until marriage, teenagers who engaged in sexual activity – girls especially, though boys as well – played dangerously with their own social value and categorization. We saw in the last chapter the consequences of unwed motherhood and the way that the delinquency label could be applied to girls who asserted themselves sexually. To meet their own needs and desires for sex as well as social requirements for at least the image of chastity, teenagers engaged in complicated negotiations around the categories of sexual activity. Can you kiss on the first date? the second? the third? What after that? What is the correct relationship between the cost of a date and the percentage of her body a girl must share with a boy? What stretch of a hand or a mouth turns necking into petting? Sexual activity took place on a graduated scale that culminated in 'going all the way.' So long as a couple went up the scale in the proper order, at the proper stage of their dating relationship, the dating system could contain and sanction their intimacies. As an institution, going steady allowed both girls and boys to maintain their reputations while permitting them access to sex, in some cases, even intercourse, so long as they didn't get caught. Pregnancy was an incontestable marker of having crossed the line between normal/moral/good and abnormal/immoral/bad. Even homosexuality was easier to hide.

Early marriage was the ultimate solution to teenage sexual behaviour. In the 1950s the average age of marriage dropped to twenty-two years of age for Canadian women,[80] and not just because of 'shotgun weddings.' Marriage was a legitimate avenue of sexual expression for those young men and women who felt caught between the incitement to sex in the culture at large and the proscriptions against their own engagement in it. Early marriage was one way to bring changes in sexual behaviour into line with the established moral order; it could realign the boundary between abnormal and normal behaviour. As Williams and Kane put it, 'After going steady comes marriage, if life is to progress in an orderly fashion and it generally does.'[81] And while they, like other advice writers, hadn't intended that final step to come as early as it sometimes did, the vision of the sexual world that they promoted and helped to instil in popular culture made marriage the most obvious way to a positive resolution of the contradictions of young heterosexuality. As a *Chatelaine* editorial writer put it, 'Fortunately there continues to be something within all normal young people that makes them feel that marriage is good and meant for them.'[82]

The space between normality and its abnormal opposite was a powerful organizer and regulator of postwar life. As a category that could mark one's acceptability and cast one's future, normality had to be constantly fought for, despite ideological constructions of it as 'natural.' But while the classificatory power of normality had tremendous influence, it did not entirely determine the way people lived their lives, as Kinsey's figures suggested. As a discursive construction, normality was perhaps less responsible for shaping teenagers' daily activities than it was for curtailing the possible range of meanings that could be ascribed to them. Whether one felt normal or aspired to normality or not, it was always there for you and others to check yourself against.[83] At times, the consequences of not measuring up were considerable. So-called abnormality was expressed at a terrible price, be it ostracism, incarceration, or psychiatrization. Homosexuality, unusual expressions of gender identity, promiscuity, and pregnancy were all evidence of an unsuccessful struggle to keep firm boundaries between outside threats to one's own psychosexual development and internal, 'natural' possibilities. As sexual beings in process, teenagers were assumed to be especially vulnerable. Hence, they were particularly singled out as targets for intervention by adults – if they were normal, the future would be normal too.

6

Sex Goes to School: Debates over Sex Education in Toronto Schools

In 1944, and again in 1948, Trustees at the Toronto Board of Education debated the implementation of sex education curricula. In both cases, sex education had been proposed as a means of combatting pervasive social problems: venereal disease and sexual deviation. While schools were already involved in the production and regulation of sexual norms and in educating young people about sexuality (for example, through the selection of specific novels or poems and not others, the regulation of co-ed activities, and the gendering of subjects like home economics), there was little agreement on how this task might be approached in a deliberate manner or whether it was appropriate for an institution of the state to do so. Underlying this disagreement were diverging opinions on the nature of adolescent sexuality, on the rights of the family and on the limits of state responsibility for moral questions. Two assumptions grounded the whole debate: first, that intervention into teenage sexuality was necessary and, second, that society could only benefit from the normalization of sexual behaviours and identities. What was at issue was how and by whom the processes of intervention and the rendering of normality were best carried out.

In their consideration of sex education curricula, municipal officials were struggling to find local solutions to national problems. Venereal disease, for instance, was regularly claimed by the press as 'Canada's number one health scourge,'[1] our 'no. 1 saboteur.'[2] During the war, the number of VD cases in Canada had increased significantly.[3] In newspapers and magazines and in materials put out by health organizations, it was 'youth' who were placed at the heart of the problem, those at greatest risk of infection, and those most responsible for its spread. The Health League of Canada alleged that the VD problem was 'largely one of youth,' although, they added, it was a youth problem that had been 'exaggerated by the war.'[4] But 'youth' was a slippery category. In 1945, where 70 per cent of VD cases were in the age group between sixteen and thirty, only 10 to 11 per cent of those cases were teenagers, the group of young people most likely to be pinpointed when the terms 'youth' and 'problem' appeared in close proximity.[5] The overemphasis on the 'youthfulness' of those with VD meant that teenagers came to be seen, alternately, as responsible for the health crisis and as victims of it. In either case, they were identified as one of the primary targets of VD-prevention efforts.

Despite widespread pronouncements about the urgency of educating young people about sexuality – especially its dangers – only Ontario, Manitoba, and British Columbia made provisions for instruction about sex in schools during the postwar period. In Ontario, the city of London had a small VD-prevention program, while Toronto's was the only school board to consider the implementation of a comprehensive sex education curriculum. There were a number of reasons for Toronto's unique position. First, some board officials prided themselves on taking a proactive approach to social problems. The Toronto Board of Education, like other Toronto institutions, liked to consider itself at the leading edge of its field. Second, and of much greater importance, Toronto was home to many of the national organizations that argued publicly in favour of sex education. Officials of these organizations had access to the local media and to school board officials, and their influence was critical to the introduction of sex education at the board. Finally, the Toronto Board was a huge, well-funded institution. The independent development of new curricula was something that few smaller boards could have undertaken. Smaller boards were forced to wait on provincial guidelines and prepared materials. In terms of developing a sex education curriculum, it was not so much a question of money as of access to resources and expertise. Toronto teachers and Board Trustees were surrounded by concerned doctors, mental health professionals, and social workers who were only too willing to extend their influence over the country's largest school district. They attended committee meetings, helped write reports, presented lectures. They helped put sex education on the Toronto board's agenda.

Discussions about sex education in Toronto had very little to do with the sexual concerns or the sexual well-being of young people themselves. In these discussions, young people were simply the means through which adults attempted to fashion solutions to postwar social problems. Teenagers were a route to the tightening of moral standards that had been relaxed during the war, a route to a reconstituted normative heterosexuality that would carry Canada securely through the modern era.

Social Hygiene

In February 1944, E.L. Roxborough, a trustee of the Toronto Board of Education and vice-president of the Toronto Big Brothers Movement, proposed that a place be found for social hygiene in the secondary school curriculum. VD rates had increased dramatically during the war, and youth were widely perceived, rightly or wrongly, to be the group most affected. That they should be exposed to prevention education was not an unreasonable suggestion, if one's main concern was with the health of the students. As we will see, however, student health was far from central in debates over Roxborough's proposal.

Social hygiene was an approach to venereal disease prevention and sexual and moral education that had been developed by middle-class reformers in the early decades of this century. As Lucy Bland writes, social hygiene involved a union of 'medicine and morals.'[6] By the mid-1940s, Roxborough's proposal notwithstanding, social hygiene was rapidly approaching outdatedness as a term and an idea. The Canadian Social Hygiene Council, originally called the Canadian National Council for Combatting Venereal Disease, had been active after the First World War in a variety of sex education efforts, some of them informed by the work of Canadian eugenicists.[7] Social hygienists had a history of trying to tackle VD by targeting 'foreigners,' prostitutes, and the 'feeble-minded' as sources of infection. The prevention efforts they had organized were largely a matter of advocating purity and denouncing promiscuity and prostitution.[8]

By the mid-1940s, the overtly racist strategies of eugenics had grown increasingly out of favour, and such moralizing tactics for disease prevention were being dismissed as dated and unscientific. During the Second World War, VD-prevention efforts were based more on 'scientific facts' than on moral admonitions. For instance, two NFB films made in 1945, one for young men and one for young women, are full of diagrams, statistics, and charts.[9] They show images of syphilis and gonorrhoea under the microscope. They are narrated by a male physician. But what most sets them apart from the materials developed after the Second World War was their emphasis on treatment. Medical science, rather than moral rectitude, is the hero of these films. We see VD clinics and hear about doctors' commitment to confidentiality. We learn that venereal disease is a solvable problem.

In proposing social hygiene, rather than sex education, Roxborough was flagging a conservative approach to VD prevention. Roxborough was not the first to raise the subject of social hygiene at the Toronto Board of Education. In 1926, the Toronto Home and School Council and the Canadian Social Hygiene Council had tried to distribute pamphlets about sex education to the parents of children in the public schools. But at that time board officials considered the project too controversial and refused to cooperate.[10] Then, in 1941, concerned about wartime venereal diseases, trustees passed a motion urging the Dominion and provincial governments to 'embark on a nation-wide programme of public education on these [public health] matters which so vitally affect our present war defence programme and our future post-war strength as a great people.'[11] What the overall impact of the motion was is hard to say, but certainly there was no mention of venereal disease in the 1942 provincial high school defence course curriculum. The closest that course came to any sort of sex education was in a section called 'social adjustment.' Under this heading girls were permitted to discuss: 'associating happily with boys; being attractive; entertaining boys; keeping a boy's friendship; love ...'[12] Boys, however, did not learn about social adjustment; they attended classes on internal combustion engines, signals, and woodcraft instead.

Despite its allusions to health and cleanliness, social hygiene was inextricably connected, in popular discourse, to venereal disease and 'dirty' sex, aspects of life that were assumed to be both too private and too distasteful for public attention. The fact that both these topics were regularly the subject of public discussion during the war, in newspapers and magazines and on the radio, had not been enough to distinguish them as suitable topics for schoolroom lessons. Thus, even in the face of the wartime VD crisis – in 1943 there were 10,000 more cases of venereal disease in Canada than there had been in 1942[13] – Roxborough's motion was treated cautiously by the rest of the board. 'We should go slow,' trustee Dr J.P.F. Williams told reporters. 'If we go at all,' added his colleague, trustee Frank Chambers.[14] The matter was left open for 'further consideration' by the board's Management Committee.

A month later, Dr Charles Goldring, Superintendent of Schools, presented Management Committee with a report on the subject.[15] Goldring told the trustees that the provincial Department of Education had yet to develop provisions for the teaching of social hygiene. Nevertheless, a program for secondary school girls had been in existence in London, Ontario, since 1942. A similar boys' program had been postponed when the male doctor who taught it was called away on active service. But Goldring was disinclined to make such an unauthorized move at his own school board. Instead, he wanted the provincial Department of Health to determine whether such a course on VD prevention was necessary. If it was, he then wanted the Department of Education 'to secure from the Department of Health authentic information to serve as a standard lesson or lecture to be given by the Health teachers on the various high school staffs to their students.'[16] Goldring thought that this lecture should be given to boys and girls separately and that it 'would be advisable to have the Guidance officers present.' While the lectures would be given 'as a matter of routine ... and should be considered a normal part of the school course,' it was obvious that Goldring himself didn't feel that way about them. A month before presenting his report, Goldring was quoted in the *Toronto Daily Star*, saying that social hygiene classes could not be taught by regular teachers but only by 'men or women qualified through medical skill and knowledge.'[17] While this suggestion wasn't included in his report, he did claim it would 'be an advantage to have a medical doctor talk to the Physical Education teachers on this subject.' For Goldring, social hygiene was a sensitive topic.

Members of the Management Committee seemed to share Goldring's hesitations about taking social hygiene on board. Although they decided to endorse the proposal to teach social hygiene – on the condition it be approved by the Department of Education – they made no suggestions about what types of material would be introduced into the classroom. Such matters were better left to the province.

Support for Sex Education outside the Board

In 1944, the national Junior Chamber of Commerce and the Health League of Canada (a group whose mandate carried on from the work of the Canadian Social Hygiene Association) did a significant amount of organizing around sex education in the schools. They sent out resolutions for endorsement to many other organizations and to government officials. They contacted American organizations for materials. They discussed the issue in special committees and drew up policies based on their findings.[18] The Toronto board's consideration of social hygiene may well have been prompted by this community activism. And, as the

Toronto board's discussions were publicized, other organizations also began looking into matters of VD prevention and the responsibility of the schools in fighting VD. A number of these other groups, like the Ontario Educational Association (OEA) and the Canadian Teachers' Federation, had definite links to the Toronto board. In general, discussions by non-state agencies were less narrowly framed than those at the Board of Education. External groups were concerned not just with venereal disease but with morals. They talked not in the couched terms of social hygiene but about sex education, a subject that went beyond the prevention of venereal disease and was conceived by some to be a form of 'character building' that could improve the calibre of adolescent morality.[19] For instance, at the 1944 convention of the OEA, a resolution to include sex education as part of the provincial school curriculum passed by a vote of ten to one in the Trustees' Section of the meetings. Arguments in favour of the resolution claimed that sex education would help to check not just social disease, but juvenile delinquency as well.[20] Dissenting opinion argued that 'parents or preachers were the people to give sex counsel and that [the issue] was a moral question'[21] and therefore outside the jurisdiction of the schools.

This counterposing of parental/church and school/state responsibilities marks a recurring theme in the sex education debates. Underneath it lay questions about the ownership of moral issues, the capabilities of parents to cope with modern circumstances, the incursion of the state into the private realm, and the perceived wane of religious influence, generally. As a *Globe and Mail* editorial said, the state is 'a useful instrument of the public will, but there are aspects of life which it cannot enter with impunity.'[22] Apparently, sexuality was one of them.

Religion operated in the sex education debate in various ways. To some commentators, religion was a general antidote to moral decline.[23] Others saw religion as providing a moral counterpoint to scientific sex education in the schools.[24] Still others found in religion the moral justification for keeping sex education in the home.[25] But apart from such general references, few 'official' religious positions on the subject appeared in the mainstream press. Shortly after Roxborough's proposal, the Anglican Church endorsed a resolution supporting sex education in homes, churches, and schools 'in order to stop the spread of venereal disease,' a problem the diocesan council attributed 'to a breakdown of moral standards, a general decay of faith, and economic causes and widespread dislocation of society.' But the church would only agree to the teaching of sex education if a 'Christian point of view' could be safeguarded.[26]

More often than not, it was Catholic organizations (as opposed to the Catholic Church itself) that publicly opposed sex education teaching on religious grounds. When the Canadian Youth Commission was preparing its report on *Youth, Marriage and the Family*, Catholic opposition to sex education greatly complicated the process, or as the director of the CYC, R.E.G. Davis, put it: 'We have had an unbelievable struggle in getting agreement ...'[27] At issue was a bibliography that was to include information on sex education. Members of the committee debated (by post) whether or not to drop the references to sex education. One woman wrote, 'If only there was another word for "sex" we might not have to step so gingerly.'[28] In the end, they decided to replace the term with the less controversial 'mental hygiene.'

Overall, little opposition of any kind to sex education was reported in the press. News reports gave coverage to groups, like the OEA that passed resolutions in favour of sex education in the schools. National magazines published feature articles supporting sex education. Psychologists and others concerned with youth proclaimed its usefulness as a cure for a variety of social ills. In a June 1944 Gallup poll, 93 per cent of respondents wanted Canadian high school students to be exposed to lectures on the prevention of venereal disease.[29] This is not to say that there was no opposition to sex education; rather, a public discourse had been constructed around it in various media which, deliberately or not, made the school board seem to be more cautious than its constituents. If Canadians in general wanted their children educated about sex, why was the Board of Education in one of the country's largest cities reluctant to act? It was a question of bringing sex into the public realm, of negotiating the boundary between state and private concerns.

Provincial Guidelines on Teaching VD Prevention

By July 1944, five months after Roxborough's initial proposal, and at the request of the Toronto board, venereal disease had been approved as a topic for inclusion on the Ontario curriculum for grades 10 and 12. However, it would be two years before students actually encountered related material in their classrooms. Provincial guidelines drawn up to govern teaching about venereal diseases emphasized a variety of precautionary measures that were intended to drain the topic of controversy. The guidelines stipulated that, before any mention of VD was made in the classroom, parents would receive informational letters from the Department of Education and teachers would be provided with special manuals. Lessons on VD would be introduced in regular (non-coed) physical education health classes where they would be part of the general discussion about communicable diseases. Students would be asked not to make any notes on the subject (which might have gone beyond the bounds of decency). They would be given provincially produced booklets at the end of their lessons. And, finally, teaching about venereal disease, though permitted, would not be mandatory.

Written under the shadow of bureaucratic anxiety, the guidelines had no clout. They were an effort to negotiate concerns around venereal disease and fears about what might happen if sex was discussed in schools. Would parents rebel? Would students be enticed into sexual activity? Would the more sheltered girls and boys be turned away from sex by frank discussion? Where other curriculum guidelines detailed the exact number of hours to be devoted to a topic and the desired outcome of the lessons, the substance of VD teaching was left to the whim of particular school boards. Concerns about public health and the infection of teenagers by syphilis and gonorrhoea were obviously secondary to moral concerns about who could talk to teens about sexual matters and what the result of such discussion might be in terms of teenage sexual knowledge and behaviour.

Evidence of the acceptability of VD education to most Canadian parents had had little impact on provincial education officials. To introduce sexual matters into publicly funded classrooms was to put the school into competition with the home and the church as the primary sites of young people's moral and, in the former case, sexual development. It was to upset notions of family privacy and of the division of labour between the home/church and the school. To make that shift was to acknowledge that those institutions were no longer capable of fulfilling their assigned responsibilities.

Some people were unconcerned by this potential realignment of moral constituencies, wanting the state to play a stronger role in influencing the moral development of adolescents. A number of Toronto teachers had hoped that concerns about venereal disease would be able to justify the place of a more broadly defined sex education in the secondary school curriculum. The 'menace' of syphilis and gonorrhoea was a potent hook for arguments that education about sexuality was socially relevant and therefore within the jurisdiction of the school. A 1944 editorial in the *Star* proposed a model of sex education that depended 'largely on the education of young persons in the responsibilities of social living. It requires that boys and girls should receive scientific education about the origin of life and their responsibility for life. It requires that young men and women should be inspired with a wholesome attitude toward one another.'[30]

Clearly, the *Star*'s definition of sex education had implications which stretched beyond disease prevention. *Saturday Night* published a similar call for a broadly defined sex education to be taught in schools. Author Miriam Chapin argued that such a program needed to consist of two things: (1) 'instruction in the physiology of sex,' and (2) 'guidance to young people working out a code of conduct which is socially approved.'[31] But while Chapin thought that sex education was important, she also seemed to consider it a special or delicate case, arguing that instruction in this area was outside the capabilities of not only the average parent but also the average teacher. Chapin shared this latter position with Goldring and others who were convinced that sex education teaching could have a tremendous influence, for better or worse, on teenage conduct.

Arguments both for and against formal sex instruction revolved around parents, their rights and obligations, and their capabilities. In early 1945, the Toronto Teachers' Council endorsed a report that advocated sex education in elementary and secondary schools as well as courses for adults in night schools. The report addressed concerns that 'Venereal diseases have reached an alarming level and menace the present and future welfare of Toronto and Ontario generally ... Many parents neither know the facts of sex nor the proper technique of imparting them to their children. Among adults and parents there is widespread ignorance. Organizations fighting venereal disease need the support of an educational program designed to assist in removing its causes.'[32] In suggesting classes for parents, the Teachers' Council was lending support to popular middle-class sentiments that 'bad,' usually working-class and immigrant ('foreign') parents, more than the prevailing wartime social conditions, were responsible for youth problems, especially VD and juvenile delinquency. Just a few weeks before the council's endorsement of the report, the Management Committee of the Board of Education had discussed the possibility of setting up mandatory 'parenting' classes for the parents of delinquent children.[33]

But the discussion of parental inadequacies in terms of sex education wasn't limited to working-class parents. While many assumed that working-class and 'foreign' children were exposed to too much sex, middle-class children were thought to be too protected. Their parents were accused of being prudes or too easily embarrassed by frank discussion.

In 1945, psychologist W.E. Blatz (of the Toronto Juvenile and Family Court and the Institute for Child Study) wrote in *Maclean's*: 'many parents side-step their responsibilities in the education of their youngsters in sex matters ... Parent shortcomings in this respect are further complicated during wartime because so many fathers, so many elder brothers, are included in the 730,000 Canadian men who are in the armed forces and away from their homes.'[34]

It bears noting that Blatz was a major proponent of the importance of parent education in the development of the 'normal' child. His work with the Institute of Child Study in Toronto and, in the 1930s, as educational consultant for the Dionne quintuplets, had helped to establish his own international reputation as an expert in mental hygiene, and the central importance in Canada of psychology for 'building and preserving well-adjusted children.'[35] But while Blatz had helped to forge strong links between psychologists and the educational system, he was not in favour of passing on the responsibility for sex education to the schools or the church or medical doctors. It was, he claimed, the responsibility and privilege of parents to do the job. That they were doing that job badly, as Blatz concluded, must have seemed to him an opportunity to extend the influence and scope of psychological expertise. While the education of children was accomplished by the school, the education of parents was an open field. Psychologists were as likely as anyone to fill it.

One of the ways in which parents were encouraged to contribute to sex education, whether it was part of the school curriculum or not, was by providing an example of the 'serene and happy companionship between husband and wife [which would] have a definite influence on the emotional attitude of the child.'[36] Parents were to model socially desirable forms of heterosexual, monogamous relationships. If, by chance, there were parents who didn't fit the mainstream image of a successful couple, here was a way of bringing that point home both to them and to their children. In this sense, sex education was not simply a means of moulding children's sexuality. As Blatz said, 'we aim not only that individuals conform to our social standards, but that *they enjoy marriage and its sexual aspects to the full in legitimate circumstances*'[37] (emphasis mine). This linking of conformity and pleasure is what sociologist Nikolas Rose would identify as one of the 'distinctive features of modern knowledge and expertise of the psyche.' Expertise, says Rose, has come to shape our desires. Our lives 'become worthwhile to the extent that they are imbued with subjective feelings of meaningful pleasure.'[38] Sex education was an effective way of bringing this expertise into the daily lives of ordinary people, where it could contribute to the sexual regulation of both children and their parents.

Advocating for Sex Education at the Toronto Board

For the most part, magazines and newspapers presented sex education as a far-reaching and necessary project which could help to build exemplary citizens. But in the pages of the Toronto *Globe and Mail* and in the offices of the Ontario Department of Education and the Toronto board, the matter was persistently treated as one of delicacy and potential danger. In November 1945, the provincial Department of Education produced a teacher's guide about venereal diseases that focused only on their scientific aspects – the process of infection, progression of the disease, and treatments. Some teachers felt that in ignoring social and 'spiritual' concerns, the booklet played it too safely, trying to de-emphasize the sexual and moral aspects of VD transmission in a bid to avoid controversy. At the Toronto board, two committees formed, one of male teachers and one of female teachers, to consider ways the booklet might be modified. Their recommendations were included in a 1946 document, 'Guiding principles in the presentation of the subject of venereal disease' prepared by the Director of Health and Physical Education for Toronto schools. [39]

The male teachers' committee concluded that information about venereal disease needed to be preceded by discussions about sex education more generally. 'In this way,' their report said, 'first impressions will be positive and stress the normal ... The need for a high standard of moral conduct, the normal girl and boy relationships, the significance of marriage and the conditions upon which happy family life is built will all be emphasized in a normal and objective way.' [40] The male teachers thought that in any discussions of venereal disease, it was better to stress its 'hopeful' aspects rather than its morbid ones. They wanted to avoid compromising the 'higher aims' of sex education and its focus on 'healthful living,' and so they counselled against using VD as a means of frightening young people to change their sexual behaviour. The men also decided that 'the most normal place' on the curriculum to insert sex education would be in grade 10 after the study of the ductless glands. At the time of their writing, there was still no place on the curriculum where a teacher could deal with human reproduction.

The ductless glands and the 'secondary sex characteristics' were as far as teachers were permitted to go in the discussion of sexuality. And these topics were to be covered quickly. The following is the entire treatment of the 'Glands of the Secondary Sex Characteristics' in a provincially authorized health text book:

These glands, partly ductless, make hormones which are absorbed into the blood and induce the qualities of manliness and womanliness. In the male they produce hair on the face, deeper voice, broader shoulders, bigger frame and muscles, love of combat and strenuous life and the instinct to protect and defend women and little children. The changes in girls are not quite so spectacular, but are nevertheless quite definite. The figure becomes more rounded and fuller. Fatty tissue is distributed under the skin, making it soft and delicate. The voice remains relatively high-pitched but softer. New feelings of tenderness for children are experienced as well as an increase in interest in the opposite sex.[41]

What stands out here, besides the gender ideology, is a conflation of sexuality and gender that would have left many students totally unprepared for the introduction of material on venereal disease. How to move from a discussion of sex as tender feelings to a discussion of sex as the cause of debilitating illness? How to understand the mechanics of transmission, with no sense of body parts or how they might be used?

Neither of the teachers' committees addressed these kinds of questions. They were far less concerned about physiology than about morality. The women teachers' committee wanted to help students understand venereal disease in the 'proper perspective': 'Although we recognize the importance of instruction in Venereal Disease, we consider that of even greater importance is the development of a healthy, sane, and moral attitude toward sex matters in general.'[42]

Teachers, the women's committee said, had to be concerned with the development of 'proper attitudes to all matters pertaining to sex.' However, they made it clear that it would not be proper for a teacher to discuss sexual relations – a directive that might have proved difficult for someone striving to offer, 'convincing reasons against the practice of promiscuity.' The women's committee suggested that 'the discussion [of sex education should be] guided in such a way that it will be of real value to [the students] in establishing a standard of conduct which will ensure rather than jeopardize their future happiness.'

Here, sex education is understood to be much more than the dry transmission of scientific facts that had been envisaged by provincial bureaucrats. The women teachers' model was intended to be an effective form of moral regulation that would encourage adherence to prevailing cultural norms. And, to ensure that the program reached the largest number of students, the women teachers thought, as had the men, that sex education needed to be introduced in grade 10. In the 1940s, many working-class students left high school to find jobs when they turned sixteen; if sex education were to begin in grade 10, the majority of high school students, including the predominantly working-class kids who had to leave, would be exposed to the material.

The result of these two committees' having met was not an expansion of the students' curriculum but a series of five lectures on the topic of Family Life given separately to men and women physical education teachers. Whether this segregation was for reasons of propriety or because of gender-specific subject matter is not clear; there exists no documentation of their content. The lectures for the male teachers were prepared by a Dr Bernhardt (presumably Karl Bernhardt of the Institute of Child Study, although there is no confirmation of this assumption in board documents). The women's lectures were given by Dr Jean Davey of Women's College Hospital. According to Charles Goldring, all the lectures were well attended.[43]

What happened after the lecture series is not altogether clear from surviving board documents. In a report written in 1948, two years after the teachers' committees met, Goldring says that the lecture series was followed (he doesn't say when) by a meeting of members of the board, the board's Advisory Vocational Committee, and 'some of the secondary school principals.' The officials met to screen four films, three of which focused on the basics of reproduction (illustrated in one film by rabbits), and one which explained menstruation.[44] Goldring says that 'the members of the Advisory Vocational Committee ... were sufficiently impressed by these films to authorize the showing of some, or all, of them in the vocational schools.'[45] Whether 'some or all' of the films were actually shown is not clear. Why the same films were not authorized for the collegiates is also unclear. One can speculate that the topic of reproduction may have been deemed too sensitive for the predominantly middle-class students who were enrolled in the heavier academic programs; or that middle-class students were thought not to need the films as badly as the predominantly working-class students at vocational schools; or that middle-class parents were more likely to complain that such films represented the encroachment of the school into family life.

It is impossible to know how many Toronto physical education teachers took up the subject of venereal disease or sex education with their students or how many followed the recommendations of the two teachers' committees. While it had been approved as a topic of instruction in 1944, venereal disease did not actually appear on the Ontario course of study for health and physical education until 1946, when it was listed as just another communicable disease, alongside tuberculosis and smallpox. Certainly, teachers had few resources to draw on in helping them to adopt a more wide-ranging perspective than that proposed by the province. Nor had they been given any substantial direction from their board to do so. After Trustee Roxborough's 1944 motion about social hygiene, the board did not discuss sex education, in any form, until 1948, and then only in response to public pressure.

While concerns over VD motivated this first round of debate about sex education at the Toronto board, discussions about its implementation show that disease prevention was just one of several ways to understand the initiative. Some, like William Blatz, saw in sex education a means of regulating parents. Others, like the men and women on the teachers' committees, saw sex education as a vehicle for regulating the moral and sexual development of their students. However, neither of these positions gained a strong foothold at the board, where control of sexuality was more likely to be exercised via the suppression of information than through more productive, positive forms of regulation. In part, the limited inroads made by sex education advocates reflected fears about the volatility of teen sexuality and what the consequences might be of talking about sex in front of teenagers. But the evidence suggests that the hesitations around social hygiene were primarily related to questions about the role of public education. Concerns about bringing sex into the public realm, about making it an explicit concern of the state, meant that these first attempts at introducing sex education into the schools had limited effects in terms of the regulation of teenage behaviour and teens' sexual identities. Certainly, in the entire discussion of social hygiene, little concern was evident for teenagers themselves or the fact that VD was, for some young people, already a painful reality of daily life. On all sides of the debate, the immediate needs of young people for information about sexual activities and VD prevention and treatment were overlooked.

If VD was the object of the first round of sex education discussions at the board, teenage sexual development was the object of the second. In both cases, actual teenagers were nothing more than the vehicles carrying 'concerned adults' to their desired goals.

Preventing Sex Crime

While fears about the spread of VD had been the catalyst for wartime discussions of sex education a different social menace was occupying public attention by the late 1940s. Sex crime and sexual perversion were the social threats that put sex education back on the school board's agenda. Alarm over sex criminals reflected a more generalized postwar concern about so-called sexual deviations or sexual abnormality. For instance, news articles about sex crime frequently slipped into discussions of perversion and sex variance, rarely making a distinction between criminal and non-criminal behaviours. A 1947 article by Sidney Katz in *Maclean's* shows the conflation of the various categories:

One of the chief reasons sex criminality has grown to such proportions is that we have miserably failed to approach the problem intelligently. Sexual abnormality has always been a hush-hush subject, and the sex pervert is probably the least understood of all our citizens.

The sex variant is much more common than is generally realized. Fortunately only a small percentage of perverts are criminals ...[46]

At a time when ideologies about the nuclear family and the benefits of domesticity – personal and collective – were gaining strength, sexual 'abnormalities' were seen as a serious threat not only to women and children but to social stability.

In the postwar period, the trend to social conformity reflected a general need for security. In the aftermath of global conflict and in the face of the cold war and 'creeping Communism,' middle-class North Americans took refuge in the safety and comfort of sameness. Part of this homogenization required the sublimation of what were perceived to be potent sexual energies, a process that American historian Elaine May calls 'containment.'[47] Social conventions limited sexual expression to the bounds of heterosexual marriage; anything else was not normal and might be dangerous. In this context, so-called sexual perverts, a category which included groups as different as homosexuals and rapists, were a threat not simply because of any potential harm they might cause to individuals, but because they showed up the impossibility of ever achieving complete social accord.

Historian Estelle Freedman has written about the moral panic over sexual crimes that emerged in the United States in the mid-1930s. Dropping off during the war, it re-emerged in the late 1940s and 1950s.[48] The two main features of the panic, noted by Freedman, were: first, it was not necessarily related to an increase in the statistics for sexually related crimes; and second, in many places in the United States, it led to the implementation of laws to curb so-called sexual psychopaths and to the 'transfer of authority over sex offenders from courts to psychiatrists.'[49]

Local variations notwithstanding, the situation in Canada was quite similar. In this country, fears over sex crime were given shape in the Criminal Code amendments of 1948, in a 1952 Senate Committee concerned with Salacious and Indecent Literature, and in the 1954 Royal Commission on the Criminal Law Relating to Criminal Sexual Psychopaths. Women's, church, and labour groups addressed the issue of sex crime in their meetings. Social service and community groups undertook research projects and prepared reports. In 1955, a group of Toronto housewives established the Parents' Action League to combat sex crime, a kitchen-table organization that achieved the endorsement of a whole range of national organizations and prominent 'experts.' Throughout the decade, magazines and newspapers repeatedly published features warning parents of the threat to their children and advocating stronger legal measures. Yet all this unfolded without there being any appreciable increase in the rate of sex offences in Canada,[50] which, according to figures from the Toronto city police, accounted for less than 2 per cent of all criminal offences.[51]

In the 1948 Criminal Code amendments, a criminal sexual psychopath was defined as anyone who 'by a course of misconduct in sexual matters, has shown a lack of power to control his sexual impulses and who, as a result, is likely to attack or otherwise inflict injury, pain or other evil on any person ...'[52] Such persons could be sentenced to an indeterminate term in a penitentiary where their cases would come under review every three years. The idea behind the law was that sex criminals could be kept off the streets as long as they remained a threat to others.

Public support for the new law, as reported in the Toronto dailies, was overwhelming.[53] Many had argued for positions much more severe than that passed by the government – for instance, that sex criminals be dealt with entirely outside the judicial system (and its various routes of appeal) and kept in mental hospitals until they showed evidence of having been cured. Surprisingly, psychiatrists, a group that would have had much to gain from the medicalization of sex crimes, were not in favour of such changes.[54] Nevertheless, extreme measures were portrayed frequently as the only reasonable methods of protecting public safety. 'Sex maniacs,' 'monsters,' or 'freaks of nature,' as they were called in the popular press, were considered to be on a slippery slope of degeneracy that could eventually lead them to murder.[55]

Part of the impetus behind sexual psychopath laws was an understanding of sexual deviation as an uncontrollable aspect of a man's (they were always men) personality, as an illness or defect that was difficult, if not impossible, to cure. A letter from a women's labour organization to the Ontario minister of health said, 'These persons are sick, both mentally and physically, they are NOT normal human beings.'[56] It was a view that made it that much easier to advocate locking them up for good. Deviant sexuality was a powerful social symbol.

It was in this context that, on 21 April 1948, the Canadian Penal Association presented the findings of a study on ways to curb sexual offences. Sponsored by the Kiwanis Club, the report was widely quoted in the daily press, where the conflation of sex offenders, sex perverts, and sex deviants was widespread and moral outrage was prominent.[57] The report itself adopted a more detached, objective tone: 'There is increasing evidence to show that part at least of the violent and often vindictive prejudice and contempt which is so commonly expressed by the public for those known to be sex offenders stems from tension and anxiety representing a kind of collective guilt. Thus the more loudly we protest the beastliness of the sex offender, the more surely do we convince ourselves that we at least are free from taint.'[58] The authors tried to debunk the notion that sex criminals were likely to commit greater and greater crimes; they claimed that their recidivism rate hovered around 9 per cent as compared to the more usual 65 or 70 per cent for non-sexual crimes.

In general, the Penal Association report made a strong argument for prevention of sex crime, as an alternative to treatment after the fact. 'Educational expert' Kenneth Rogers of the Canadian Welfare Council (and of the Big Brothers) wrote: 'Sound moral and character discipline can prevent the physically-based sexual deviate from becoming a sex-offender. Sound child-training can prevent the normal boy and girl from becoming a psychogenic sexual deviate, a sex-offender or from being influenced or seduced by an aggressive sex offender.'[59] In a lengthy and impassioned discussion, Rogers underlined the importance of the schools' involvement in this work:

The fact must be faced that ignorance on the subject of sex education is abysmal – even in these days ... As one writer has put it, this whole matter of sex ignorance 'has been a legacy of darkness, compounded of shame, handed down from father to son.' This insightful observation is a challenge to our 'tradition' that all sex matters – especially sex education – belongs in the home. If a tradition is so rigid that it prevents society from correcting its own faults, then it may be necessary to break that tradition.

Let the fact be faced that many, many parents are themselves very ignorant in this matter. Marriage and having children have taught them a few simple, and often quite unrelated, facts regarding the mechanics and causes of procreation. These are either rarely talked about, or if talked about are talked about quite loosely. So when their children are of an age to receive home instruction their ignorance is often complicated by their embarrassments. The crux of this problem lies just here, that when those children become parents they are not likely to be any better prepared for their responsibility than their parents were! If telling the true factors is always to be left to parents under these conditions the rising tide of sex-crimes, sex delinquencies and disease may never be stemmed.[60]

Rogers was unwilling to entertain the usual arguments against sex education in the schools, arguments similar to those that had been used earlier to forestall social hygiene teaching in Toronto classrooms. Contemporary social problems were, to him, evidence that those arguments had outlived their usefulness. 'By our ignorant, short-sighted and blundering relationship to the business of normal heterosexual relations and social living,' Rogers wrote, 'we manufacture perverts.'[61]

For Rogers, sex education meant more than a one-off lecture or a bit of private counselling by the guidance teacher. He envisaged 'mass' programs of 'carefully prepared classroom instruction,' beginning in elementary school and continuing into high school grades. Children needed to learn about sex, Rogers concluded, to keep them from drifting 'into one of the abnormalities which appear to be on the increase lately. We should not be called upon to pay the increasing toll of ignorance; a wretched toll summed up in separations, divorces, promiscuity, venereal diseases, homosexuality and sex crime.'[62] Here 'sex crime' operates as only the most frightening possibility in a chain of troublesome sexual issues. To prevent sex crime would be to prevent these other, lesser problems as well.

On the day after the Penal Association released its report, school board trustees passed a motion requesting Goldring to prepare a report on what the board had done, or could do, to help implement the Penal Association's recommendations regarding education. Goldring took less than two weeks to prepare his report. In it he detailed the sequence of events around the implementation of the units on venereal disease, concluding that schools were already doing everything in their power to deal with sex education: 'It should be remembered that the scope of the instruction in this or any other subject of the curriculum is determined by the Department of Education ... [I]nstruction in this phase of helpful living is probably as extensive as is permitted under existing [provincial] regulations.'[63]

Goldring suggested that the interest generated by the Kiwanis project might prompt *the province* to make some changes to the curriculum. But he offered no suggestions as to what direction those changes might take or what part the board might play in helping them along. His position on sex education was no less cautious than it had been on social hygiene. No matter how socially valuable they might be, Goldring was no advocate for discussions of sex in schools. Nevertheless, at the end of May, the Management Committee appointed a special committee to consider sex education. Committee chair Charles Edwards told the *Telegram* that sex education in the schools might keep children from picking up misinformation on the street. And an enthusiastic superintendent of secondary schools, C.W. Robb, claimed that 'No more important subject exists today,'[64] an unusual public endorsement by a board official on what was still perceived by some to be a sensitive topic.

Family Life Education: The Theory

Before the special committee met for the first time in early September 1948, Charles Edwards wrote to an American authority on sex education, Dr Adolf Weinzirl of the University of Oregon, asking for information about providing sex education in public schools. In his lengthy reply, Weinzirl outlined the kind of 'character building' program that had been proposed by a number of American groups in response to the limitations of VD education programs. According to Weinzirl, a sex education program, best referred to as 'family living,' had to respond both to the need of parents to have their children educated in 'morals' and the need of students to learn about sex and 'family living.'

Broadly speaking, parents do not have a clear idea as to how 'morals' are 'taught.' From our standpoint, we can understand that what is meant here is the transmission of our cultural attitudes with respect to the exercise of reproduction in connection with monogamous marriage to the oncoming generation. It really means the establishment in children of feelings and emotions that will compel attitudes and behaviour leading to a minimum of promiscuity and to restricting sex to monogamous marriage with the expectation of having and raising children.[65]

A more explicit description of moral regulation would be hard to find. Implicit in Weinzirl's explanation was the assumption that these feelings and emotions were not necessarily natural, or inevitable, but that they had to be taught. Mothers and fathers had an important role to play in all this, teaching by example that monogamous marriage 'is the ideal relationship.' Weinzirl suggested that the various components of a program in family living – scientific information, materials confirming the family 'as the basic unit of society,' discussions on family relations – be integrated into the curriculum as a whole – for instance, into biology, social science, and home economics classes. With such an approach, he wrote, opposition from conservative members of the public is minimized. (Surveys in Oregon had apparently calculated the rate of opposition to be no more than 2 or 3 per cent.)

The 'family living' approach to sex education marked the evolution of earlier social hygiene efforts. Social hygiene had been narrow in scope, justifying itself as the solution to a specific social problem – venereal disease. While family life education would address problems like VD and juvenile delinquency, it was also intended to shape a new kind of youth, to contribute to the production of young women and men who were well versed in and committed to the moral values of their communities. As American sex educator Frances Bruce Strain wrote in her 1942 book, *Sex Guidance in Family Life Education: A Handbook for the Schools*, family life programs were 'directed toward the furtherance of normal sexual development and stability in children in an ordered world ...'[66] They were about the regulation of sexual behaviours and identities, a technique for moral governance that capitalized on the fact that youth were unfinished products.

For Strain, education for family life was a project that went far beyond the control of disease. Her own guidelines listed no fewer than eleven topics that needed to be promoted in a comprehensive program:

1. Satisfaction of the love impulse throughout its various stages of growth
2. Association of the sexes in work and play
3. Adoption of acceptable terminology
4. Utilization of innate pride in function for good living
5. Knowledge of mammalian reproduction, including human
6. Correlation of sex knowledge with everyday experience

7. Preparation for sexual maturation
8. The balancing of sexual and non-sexual (egoistic, social) satisfactions
9. The removal of causative factors in sex delinquency
10. The substitution of acceptable for unacceptable modes of sex expression
11. The fostering of the creative and recreative arts and sciences[67]

Strain's program covered sex education from biological, social, and moral perspectives in order to prepare students for the 'immediate world of reality.' It would produce properly gendered, normal teens, who could use their sexuality to help them meet prevailing social conventions and reap the rewards of conformity.

Strain understood sex education to be a progressive project that needed tempering by good judgment and conservatism in its implementation: 'if one becomes a radical, one loses step with both the conservatives and the progressives. Especially one loses influence with young people, for much as they scoff at "being old-fashioned" and "stuffy," they are critical and exacting, especially of those who are in positions of dignity and authority.'[68] It was certainly not the role of the sex educator to challenge those exacting positions.

Strain's desire to keep a conservative face on sex education in the schools was a pragmatic response to the kind of resistance to sex education that, for instance, had been apparent at the Toronto board in 1944. And, indeed, in Strain's text, conservatism is everywhere evident in her absolutely rigid faith in gender difference and her promotion of a single acceptable standard of sexual expression. Thus, Strain's notion of the ideal teacher was someone who was young, married, a parent of one or two children, a 'pleasing dresser,' of medium height and weight: 'To have lived a normally married life, to have loved, mated, had a family, and reared them year after year in one's home – this is undoubtedly to have one of the best qualifications for leadership in this field.'[69] A man and a woman working together as a team would provide the best calibre of sex instruction, for 'one must know both masculine and feminine nature,' Strain said. If a school could allocate just one teacher, a woman would be more desirable than a man. Single people and divorced people could, if necessary, be satisfactory choices if they were not bitter, or antagonistic towards the opposite sex. For any teacher, strict adherence to the appropriate gender role was critical: 'Men must be definitely masculine with that quality which used to be called manly, and women must be feminine with that quality which used to be called womanly. It won't do to shade even slightly in the opposite direction.'[70] Clearly, what was 'progressive' about family life education was not its stance on sexuality *per se*, but its position on where sexuality might be discussed, by whom, and for what ends. Given the eventual outcome of matters at the Toronto board, as we will see, even this position was a controversial one.

Family Life Education: The Toronto Curriculum

At its first meeting, the special committee appointed by the Toronto Board of Education asked Charles Goldring to prepare a report on a possible program of sex education suitable for students in grades 7 and 8, a request that already showed how trustees' attitudes to sex education had changed – social hygiene proposals had targeted older students in grade 10. Goldring passed the task on to a committee of teachers under the leadership of N.R. Speirs, director of physical training. This eight-member committee was joined on occasion by three consultants: Dr J.D.M. Griffin, psychiatrist and member of the Canadian Council on Mental Hygiene; Dr Kenneth H. Rogers, psychologist at the University of Toronto and staff member of The Big Brothers movement; and J. Alex Edmison, KC. Each of these men had been involved in the study on sex offenders done by the Canadian Penal Association. Their status as experts and the fact that their study had received widespread attention helped to establish the integrity and importance of the teachers' committee.

The report on family life education produced by this teachers' committee took its cues from Weinzirl and other prominent American and British sex educators. It took a far different direction from the limited 1944 provincial guidelines on social hygiene. Indeed the whole 'family life' approach precluded 'morbid discussions' of venereal disease. The report went so far as to suggest that perhaps venereal disease did not need to be mentioned at all in the classroom. The aims of the program would be much better served by motivating students to fashion themselves after the ideal rather than frightening them with proscriptive talks about nasty topics like syphilis and gonorrhoea. The aims of the grade 7 and 8 programs proposed by the teachers were:

1. To enable pupils to appreciate and value the normal, natural husband-wife-child relationship in the home and recognize in that the sustaining of successful, happy family life.
2. To give pupils standards of values that will enable them to distinguish what is good in sexual life from what is sordid, selfish or perverted.[71]

Classes would be coed in grade 7 and segregated in grade 8, when reproduction would be discussed.

Teachers of this innovative course were to be guided by principles in
the provincial curriculum on health education. Of particular importance was a directive claiming that 'The establishment of habits, attitudes and ideals of life, is more important than mere physiological
information.'[72] Thus, the family life curriculum de-emphasized biology
in favour of teaching about moral and social perspectives on sex. Children were to be instructed in the mores and conventions of their society, especially as they demanded the control and direction of sexuality
into the one sanctioned form of expression – heterosexual monogamy.
Children would learn 'that there are good and justifiable reasons
behind the conventions governing sexual behaviour and that they protect the home and particularly women and children.'[73] Alternatives to
marriage would not be presented, nor would the difficulties and problems of family life – they were not positive enough. Material about sex
delinquency was also deemed unfit for children. Instead pupils
'should be made to feel the excellence of sex and its immense potential-
ities.'[74]

One of the ways of showing this perspective was by demonstrating
the superiority of the human being over other life forms. The definition
of superiority here is tied not to human biological complexity but to our
ability to form heterosexual, nuclear families. So, in a discussion of
amoebas, for instance, it is not enough to know how they go about
reproducing; we also need to know that: 'there is [for them] no infancy,
no dependence, no care and no family.' Same thing with fish: 'two parents required - some family life - mother lays eggs father fertilizes. There
is some slight protection of the eggs until they are hatched and in some
cases even a protection of the young fish, but there is little indication of
any family life - no affection - sometimes young are eaten by parents.'[75]
And so we go until we get to human beings:

The child is born into a family unit with a mother and father who were married and agreed to love and cherish each other and care for their children.
Human mating is not merely seasonal or purely instinctive. It can be affected
by intelligent choice and governed by long-term considerations. It takes two
parents living together to provide a happy place for a child to be born, be
cared for, and to grow up into a happy, healthy person. That is why down
through the ages we have had the institution of marriage and the family as a
setting for babies.[76]

And this right after the war, with the increase in single-parent families caused by divorce, desertion, and death.

Clearly, domestic ideology was more important in this instance than the representation of 'real life.' This point is fundamental to the whole process of constructing social norms and of normalizing particular forms of expression. As Kinsey found, norms are definitely not about what people do. There is little room for the expression of power in a social landscape where all are accorded equal access to the norm. And normalization is very much about the distribution of power. It is about making distinctions, performing exclusions. The more narrow the definition of normality, the more powerful its potential to subordinate and suppress.

Reactions to the Curriculum

Family life education as proposed in the teachers' report was accepted with strong commendations from the special committee of the board. But Management Committee was less enthusiastic, holding back on its endorsement until the province gave its go-ahead. When provincial approval did come, it was conditional: family life was to be offered only on an experimental basis; family life teachers would have to receive special training; and department officials would have to be permitted to observe family life classes.

Media reaction to the idea of family life education was mixed. An editorial in the *Telegram* claimed that while the board was 'trespassing upon an obligation of parents,' it was 'taking a progressive and necessary step.' It was natural, the editorial continued, 'even necessary,' for young people to exhibit an 'innocent curiosity' about sex. The problem for sex education instructors would be to respond to that curiosity with information that could 'obviate false notions and subdue unhealthy trends, but in a manner which ... does not stimulate premature interest ...'[77] Young people could learn about sex, but they were not to engage in it. It was assumed that only special teachers would be able to keep adolescent hormones in check. These, then, were not the same concerns over the school's incursion into private life that had held back discussions about social hygiene. In 1948, critics worried about the explicitness of the information students were to be offered and what students would do with it when they got it.

The *Globe and Mail*, which was not particularly responsive to the idea of sex education in the schools in the first place, was concerned about the calibre of the instruction in such a course. If one of the goals of sex education, by whatever name, was to forestall the development of sexual perversions, to assist children in achieving 'normalcy,' then it was crucial for instructors to be sanctioned representatives of the norm. As a *Globe* editorial put it: 'It is not just a question of knowing facts and being able to recite them to a class, but a teacher of sex must have the manner, moral attitude and psychological balance which are absolutely essential [to this topic].'[78] While teachers of mathematics or spelling were not required to embody their subject matter, teachers of family life would be. Likewise, students were thought to be either suitable or not suitable to receive sex education. Trustee Isabel Ross (who also sat on the moral issues committee of the local Council of Women) asked, 'What about the boy or girl who is not ready for sex education in grade 7 or 8? ... I would hesitate to give the information to some children. It would be necessary to pick and choose, and carry some over into later grades, before they are taught the subject.'[79] What 'not ready' actually meant in this instance is not clear. Presumably it ran the gamut from immature to already 'oversexed.'

As an untried phenomenon, the family life curriculum took on the exaggerated powers of things unknown. It had been designed to shape youth into morally correct citizens. If, indeed, it was capable of achieving that end when taught well, what might happen to young people if it was taught, or learned, badly? Fears were that its powers might occasion the undesirable effects it was meant to forestall, such was the assumed volatility of teenage sexuality. This assumption, when coupled with notions that young people's sexual development was fragile and vulnerable to derailment, made sex education a potentially hazardous undertaking.

In March 1949, N.R. Speirs, director of physical training for the Toronto board, presented the first in what was planned to be a series of instructional lectures on family life for the supervisors of physical education and about 250 teachers. Over the course of the afternoon meeting, the family life curriculum was outlined and teachers were given an opportunity to view a number of films that were being considered for the course. The main purpose of the introductory lecture was to reassure teachers of the importance of the project and to allay any doubts about the suitability of the material for young students. In this vein, Speirs began by citing the results of '[unnamed] studies made in Toronto' which showed that only 13 per cent of students received sex instruction from their parents. Clearly, he suggested, there was a need for the school to intervene.

Speirs addressed various concerns that parents might be expected to raise, all the while stressing the high calibre of the teachers themselves, and the quality of the program. In particular, he put distance between these chosen instructors and those he called the 'emotional quacks' who had been behind earlier, old-fashioned, embarrassing efforts at sex education and social hygiene. The family life curriculum had been developed in contrast to those dated enterprises, most of which had been organized through church and other charitable organizations concerned with social and moral purity.[80] Turn-of-the-century sex educators had tried to scare young people away from masturbation; their teachings were laced with religious doctrine. Family life education, by comparison, was said to be a modern, 'scientific' program, based on contemporary pedagogic principles. It emphasized positive values not fear or shame. 'Instead of appealing to adolescent altruism and idealism, the [earlier] approach was apt to be either cynical or sentimental. Most of these historic misadventures are now hoary with age and deserve to be forgotten.'[81] Family life education would help speed their relegation to the history books.

In spite of the 'excellence' of family life education, Speirs made frequent references to the need for caution and tact in its implementation. 'Nothing should be done,' he said, 'to suggest that family life education is "risky" or "questionable" in the opinion of teachers or authorities,' though 'questionable' is the exact word that some trustees and some members of the public applied to the whole experiment. It may have been fear of the public's wary appraisals that prompted Speirs to declare that 'nothing is to be given to the pupil that could be taken home – no notes – no examinations – no pamphlets or books and, of course, no advertising matter [for the program itself].'[82] At home, sex education materials might find their way into the hands of younger children, or they might lead to nervous questions from concerned parents.

Speirs also warned against discussions of sex delinquency: 'We do not want to lay ourselves open to the rumour which circulated in Forest Hill that they were using the Kinsey Report as a text book.'[83] He wanted the course to be run along conservative lines: 'When in doubt – don't.' His fears were well-founded. Two weeks after the lecture, Goldring was called to report to the board on the 'nature and suitability' of the films that had been screened for the teachers. On 7 April, the board met behind closed doors to discuss the entire project. Apparently, some of the teachers at Speirs's lecture had objected to the nature of the material presented. One told the *Globe and Mail* that the family life course had 'no morals.'[84] Some trustees agreed with the complaint, saying that children in grades 7 and 8 were too young to be exposed to the course.[85] In the end, the proposed course, which was to have started after Easter, was postponed and referred to Management Committee for yet more discussion. The *Globe and Mail* applauded the decision to hold off: 'To oblige teachers paid by the State to take over this intimate function of parenthood ... is an unjustified intrusion into the privileges of the home ... Now that the Board has come to see the problems [of the family life course] more clearly, it might be a good time to drop the business.'[86]

But the trustees didn't drop it. They discussed it again, at length for the first time, in another session behind closed doors – the only appropriate place, some of the trustees thought, for the consideration of sexual matters. Then, they screened three of the movies that had been shown to the teachers. The result of the hush-hush meeting and the long-overdue discussion was that Goldring was asked to prepare yet another report on a modified version of the original family life program. He was to keep 'in mind that the instruction to be given be chiefly that which is outlined in the course for Grade 7,'[87] meaning that the grade 8 curriculum was to be scrapped. It also meant the end of anything sensitive enough to demand boys and girls be separated, such as any information dealing with the actual human bodies that lived in the families being discussed.

The grade 8 program had included topics such as: 'the hygiene of adolescence, including menstruation and nocturnal emissions'; sexual vocabulary; social behaviour, including 'sex-releasing activities'; and, most importantly, 'the meaning of growing up,' a section about reproduction and bodily functions. The grade 7 curriculum – suitable for coed classes – was focused on the family (including fish and amoeba families) and 'getting along with others.' Some of the critical topics suggested for discussion were: 'hogging the phone' – a particularly middle-class concern – cheating, tattletales, 'turning down a date gracefully,' 'taking sister to the party,' and chores. A short section on boy-girl relationships would stress that 'interest in the opposite sex was normal,' and that 'rough play [was] undesirable.' A much longer section on community life would discuss 'loyalty to family ideals,' 'conventions and customs,' and 'development of a scale of values.' In some schools, 'where girls mature earlier,' menstruation would be discussed (by girls only) in grade 7. The qualification was class-based. As a Big Brothers worker had claimed in his investigations of a working-class neighbourhood, 'The girls mature rapidly and the moral problem is real even with girls of public school age.' They were, he said, 'worldly-wise.'[88]

In stripping the grade 8 portion of the program, the board was taking the sex out of the sex education course. It was reverting to its earlier method of regulating teen sexuality by restricting access to information. After the revisions, family life education ceased to be a euphemism for sex education and came to mark the limitations of the course. Students would receive little guidance around the physical and emotional changes they would experience during puberty, nor would they learn about their own sexual capabilities and what they might mean if they began to date. Instead, students would become well versed in the ideology of the Canadian heterosexual nuclear family. They would learn the importance of rules and standards of conduct, and they would come to understand the significance and the face of normality. In the 'cleaned-up' version, family life education was about being a middle, class teenager under the authority of parents and community. In its original version, it had been about growing up and anticipating adult roles. Even in its reduced state, the final family life package remained an offence to the sensibilities of some trustees. Nevertheless, the board passed the course with a narrow vote of ten to eight.[89] But over the next decade, there was not a single reference made to sex education in the board's records. Similarly, on the provincial level, mention of venereal disease disappeared from the 1950 course of study for health and physical education.[90] According to the *Telegram*, the family life program was dropped from the Toronto curriculum, without comment, in the fall term of 1952. It wasn't until the mid-1960s that the whole debate began anew. Experts were engaged, the Department of Health was lobbied for permission, and trustees quarrelled over their opposing viewpoints. Finally, in 1966, a comprehensive program on family life was introduced to students in grades 7 to 12.

One of the things we learn from this story is that the introduction of discussions about sex into the public realm does not always represent progress; nor is it an easy process, as Foucault argues in *The History of Sexuality*. Public discourse is a powerful site of and mechanism for the regulation of sex. While we might deplore a social climate that prohibited the open discussion of the physiology of sex in schools, we might find equally offensive explicit attempts to mould children via their desires for sexual knowledge.

The initiatives around sex education at the Toronto Board of Education in 1944 and 1948 took their starting point from social needs as determined by particular groups of adults during a particular historical period. Discussions over sex education were rarely *about* youth. Instead, they considered the relationship between families and the state; they were about the mandate of the school board and the calibre of teachers. When teenagers were inserted into these debates, they were the raw material for the development and reproduction of normative heterosexual standards, a process that could be based either on a lack of knowledge or on the production of it, depending on one's perspective. Teens were never present in these discussions as individuals who might themselves already be participating in sexual behaviours, or who might already have contracted a venereal disease or been exposed in some way to 'sex crime.'

In both the social hygiene guidelines and the family life curriculum, young people were on offer to assuage the fears of the postwar middle class. Fears about social change and about future security were crystallized in discourses about sexuality that took teenagers as their objects. Certainly, without national public discussions of VD and sex crime, sex education would never have been raised on the board's agenda. That the family life program lasted only a year indicates the weakness of the board's commitment to even the watered-down version of the subject.

What is interesting here is the way that young people could symbolize social problems – the VD carrier, the potential sex criminal – and their solution – the morally responsible boy or girl, the parent of the future. This meant that as the board attempted to solve one set of problems, like sex crime, it risked creating another, by bringing teenagers and sexual knowledge into too-close contact. It was a catch-22 situation for the trustees. Because it was assumed that teens had yet to develop a mature moral sense or a mature sexuality, they were perfect candidates for sex education; indeed, they were clearly in need of it to help guide them towards accepted social norms. But the disjuncture between moral competencies and sexual potential was tremendously difficult to negotiate. Who could say that a teenager's moral sense would stay ahead of her libido? In this regard, a little sexual knowledge might prove a dangerous thing.

7

Manipulating Innocence: Corruptibility, Youth, and the Case against Obscenity

In 1949, a Toronto man wrote to the Ontario Government Censorship Bureau (a bureaucratic entity that, in fact, did not exist) to protest the availability of cheap pulp paperbacks. 'These books,' he wrote, 'many of them filthy in the extreme, have alluring colour covers, and any adolescent can buy publications for 25 [cents], that his parents would be shocked to read.'[1] His complaint was one of many received by the Ontario attorney general's office in the post-Second World War period when, after years of paper shortages and restrictions on trade, Canadian newsstands were opened to a huge range of mass-market publications from the United States. Concerned citizens, as individuals and as members of a wide spectrum of organizations, condemned the 'licentiousness of magazines,'[2] the 'flood of objectionable literature,'[3] 'porno-graphy for profit,'[4] and, among other things, the transformation of Canada into 'an open end[ed] sewer' for filth from the United States.[5] For the most part, these objections were articulated through a discourse of concern for youth who, it was assumed, had relatively unlimited access to inexpensive printed material over which their parents and teachers had little control.

In the 1930s and 1940s, mass-produced literature had flourished, especially in the United States. The creation of new genres and new approaches to marketing and distribution combined with improvements in printing techniques to make the publication of comics and paperbacks increasingly profitable.[6] After the war, Canadian newsstands felt the full impact of this growing sector of the U.S. publishing industry. The market for so-called 'real literature' was swamped by thirty-five-cent pulp novels, fifteen-cent magazines and 10 cent comics that were readily available in drugstores and cigar stores. In Ottawa, for instance, a single news and magazine distributor received 3800 copies of *Women's Barracks*, a 1952 pulp novel title.[7] In 1950, a researcher for the Toronto Board of Education counted 135 different comics for sale in that city, and he estimated their readership at more than 500,000 individuals each month.[8] To put these figures into perspective, the Canadian distribution of hard cover-books was limited to 2000 bookstores, while magazines and pulps could be bought at more that 9000 outlets.[9]

Alongside this boom in pulp publishing, so-called sexy magazines were also becoming increasingly visible. As a 1952 *Reader's Digest* article said, such questionable material was nothing new; what had changed was its accessibility. In the years before the Second World War, 'girlie' magazines had been available only in (male) adult environments like 'barbershops, saloons and army posts.' By the 1950s, however, these magazines were being sold right at the corner drugstore, on the same shelves as family magazines and 'useful books.'[10] In 1953 the launch of the 'tasteful' and expensively produced *Playboy* solidified the trend.

Fears about the power of mass media to divide parents from children were not unique to postwar North America.[11] They had followed the emergence of novels in the nineteenth century, and of silent films in the 1910s and 1920s. They would re-emerge over television in the late 1950s and the 1960s. We see them today in discussions about rock videos, Nintendo games, and the Internet. Writing about the British campaign against horror comics of the mid-1950s, Martin Barker says that 'each rising mass medium in turn has been targeted in the name of revered values.'[12] But, he adds, parental and social concerns are less a factor of the medium that spawned them than they are of the values assumed to be threatened by it. Where turn-of-the-century working-class parents worried that commercial entertainments such as cheap movies undermined traditional gender roles and put their daughters in too close proximity with boys,[13] middle-class parents of the 1950s worried about standards of sexual behaviour and whether the pulps encouraged their children towards deviance. In both cases, the medium was an easier target of popular protest than the general social context which spawned it.

Postwar discourses about the 'corruptibility' of youth, and their need for protection from sex as it was portrayed in various forms of pulp literature, were able to provide the impetus for broad-ranging initiatives of moral and sexual regulation that targeted adults as much as they targeted young people themselves. Discursive constructions of youthful innocence helped to set the boundaries of normative sexuality, thus marginalizing non-normative forms of sexual expression by people of all ages. Without the concepts of youth they were able to mobilize, these regulatory discourses would never have been so widely circulated.

Postwar discussions about the effects of indecency and obscenity on young people occurred in a variety of contexts. Here I pay particular attention to three of these: efforts in the late 1940s to restrict the circulation of comic books, especially crime and horror comics; the proceedings of the 1952 Senate Special Committee on Salacious and Indecent Literature; and a 1952 trial over obscenity that took place in Ottawa. Each of these illustrates the way 'youth' was used as a rhetorical trope in attempts to maintain dominant sexual and moral standards.

While the Ottawa trial contributed to the production of official legal discourse about obscenity, the public debate over comic books and the special senate committee were key to the constitution of more popular English-Canadian discourses. They provided a focal point for public consideration of what was constructed in many media reports as a national problem. And, indeed, obscenity was taken up as an issue across the country by a diverse range of constituencies with agendas that were not always entirely compatible. For instance, presentations were made to the senate committee by women's and labour organizations, children's advocates, and youth groups from all provinces, by anglophones and francophones, and by representatives of Protestant and Catholic churches. Nevertheless, the problem evoked a different response in Quebec than it did in the rest of Canada simply because most of the material deemed to be indecent came from the United States and was published in English. I focus specifically on the construction of the problem in English Canada.

Given the U.S. origin of the pulps, I was surprised by how few attempts were made to counterpose a Canadian moralism against some version of American licentiousness. At the turn of the century, the relationship between the two countries was often sexualized in popular discourse. In her book on turn-of-the-century heterosexual conflict, Karen Dubinsky shows a wonderful example of this discursive strategy with an 1891 cartoon about a Canadian election fought over free trade. In the image, Miss Canada is being chased by a menacing Liberal (in favour of free trade) while Uncle Sam looks on approvingly. Tory John A. Macdonald (anti-free trade) steps in to save the virtue of the lady and the nation.[14] In the early cold-war era, the tendency was against such a polarization of Canadian and American interests. On the one hand, Canadian and American political ideologies were developing along somewhat similar cold-war-inspired lines; in the ideological fight against Communism the United States was an increasingly important ally, not one to be vilified as a moral threat. On the other hand, Canadians were increasingly exposed to various forms of U.S. popular culture.[15] It is likely that many Canadians would have been familiar with and felt affinity towards the many campaigns against immorality and obscenity that were taking place in the States. There was, in fact, a sharing of resources and personnel that took place among activists and organizations on both sides of the border. In this sense, the Canadian anti-comics campaign was decidedly different from the one that was unfolding in Britain, where the initiative was spearheaded by the British Communist Party as part of a general fight against American cultural imperialism.[16]

The Threat of Indecency, or Why the Concern about Obscenity?

What counted as harmful literature in the late 1940s and the 1950s was a wide range of material, although the exact details of its content is not always easy to ascertain. As they do today, standards of decency and propriety varied widely – even within class and ethnic groupings. Certainly there did not exist agreed-upon definitions – even in law – of either indecency or obscenity. What I am concerned with here, however, is not so much the actual content of materials that were thought to be indecent or obscene, but the language and discursive strategies used to present them as such. How was it that social critics were able to generate concern about particular types of publications? My findings are similar to those of Martin Barker in his analysis of the British campaign against horror comics. Barker found that arguments against the comics were based more on popular ideas about the young people who were assumed to be reading the comics than about the content of the books themselves.[17] In Canada, postwar debates about the moral effects of mass-market publications crystallized concerns about the nature of youth, their relationship to sexuality, and the place and character of sexuality in Canadian society.

Two distinct, but related, efforts to clean up Canadian newsstands suggest that different media came under scrutiny at different times. In the late 1940s, crime comics were the major concern, until a 1949 amendment to the Canadian Criminal Code almost completely eliminated them from the newsstands. In the 1950s, cheap paperbacks and what were referred to as 'girlie magazines' took their turn as targets of public protest and condemnation. Disapproval of these publications was insti-

tutionalized in the 1952 senate special committee. While these two episodes of moral concern exploited a variety of regulatory strategies –
some shared, some not – the ideologies that helped to construct them
were remarkably similar.

Anti-indecency campaigns (I use the word campaign with hesitation –
it suggests perhaps too organized a shape for what were often contradictory efforts) relied heavily on representations of young people as in need
of both protection and control, particularly in the realm of sex and
morality. Teens were assumed to be impressionable – 'born imitators' –
in ways that adults were not. Adolescence was seen as a time of both
sexual and moral development,[18] the success of the former depending to
a great extent on the success of the latter. With the proper guidance, teenagers could learn to control their unfolding sexuality. However, this
belief that teenage morality was a blank slate meant that teens were
open not only to 'proper' influences but to 'improper' ones as well.
Their moral immaturity – or moral innocence, as it was more likely to be
called – was said to leave them vulnerable to harmful sexual attitudes
that might lead to degeneracy and delinquency. As one magazine journalist claimed, 'The love comics are to the girly magazines what elementary schools are to high schools. If a child's taste is formed by love and
crime comics, he or she will continue to crave lurid, unreal, violent and
sexy material in print.'[19] And such material, apparently, could skew an
adolescent's understanding of her own social climate: 'The mass production and distribution of sensational novels depicting lewd, repulsive and
perverted behaviour of the characters as a normal way of life has super-
seded all other worthwhile publications offered for sale in Canadian
stores. Men and women are portrayed as monsters of perversion and the
women pictured as Lesbians and modern Messalinas. Added to this is
the continuous suggestion that crime and perversion is [sic] normal ...'[20]

More than anything else, it was normality that was deemed to be
under threat from the pulp publications. They were accused of making
immorality seem normal, of shifting the boundaries of what was seen to
be acceptable: perverts might cease to be perverse; abnormality might
fail to operate as a negative marker of sexual and moral difference from
the norm; monogamous heterosexual marriage might end up as just one
of many forms of sexual expression. Arguments about the dangers of
indecency suggested that a whole process of moral degeneration would
be put into effect if 'immature' teenagers read pulps, absorbed their sordid values, and carried them into the 1960s.

Young people were widely regarded as products in which adults

invested sums of time and money, along with material, emotional, intellectual, and spiritual resources. Parents considered it their right to make
these investments exclusively or to have them made by other adults of
their choosing. In this context, teenagers' reading of comics or dime-
store novels turned the publishers of this literature into trespassers and
usurpers of parental prerogative. The publishers were guilty of competing with and disrupting the influences of the home, the church, the
school. A widely circulated 1952 resolution from the town council of
Timmins, Ontario, included the following justification for regulatory
measures against obscenity: 'AND WHEREAS, millions have been spent
on excellent universities, high schools and public schools to educate our
children to become law-abiding, productive and lovable citizens, who
are our most sacred investment, and who should not be exposed to an
education, through the reading of filthy literature, stories of compromising situations, and details of sex crimes, which tend to undermine our
whole educational system ...'[21]

Some thought that bad literature was powerful enough not just to
threaten but to cancel the efforts of church, school, and home to educate
young people about proper forms of sex and family living. Members of
the Canadian Committee for the International Conference in Defence of
Children worried that indecent literature might turn young people from
the goals adults had set for them: 'high ideals, noble emotions and con-
structive action directed to the general good.'[22] Pulp literature was seen
as competition for approved forms of sex education (however limited
these were) that promoted the normalization of sexual and moral standards. The outcome of this contest could affect 'the whole moral tone of
the nation.'[23] 'Civilized life,' 'democracy,' and 'freedom' were all
thought to be dependent upon a particular, dominant version of morality. As long as this was challenged by the salacious materials on the
newsstands, the future itself seemed to be threatened.

During the early years of the cold war, statements about 'threats' to
the nation often concealed fears about Communism, and the discussion
about printed indecency was no exception to this. A direct relationship
was assumed between a particular version of moral health and Canada's
strength as a nation. Demoralization, in both senses of the word, was
assumed to be a prime strategy of infiltrating Communists. In their 1953
report, members of the Senate Special committee on Salacious and Indecent Literature stated that 'in the world-wide struggle between the
forces of darkness and evil and those of good, the freedom-loving, democratic countries have need of all the strength in their moral fibre to com-

bat the evil threat, and anything that undermines the morals of our citizens and particularly of the young is a direct un-Canadian act.'[24]

During the proceedings of the committee, chair J.C. Davis (who took over after the death of J.J. Hayes Doone, the instigator of the project) expressed his own racist version of this position, without any opposition from his colleagues: 'This is a Christian country, and we have to fight the powers of darkness from non-Christian countries. The morals of this country have to be strengthened to keep us strong. We are being attacked at the very roots by the influx of indecent literature and we have to stop it one way or another.'[25]

Notions of 'threat to the nation' operated discursively in much the same way as the more frequently cited 'threat to youth' – by stirring up moral indignation that might lead to calls for protective regulation. Moreover, each of these phrases could be used to underscore the gravity of the other: a threat to the nation was perceived to be a threat to teenagers and youth. Who could not be moved by the vulnerability of young people, struggling towards maturity? Who did not want them to develop to their full potential? Who could abandon the goals of those who had died so recently on European battlefields? Who could abandon their sons and daughters to an atmosphere of immorality and indecency that was assumed to be the antithesis of a democratic society? The crusade against obscenity and harmful literature was built on, and gained its momentum from, these kinds of discursive attachments. Notions of patriotism and 'Christian values' were called on to underscore arguments against the mass-market publications. They lent weight to an issue that might otherwise have appeared to be trivial.

The Canadian Fight against Crime Comics

In Canada, the fight to ban crime comics, although not entirely cohesive, was broadly based. As the product of well-organized efforts by individuals and groups it certainly had significant effects. The man most often identified with the crime comics campaign was E. Davie Fulton, Tory member of Parliament from Kamloops, British Columbia. Fulton claimed that national interest in the matter had been 'aroused' by the Federated Women's Institutes, the Federation of Home and School Associations, the Ontario Teachers' Federation, Parent–Teacher Federations, and the Imperial Order Daughters of the Empire (IODE) – all of them middle-class and predominantly female organizations.[26]

Comic books were by no means new in the late 1940s, but their content had undergone substantial change since they first appeared in the 1920s as bound collections of newspaper strips. In 1938, readers were introduced to Superman, the first super hero (created by Jerry Siegal and Toronto-born artist Joe Shuster). By 1941, American publishers were putting out 168 different titles, and by the middle of the war, National Periodical Publishers claimed sales of more than 12 million comics per month.[27] At its peak, in the postwar decade, it is estimated that the U.S. comics industry was producing 60 million comics per month.[28]

Before the war, Canadian comic book fans had developed their reading habits on a steady diet of American publications. But in December 1940, faced with a growing wartime trade deficit, Prime Minister Mackenzie King restricted the importation of non-essential goods from the United States. Comic-books were banned along with other fiction periodicals, opening the way for an indigenous comic book industry. According to historian John Bell, four Canadian publishers quickly made moves to take advantage of the trade restrictions. Bell says that while all four (Maple Leaf Publishing, Anglo-American, Hillborough Studios, and Bell Features and Publishing) published in various genres, they were particularly eager to make up for the absence of American superheroes.[29]

Canada's first two superheroes, Iron Man and Freelance, both debuted in 1941, and both had their origins in the 'Southern Hemisphere.' Iron Man was found living alone in a 'sunken bubble-city,' the only survivor of a civilization that had been wiped out by an earthquake. On returning to the surface-world, he used his indestructibility and superhuman strength to fight Nazis and other bad guys. Freelance, by comparison, grew up with a lost tribe in a tropical valley (!) in Antarctica. While he had no special powers beyond his amazing athletic ability, he too battled the Axis powers. Neither, says John Bell, had anything particularly Canadian about him. Thus it was Nelvana of the Northern Lights, issued in August 1941, who became Canada's first truly national superhero.

Based on a character from Inuit mythology, Nelvana was, nevertheless, portrayed as a white goddess, the personification of the North. She drew her supernatural powers from the Northern Lights and dressed in a short, fur-hemmed skirt, tall boots, and a cape. She had just about everything a superhero could want: she was immortal, she could fly, travel at the speed of light, melt metal, disrupt radio communications, make herself invisible, and alter her own shape and that of her brother (with whom she communicated telepathically). She put her powers to use fighting supernatural villains with nasty ties to the Nazis.[30]

Nelvana's male counterparts, Johnny Canuck and Canada Jack, emerged in 1942 and 1943, respectively. Created by Leo Bachle, who was at the time a student at Toronto's Danforth Technical School, Johnny was a captain in the air force and travelled the world fighting the Axis powers. And while he had no supernatural abilities, Johnny was always triumphant. Bell identifies the critical elements of any Johnny Canuck story as: 'an exotic locale, contact with the anti-Axis underground, a beautiful woman and countless improbable escapes by "Canada's answer to Nazi oppression."'[31] Canada Jack was similarly without supernatural powers. His adventures took place on the home front, where he battled saboteurs and Nazi spies, clad in a tank top and gymnast's tights. He was assisted by a group of children known as the Canada Jack Club which, Bell says, 'was quite unique in that it existed both in the pages of the *Canadian Heroes* comic book and in the real world.'[32]

The success of Canada's wartime superheroes was short-lived. In 1945, the borders opened again to U.S. imports, and the Canadian comics industry began to collapse.[33] A 'Canadian Comic Report,' compiled by Superior Publishing Limited in Toronto, claimed that between November 1948 and October 1949 the total number of titles on Canadian newsstands grew from 95 to 176. The number of Canadian titles listed in the document was only 23.[34]

After the Second World War, the patriotic superheroes took a back seat to new narrative genres. Crime, horror, and love comics became especially popular, launching a wave of public concern. New titles appeared regularly, and many readers increased their consumption by exchanging copies with friends. As Fulton said, the whole process of buying, reading, and trading could occur outside parents' control. Newspaper and magazine articles frequently played up the fact that comics were not a large part of adult culture. Parents and teachers were often described in the act of 'discovering' a 'hidden stash' in a child's room or school desk. Apparently many were 'shocked' by what they found: drawings of women that emphasized their breasts and buttocks; detailed stories about crime, including murder and rape; titles like *Tales from the Crypt*, *Haunt of Fears*, *Crimes by Women*, *Heart Throb*, and *Flaming Love*.

Toronto Board of Education trustee W.R. Cockburn was typical of those who spoke out against comics. In 1945 he raised concerns about them with the board's Management Committee, saying they were 'degrading and detrimental to the welfare of our youth.'[35] Complaining that biblical comics were largely unavailable in Toronto, Cockburn showed his colleagues comic books he had been able to buy in the city –

Daring, Human Torch, Black Terror, and *Boy Commandos* – saying, 'They're nothing but a lot of rot about daggers and guns.' A similar argument was endorsed in 1947 by the members of the IODE's National Education Committee who lamented the eclipsing of funny comics: 'Instead we have "Superman" and gangs of thieves, G-men and sadistic murderers who carve their way through the "funny pages" talking plain talk, and giving people "the works."'[36]

While views like those expressed by Cockburn and the members of the IODE were widely reported on, they were not shared by everyone. In 1949, *Chatelaine* ran a story by Mary Jukes called 'Are Comics Really a Menace?'[37] In an attempt to interrupt prevailing anti-comics discourse she claimed that psychologists, teachers, and parents 'do not look upon this form of entertainment as dangerous [despite] the daily papers continu[ing] to turn up stories tying juvenile delinquency to the reading of certain types of comics.' In a poll of 2000 of its readers, *Chatelaine* found that 'they are wholeheartedly in favor of real comics; they don't feel that all comics should be scrapped because of the few horror numbers.' Of course, the acceptability of 'real' (funny?) comics was precisely the point the IODE had been trying to make. Fulton, Cockburn, and the others who raised their concerns publicly didn't think all comics should be scrapped; their goal was to influence policies that separated the 'good' (what they called 'real') comics from the 'bad.' It was a position that many of the *Chatelaine* readers seemed to share, despite Jukes's attempts to construct their opposition to it. One-sixth of mothers, she said, found comics to be 'trashy, awful and undesirable,' while 'the majority object only to those portraying violence, ugliness and fantastic situations ... Another large group disapprove of the fantastic type of comic – the phantom woman whose supernatural powers involve her constantly in fisticuffs with burly men; sexy women with bodies of Lana Turner and spirits of Genghis Khan, to quote one [reader] 'Even Hollywood has never lifted the American bust to the high place it occupies in the fantastic and crime type of comic."'[38]

Portrayals of crimes, overly graphic representations of women's bodies, and a rarely defined immorality were the main concerns of the anti-comics crusaders. Today, postwar comics seem an odd mix of provocativeness and predictability. In Canadian titles, at least, the good guys and gals always won – even if it wasn't until the last frame – and, generally, crime didn't pay. But such morally acceptable endings were invariably preceded by fights, killings, and other dirty deeds, depictions of scantily clad women, and graphic or textual sexual innuendo. 'Barry

Kuda,' a story in a 1946 issue of *Unusual Comics* (Bell Comics, Toronto), shows how these 'dangerous' elements were combined: 'What made the walls of Queen Merma's palace tremble as she held a farewell banquet for Barry Kuda and Algie? Barry was soon to learn, when the banquet hall became a scene of boiling terror and Sato's awful army, with their bodies glowing red hot, fought to brand the Queen's domain with THE SYMBOL OF SIN!'[39]

As Sato's volcanic eruption destroys Merma's palace, the blond and muscular Barry Kuda (wearing a wrestling-type singlet and shorts) carries the slim, white, long-haired Merma (wearing bikini shorts and conical breast-coverings) to safety. Barry returns to the palace to fight the devilish Sato, complete with horns, and to find his friend Algie. But Barry's plan is foiled when he is frozen stiff in his tracks by one of Sato's men.

In the meantime, Sato himself has gone in search of Merma.

Merma: What do you want, Sato? Keep away! What can you gain by killing me?
Sato: But - I'm not going to kill you, my dear. It's lonely in Volcania! I'd like a real queen for a wife!
Merma: No! No! Not that! Barry – Bar –

Her cries are to no avail. Merma gets frozen too. In the next frame, she is lying helpless on a table, Sato's doctor hanging over her scantily clothed body. When her 'frozen flesh is thawed,' he gets ready to inject her with the blood of one of Sato's guards so that she will be able to survive in their underworld. 'Oh. No! No! Barry! Algie! Help!'

The scene shifts to the outside of the palace where Barry has managed to thaw himself out, find his friend, and kill some of Sato's minions. Bodies are flying in all directions. And just in time, Barry and Algie run through the carnage to find Merma who is about to receive the injection of devilish blood. 'Help No —— Oh, Barry! Thank Heavens!' Sato is vanquished, Merma is saved, and Barry and Algie are fêted as heroes.

A 'Lucky Coyne' episode, from a 1946 issue of *F.B.I.* comics, is a more typical crime story.[40] It, too, portrays fighting, a mild brand of sexual sadism, and women in suggestive clothing and poses. But again, good triumphs over evil at the end. The story opens with Lucky Coyne, a journalist and regular guy (no special powers), interviewing a recently released convict, Count Morphine. Morphine has just opened a lonely hearts club. He tells Lucky his time in prison left him sympathetic to the plight of lonely people. Lucky smells a rat. He sends his pals Kitty and

Terry off to visit the club. From their vantage point on the dance floor, they try to figure out what Morphine is really up to. But Morphine over-hears their deliberations, and the two plants are whisked to the base-ment where they are shown a woman in a torn dress, chained hand and foot to what looks like a large wooden water wheel. 'This lonely heart's beloved is a bit late in his appointment,' Morphine tells them. 'He should have returned three minutes ago.' Morphine's helper starts to turn the woman on the wheel and she screams (in huge bold capitals), 'OH, NO, NO!'

In the next frames, Terry's arms are bound behind his back as Kitty is tied beneath a large vice that is covered in nails. Morphine turns to Terry: 'Mike will take you to a certain jewelry store. Your speedy return and what you bring will determine your playmate's fate!' The bound Terry clues in: 'So that's your game! Torturing a guy's girl unless he robs for you!' Fortunately, Lucky sees Terry being forced down the street by Mike. Lucky decks Mike. Terry explains the situation to him as they run back to the club. They get to Kitty just as the nails are about to crush her. They save the woman on the wheel, Kitty phones the police, and Lucky and Terry go upstairs to corner the evil Morphine. After a few punches, the police arrive, the thieves are put out of business, and we see Kitty hanging on Lucky in the final frame.

Opponents said that the comics 'glamorize[d] crime, brutality and immorality'[41] and gave young people 'a wrong idea of the civilized way of life.'[42] Adult commentators tended to take the view that young read-ers (blank slates that they were assumed to be) passively absorbed what-ever the comics put before them and that, once exposed to crime, sex, and violence on the page, children and teens would develop a taste for it and be moved to re-enact it in daily life.

In June 1948, Fulton first introduced the issue into the House of Com-mons, arguing that crime comics were leading Canadian young people into delinquency. While this flagging of possible moral degeneration got the issue on the government's agenda, it was not enough to convince the minister of justice, J.L. Ilsley, of the immediate need for suppression. The minister claimed that his own research, including queries to the provin-cial attorneys general, had not uncovered any conclusive evidence of the link between reading crime comics and subsequent delinquent activity. Ilsley quoted Dr C.M. Hincks, general director of the National Commit-tee for Mental Hygiene, who said: 'It has never been scientifically estab-lished that crime or thrill stories either in movies, radio or comics have contributed to delinquency. Prohibiting publication is an admission of failure on the part of the family and the educational system in encouraging the development of wholesome and healthy interests.'[43]

Ilsley's stance on comics was a 'scientific' one versus the decidedly moral approach adopted by Fulton. Originally, Fulton had attempted to take a more 'rational' approach. Before introducing his bill, he requested statistics on delinquency from the minister of justice. But the figures he received, for crimes committed by people under the age of eighteen, did little to help his case. In 1945 there had been 3934 convictions; in 1946 there were 3682; and in 1947 there were 3350.[44] Despite Fulton's continued claims to the contrary, the actual incidence of delinquency was falling. According to sociologist Augustine Brannigan, this trend in delinquency rates was consistent for the years 1942 to 1949, and the figures remained 'relatively low' until the mid-1950s.[45] Still Fulton persisted, appealing to common-sense notions of what was good for young people, of how easily they might be corrupted, and of how dangerous the effects of comic books were:

I just want to give an example from the one [comic book] I have in my hand. It starts off on the inside cover with the picture of a man striking a match and staring at it. The caption over the next picture is, 'Tonight I dreamed of a blazing moon like a fiery wheel in the sky – burning trees were crashing about me,' and the caption is illustrated. The next picture portrays him walking to a slum tenement, and he says, 'I saw an old condemned building. Nobody would care if it burned down.' The next picture shows this man holding a burning match, and the caption says, 'Tonight I stole into the cellar of the condemned building and set my first fire.' That is a fine thing to put before a youngster of twelve or so, who perhaps has just struck his first match.[46]

Eventually, Ilsley conceded that legislation was necessary. Apparently, his change of position came after he received a selection of comics from Fulton – *Crime* and *Crime Does Not Pay* – comics which Ilsley characterized as a flagrant abuse of freedom of the press. But Ilsley wanted to take his time over the new law, and the conclusion of the comics debate was held off until the next parliamentary session. By the time that session was underway, Ilsley had retired from politics and been replaced as justice minister by Stuart Garson. Fulton introduced his Private Member's Bill once again, and a full-scale debate of crime comics occupied the House for several days.

MPs rallied to the call to protect youth from 'the trash you get in these dime crime comic books.'[47] In a particularly evocative, though not entirely typical, contribution to the Commons debate, Daniel McIvor, MP for Fort William, described the crime comics as a tactic of 'the devil.' He said, 'You can almost hear him saying, "Get them young. That is the time to get them." Our Sunday school teachers can work their heads off and still not succeed in combating an agency such as obscene literature. It is a curse.'[48]

Many of the MPs admitted to having made studies of crime comics at their local drugstore or in their home ridings. They argued their support for Fulton's bill on the basis of personal experience and gut reaction. They waved (unnamed) comics at their colleagues and read statements from concerned constituents. Howard C. Green (Vancouver-Quadra) read from a letter from 'a mother in Vancouver, who, by the way, is the daughter of a distinguished Canadian authoress': 'I know you are as anxious as any conscientious parent to see our Canadian children rescued from the evil effects of these criminal immoral magazines. I believe a big house-cleaning of our magazine and paper-back 25-cent books is overdue. We busy ourselves building youth centres, working in church to show our young people the guide posts to clean living, and all the time a stream of filthy books is allowed to come into our country.'[49] The MPs mobilized common-sense assumptions about shared moral principles: 'I know it would disgust everyone in the House and it would disgust the average man and woman right across Canada.'[50] There was much mutual congratulation on the 'high level' of the debate, and there were commendations for Fulton from the other MPs and for the minister of justice for bringing the bill to the House.

Bill 10 was passed in December 1949. It amended section 207 of the Criminal Code which dealt with obscene literature: 'to cover the case of those magazines and periodicals commonly called "crime comics," the publication of which is presently legal, but which it is widely felt tend to the lowering of morals and to induce the commission of crimes by juveniles.'[51] While the actual wording of the amendment was broad and vague, its inclusion in the general section on 'obscene literature' is telling. Subsection one of section 207 would be contravened by anyone who 'prints, publishes, sells or distributes any magazine, periodical or book which exclusively or substantially comprises matter depicting pictorially the commission of crimes, real or fictitious, thereby tending or likely to induce or influence youthful persons to violate the law or to corrupt the morals of such persons.'[52] Even in law the moral capacities of young people were what set the bounds of decency. Under such a broad definition, fairy tales and news articles might have been subject to prosecution. Of course, they were not. Crime comics, on the other hand, rapidly disappeared from Canadian newsstands. At the end of 1950, a researcher for the Toronto Board of Education claimed to have found no crime comics for sale in the city.[53]

Fredric Wertham and *Seduction of the Innocent*

One of the main proponents of the theory that comics were dangerous literature – the reading of which could lead otherwise normal youngsters to perform criminal or sexually immoral activities – was Dr Fredric Wertham, senior psychiatrist for the New York City Department of Hospitals from 1932 to 1952. In 1948, the year E. Davie Fulton introduced his bill into the Canadian House of Commons, Wertham published five articles in popular American magazines denouncing comics in general and crime comics in particular.[54] In the House of Commons debates, Fulton referred to Wertham and cited his American 'evidence' as support for the proposed amendment to the Criminal Code.

Wertham outlined his position in detail in his 1954 book, *Seduction of the Innocent*, which was a featured selection for the Book-of-the-Month Club that year.[55] The book mentions E. Davie Fulton and the passage of Bill 10, quotes from *Hansard*, and speaks in glowing terms throughout most of a chapter about the work against comics that had been done in Canada, both in Parliament and among ordinary citizens:[56] 'No debate on such a high ethical plane, with proper regard for civil liberties but with equal regard for the rights and happiness of children, has ever taken place in the United States.'[57]

It is impossible, here, to do a full critique of Wertham. Nevertheless, it is important to consider his work because it was so influential on Canadian activists. He was quoted in the House of Commons debates. He was referred to and cited by people writing to the Ontario attorney general. He corresponded with members of the British Columbia Parent–Teacher Federation, including a Mrs Eleanor Gray, who was mentioned by name in *Seduction of the Innocent*. In a letter he wrote to thank Gray for a Christmas card, Wertham acknowledged his own importance in the international debate on comics when he wrote, 'P.S: If you wish to, you may quote any part of this letter in any way you wish.'[58]

According to Wertham, comic books affected reading skills, desensitized young people to violence, and led to delinquent behaviour, psychological difficulties, and problems in sexual development. While delinquency, illiteracy, and sex each get their own chapter in *Seduction of the Innocent*, concerns about sexuality appear throughout the book, as does the evocative sexual language that Wertham used to build his case. For instance: 'I have come to the conclusion that this *chronic stimulation, temptation and seduction* by comic books, both their content and their *alluring* advertisements of knives and guns are contributing factors to many children's maladjustment' (emphasis mine).[59] At times he was even more blatant, writing, for instance, that children 'give up crime-comic reading like a bad sexual habit.'[60] But what operates as a literary device on one page becomes fact on another – for Wertham, reading comics *was* a bad sexual habit. In a chapter entitled, 'I want to be a sex maniac!' he says that 'an elementary fact of [his] research' is that 'comic books stimulate children sexually.'[61] Wertham took it as self-evidently bad that 'children' should be sexually 'turned on.' Reading comics, he said, impedes 'the free [sexual] development of children' and causes 'sexual arousal which amounts to seduction.'

Wertham's tendency to refer to children, while offering case studies of adolescents, was a rhetorical technique that helped to support his main argument that comics 'seduced' the 'innocent.' To have referred to adolescents would have been to refer to young people who were already in the process of becoming sexual, who were somewhat less than sexually innocent. In invoking 'children,' as an imperilled group, Wertham heightened the sense of moral outrage implicit in his writing. The slipperiness between the terms child and adolescent that is evident in Wertham's text is not unique to him, though he manipulates it to his advantage in a remarkable fashion. That adolescence was considered by many to be a transitional 'stage' between childhood and adulthood contributed to the slippery usage. Definitions of adolescence as transitional meant that while adolescents were not children, they continued to be affected by notions about childhood – for instance, the ambiguous concept of childhood innocence.

'Innocence' was put to work by anti-indecency activists in a number of ways, although it was generally employed to rouse in adults a protective 'instinct.' According to sociologists Rex Stainton-Rogers and Wendy Stainton-Rogers, various notions of childhood innocence have persisted in Western culture since at least medieval times, their roots lying in Christian ideas about infants as free from sin. The Stainton-Rogerses write that since Rousseau's *Émile* (1762), childhood innocence has remained a romantic and valorized ideal in Western societies.[62] But while this notion of innocence has been long-lasting, it remains a difficult one to pin down. We can see various senses of the word by counterposing it to a range of opposites. The Stainton-Rogers suggest 'knowingness, ignorance, savagery and animality' as some of the possibilities, along with sexuality, which they claim is 'by far the most common' opposition.[63] But the meaning that sexuality might take on in this instance is elusive in its own right. Wertham's concern about even the sexual feelings young people had was just one of many possible perspectives on what constituted evidence of corruption.

Certainly, Wertham's talk about sex would have fuelled parents' fears about their children's reading habits. The whole notion of seduction, which appears first in the title and re-emerges throughout the text, rests on a giving up of control, a giving in to temptation. It suggests a triumph of desire over rationality – not the sort of thing to facilitate children's obedience to their teachers and parents, or their allegiance to sexual and moral norms. But worse than this, seduction comes about by the allure of someone or something compelling and powerful. One is rarely seduced by the everyday; a seducer is much more likely an outsider, an unknown. A seducer is mysterious and illusive. And he or she succeeds in the seduction not by using physical force but by enticing the seducee to consent. How could parents fight such a force? How could they ensure not only their children's physical safety, but their mental and moral safety as well?

It is tempting to read anything peculiar to the 1950s as a response to, or a consequence of, anti-Communist ideology and the cold war. In Wertham's case, it is almost impossible not to make that connection. Throughout his study, he exploits the fear parents had that they were losing control of their children, that economic and technological changes were complicating the world and creating distance between the young and the old. At a time when tight, emotionally fulfilling families were promoted as essential to the pursuit of personal and political security, anything that put space between children and their parents (not only comics but also rock 'n'roll and dance, hair, and clothing styles) was suspect. And anything that 'seduced' children, that made them consent to their own lack of parental control, reeked of brainwashing (read: popular explanation for the spread of Communism). It was Wertham's ability (whether conscious or not) to give sexual overtones to this fear of the unknown and the foreign and to link the whole package to children that made his book resonate so strongly with many of its readers.

Certainly, Wertham was not the only one to believe that comics had a negative effect on children's sexuality, but he was the only one to state his concerns so explicitly. While other commentators spoke demurely of the links between comics and perversion or comics and immorality, Wertham spoke explicitly about masturbation, sado-masochistic fantasies, homosexuality and homoeroticism, prostitution, and sex crime. Though his concerns were numerous, underlying them all was the risk that young people were being exposed to things of which they apparently had no prior knowledge, things that he felt were not suitable for children (however defined), including, and especially, their own sexual feelings. He cites numerous cases where boys and girls recounted to him masturbatory fantasies which were 'aggravated' by reading comics. Even in those cases where young adults seemed to have emerged from their comics-reading years unharmed, Wertham held steadfastly to his position that they might, nevertheless, end up with sexual troubles: 'But is it not one of the elementary facts of modern psychopathology that childhood experiences very often do not manifest themselves as recognizable symptoms or behavior patterns in childhood, but may crop up later in adult life as perverse and neurotic tendencies?'[64]

Wertham's analysis rested on a simple construction of monkey read, monkey do, based on his clinical observation of troubled youth. He was particularly concerned about what he saw as the tendencies of the various forms of comics to encourage homoerotic attitudes. Would the millions of comics circulating across North America lead to an increase in the number of sex deviates? Wertham claims that certain types of comics tended to fix boys in their pre-adolescent phase of disdain for girls – what other writers frequently called the 'normal' homosexual phase of heterosexual development.[65] It seems that homo-erotic attitudes were caused, in part, by 'the presentation of masculine, bad, witchlike or violent women. In such comics women are depicted in a definitely anti-erotic light, while the young male heroes have pronounced erotic overtones.'[66]

Wertham lamented the fate of adolescent boys, who lived with their own fears of becoming homosexual. Apparently such boys were likely to become 'addicted' to the 'homoerotically tinged type of comic book,' a habit which could only lead to homoerotic fantasies, followed inevitably by guilt and shame as they learned of social taboos against sexual deviation. Certainly, homosexually inclined boys had few other sources to turn to for acknowledgment of their desires, and, given the social climate, they may have felt shame about their reading habits. But, of course, Wertham was not concerned about the discriminatory social conditions and widespread intolerance that led to those feelings of oppression; he was concerned about the tenor of the comic books. Singled out as exemplary of those needing to be cleaned up were the 'dangerous' chronicles of the Caped Crusader and the Boy Wonder.

Wertham's discussion of Batman is a prime example of 1950s moral panic about sex perversion – four and a half pages of 'expert opinion' on the 'Ganymede-Zeus type of love-relationship.' His arguments about the dangers of Batman drew on the most stereotypical signifiers of homoness and on a macho individualist version of masculinity more suited to the receding frontier than to postwar domesticity and middle-class corporate life.

At home they [Batman and Robin, aka Bruce and Dick] lead an idyllic life ... They live in sumptuous quarters, with beautiful flowers in large vases, and have a butler, Alfred. Batman is sometimes shown in a dressing gown. As they sit by the fireplace the young boy sometimes worries about his partner: 'Something's wrong with Bruce. He hasn't been himself these past few days.' It's like a wish dream of two homosexuals living together. Sometimes they are shown on a couch, Bruce reclining and Dick sitting next to him, jacket off, collar open, and his hand on his friend's arm.[67]

Moreover, Robin was often shown standing with his legs apart, 'the genital region strictly evident,' and Batman, in their crusading adventures, frequently came to Robin's rescue. By Wertham's definition, the stories contained no 'decent, attractive, successful women,' evidence of an anti-woman attitude he equated with the homoerotic theme. Boys exposed to this pastiche of codes and signifiers would, no doubt, be incited to homoerotic fantasies. And, Wertham claimed, he had the case studies to prove it.

While girls are mentioned infrequently in *Seduction of the Innocent*, they too were at the mercy of the comic-book publishers, perhaps even more so than boys. Wertham contends that female character development was more severely affected by comics than was male character development, primarily because of the nature of female superheroes.[68] He considered characters like Wonder Woman so far outside normal constructions of femininity that girls would be thrown into a spin of mental torment if they should ever endeavour to identify with their heroines.

Resting on his claim to 'professional' knowledge, Wertham 'outs' Wonder Woman, asserting that her lesbianism is 'psychologically unmistakable.' Apparently, Wonder Woman 'is always a horror type. She is physically very powerful, tortures men, has her own female following, is the cruel, "phallic" woman. While she is a frightening figure for boys, she is an undesirable ideal for girls, being the exact opposite of what girls are supposed to want to be.'[69] One could make much of the 'supposed to' in this sentence. Is Wertham responding to women's and girls' dissatisfaction with postwar discourses on femininity? Is the powerful Wonder Woman a symbolic foreshadowing of the eruption of 1960s feminism? Is this why Wertham is careful not to make any mention of Wonder Woman's sidekick, the pudgy, bon-bon eating Etta?

In the context of postwar psychological discourse, so-called normal sexuality, as we have seen, was not a given; it needed to be fought for and nurtured. 'Normal' sexuality was thought to be the culmination of a precarious developmental process that might easily be sent astray. Outside influences could stall or preclude the attainment by adolescents of sexual maturity. Comics, at least as Wertham and his followers understood them, were clearly in this category of outside threat. What was thought to make comics especially dangerous was the fact that they were deliberately aimed at a young readership. While their content was 'tame' when compared to, say, sex magazines, the moral imperative to clean comics up was considerable because of the long-term consequences they might have had on the 'immature' characters of their intended young audience. The perceived unambiguous relationship between comics and youth was critical to the success of the anti-comics activists. Certainly the passage of the Fulton bill was a major victory for them. More importantly, concerned citizens were also able to exert tremendous pressure directly on the publishers. In 1954, the publishers developed their own production code, similar to that used in the film industry. Overseen by the Comics Magazine Association of America, the code included guidelines such as the following:

- All characters shall be depicted in dress reasonably acceptable to society.
- Illicit sex relations are neither to be hinted at or portrayed. Violent love scenes as well as sexual abnormalities are unacceptable.
- Respect for parents, the moral code, and for honorable behavior shall be fostered. A sympathetic understanding of the problems of love is not a license for morbid distortion.[70]

While campaigns against the perceived immorality in other types of reading material also drew on discourses about young people's vulnerability to corruption, the frame of the discussion was not the same as it had been in the fight against comics. Unlike the market for comics, the market for sex magazines and pulp novels was not primarily made up of children and teenagers. To talk about protecting young people from the influence of these adult publications was to admit, on some level, a loss of control over young people by adults and a failure to maintain the innocence the campaigns claimed they were protecting. Would the truly innocent youth read such things? It was a contradiction the campaigners never addressed.

Targeting Obscenity: The Senate Committee on Salacious and Indecent Literature

For those concerned about the reading materials available to young Canadians, Fulton's success with the crime comics bill was a mixed blessing. Some claimed it left open a space that was filled by other, perhaps even more dangerous publications – 'by offensive substitutes no less harmful to character formation.'[71] Certainly the elimination of the crime comics left a gap on the agendas of the decency crusaders. But it was a gap that was quickly filled, as concerned citizens turned their attentions to other genres of so-called immoral literature, including pulp magazines and mass-market novels.

New Brunswick senator J.J. Hayes Doone said that Fulton's fight had prepared the path for this next step to clean up the newsstands. In May 1952, Doone presented to the Senate arguments against 'offensive publications,' saying that the (unnamed) magazines, books, and photographs provoked juvenile delinquency and adolescent crime, that they were 'dangerous to the permanence of family life,' and 'evidence of a breakdown in our social machinery.'[72] In response to what he claimed was widespread public demand, Doone appealed to his colleagues, 'particularly on behalf of children,' to establish a special committee of the Senate to investigate

1. Salacious and indecent literature;
2. Publications otherwise objectionable from the standpoint of crime promotion, including crime comics, treasonable and perversive tracts and periodicals;
3. Lewd drawings, pictures, photographs and articles whether offered as art or otherwise presented for circulation.[73]

The motion was agreed to, and in 1952 the committee met six times. They heard twenty-five witnesses and received 'hundreds' of briefs, letters, and petitions. At the end of the parliamentary session, the committee recommended, and the Senate agreed, that it be reappointed in the next session.[74] Surprisingly, given its success as a vehicle for public opinion, the committee's final report, presented in April 1953 and presumably based on the hundreds of pages of its published proceedings, covered only five pages and included but a single recommendation. Committee members suggested that customs operations be expanded in order to deal with the 'serious threat to the moral standards of Canada' that resulted from the importation of American publications.

Nowhere did the committee ever define salacious or indecent literature, though they said it came in many forms: 'The soft-covered book, selling at a small price; numerous periodicals and magazines; and a more recently threatening immense influx of the digest type of sex literature.'[75] The assumed danger in all of these, and the primary (stated) concern of committee members, was their 'effect on the Canadian juvenile mind and conscience,' even though – unlike comics – these publications were not directed specifically at young people. Nevertheless, concerns for the 'moral and mental fitness' of teenagers were said to motivate the committee's work generally, and the many, many calls for regulation which it entertained.

While the committee's report did not lead to any immediate or substantive legislative change, the effects of the committee, as generator and disseminator of a national discourse, were not negligible. The proceedings, and news reports of them, contributed to a heightened public awareness of the 'dangers' to be found on local newsstands; they helped strengthen general notions that the integrity of 'shared' Canadian moral standards needed to be protected; they underscored the discursive relationship between teen immorality (sex delinquency) and 'offensive' reading material; and they lent a significant institutional authority to the various clean-up campaigns organized by churches and community groups. In all of these senses, Doone's initiative was tremendously successful.

None of those who spoke before the committee was in favour of the continued unregulated circulation of the 'salacious and indecent literature.' Even representatives of the distributors echoed prevailing sentiments about the need 'to do something.' But ideas on what that 'something' might be varied. There were few explicit calls for censorship, and a number of presenters actually made speeches about its dangers. In terms of postwar discourses on democracy, censorship evoked images of Soviet repression and a 'threat to essential liberties.'[76] Most briefs focused on the need to tighten existing obscenity legislation and to encourage its enforcement with the weight of public opinion. The court actions that this enforcement might lead to were not considered to be censorship. Instead, they were seen as evidence of justice at work. The removal of a book or magazine from circulation was simply one of the limitations on public life that were necessary for the protection of freedom.

A central feature of the moral panic over indecency was that nowhere in these discussions were the definitions of immorality and indecency at issue, nor was the need of Canadians to be protected from them questioned. Immorality and indecency were assumed to be known and harmful categories; all that needed to be asked – by concerned senators, editorial writers, or parents – was how they could best be dealt with. This limited frame of reference is blatantly obvious in the evidence from an Ottawa obscenity case that ran concurrently with the first round of the senate hearings. In the trial evidence, one sees how this truncated debate was made possible by ideas about the relationship between youth and sexuality. Indeed, one can also see that had it been possible to step outside prevailing discourses of childhood and adolescence, the trial might never have occurred.

Lesbianism as Obscenity or *Women's Barracks* as a Threat to Girls

In March 1952, National News Company, an Ottawa distributor, was charged under Section 207 of the Criminal Code with eleven counts of having obscene matter in its possession, 'for the purpose of distributing.' Seven 'girlie' magazines and four pulp novels were named in the charges. All were eventually found to be obscene by Judge A.G. McDougall, and National News was fined a total of $1100.[77]

Among the novels was *Women's Barracks*, written by an obscure French author named Tereska Torres.[78] Its story is similar to the one told in Torres's 1970 autobiography about her time in the women's section of the Free French Army during the Second World War.[79] The novel follows a group of women who spent several years together in a London barracks. We read of their work assignments and drills, of their hopes for France, and their social and sexual lives. The characters are a mixed lot, mostly young heterosexuals, though there are two lesbians and an 'older' (forty-year-old), sexually experienced woman named Claude who has affairs with men and women. Several of the heterosexual women have affairs with married men, one of them gets pregnant out of wedlock, all of them drink. In the midst of this, the narrator operates as the moral centre of the book. She distances herself from the other women and their sexual and emotional experiments – engaging in none of her own – trying to maintain her ideals about love, fidelity, and marriage.

To the present-day reader, Torres's prose is far from lurid. Nevertheless, *Women's Barracks* was packaged in typical 1950s pulp style and marketed as 'THE FRANK AUTOBIOGRAPHY OF A FRENCH GIRL SOLDIER.' While the allusions to sex in the book are many, the details of it are few. In her foreword to the book, Torres links the sexual activity and its emotional fallout to the adversities of war; in 'normal' circumstances, she suggests, little of this activity would have taken place.[80]

When the book first came to trial, Crown Attorney Raoul Mercier's strategy was a simple one. He wanted to prove, simply, that the book had been for sale in a particular cigar store, that the store had been supplied by National News, and that copies of the book had been found on the premises of the distribution company. He was confident that the judge would find the text itself obscene when he came to read it.

In 1952, the test of obscenity used by Canadian courts was 'whether the tendency of the matter charged as obscene is to deprave and corrupt those whose minds are open to such immoral influence and into whose hands a publication of this sort may fall.'[81] Based on notions of innocent and impressionable youth, the test was a lowest-common-denominator definition of what was appropriate for Canadian readers, adults and children alike. Known as the 'Hicklin test,' it was first defined by British judge C.J. Cockburn in 1868 and introduced into Canadian courts in 1904.[82] In his ruling, in a case about an anti-Catholic pamphlet, Cockburn stated explicitly that he was concerned with the danger a work charged as obscene posed to 'the minds of the young of either sex, or even to persons of more advanced years.' Canadian judges maintained this primary emphasis on youth. In a 1957 obscenity case, *Regina v. American News*, Ontario Court of Appeal judge J.A. Laidlaw wrote: 'I have no doubt that the object of the law is to protect the youth of the nation and to guard them against the danger of exposing their morals to impure matter ... Cockburn C.J. mentioned youth in his judgment in the *Hicklin case*, and most Judges in considering whether or not a particular matter is obscene have regard to the youth of the nation.'[83]

The Hicklin test remained in effect in Canada until 1959, when amendments to section 150(8) of the revised Criminal Code (1953–4) detailed a definition of obscenity based on the 'undue exploitation of sex,' where the term 'undue' had 'regard to the existing standards of decency in the community.' In 1962, this new definition was the basis of the Supreme Court of Canada decision that dismissed a charge of obscenity against the book *Lady Chatterley's Lover*. This decision also rendered the Hicklin test obsolete. In shifting the direction of judicial concern from the 'minds of youth' to 'community standards,' the new law helped forestall a tendency to declare material that might have been 'harmful' for young readers to be harmful in general. It was this tendency, institutionalized by the Hicklin test, that made adolescent morals a major focus of the *Women's Barracks* case.

Under the law, no one could be convicted on an obscenity charge if they could prove that the 'public good' had been served by the act in question. This was the grounds of the defence strategy pursued by National News's lawyers, G.W. Ford and J.M. McLean. As they put it, even if Torres's book was technically obscene, it still might have fulfilled a social purpose.[84] Expert witnesses were called to explain just what that purpose might have been. The crown attorney, wanting equal time, revised his original strategy and called his own experts to prove the first lot wrong. All told, the trial gave rise to a substantial, public, documented discussion of lesbianism.

While lesbianism is clearly not the focus of the novel, it was the focus of courtroom debate. A copy of the novel is filed with the court transcripts at the Archives of Ontario. Inside the front cover are the initials 'R.M.,' presumably referring to Crown Attorney Raoul Mercier. Throughout the text are underlinings and annotations in both pencil and black pen. Fifteen pages are marked with tags made out of sticky tape, possibly pages from which Mercier might have wanted to read in the courtroom. On all but two of these pages, there is some reference to lesbianism.[85] In the margins Mercier has written: 'lesbianism' and 'sex act' (each of these is repeated several times); 'lesbian crave' (56); 'ménage à trois' (87); 'homosexual' (32); 'act of lesbianism' (125). The one scene of lesbian seduction is marked 'all previous chapters lead to but this one climax' (46); passages prior to this are marked 'preparation' (34) and 'build-up' (12 and 36), presumably referring to the scene of lesbian seduction. There are no tags on the parts where heterosexual women find themselves pregnant, or where they discuss their plans to sleep with married men, or where they attempt suicide. The definition of immorality at work here is too narrow to include them. For Mercier, what made this book obscene was its discussion of lesbianism.

Even one of the expert witnesses for the defence, Toronto *Globe and Mail* writer J.A. McAree, claimed that lesbianism was the 'theme' of the book.[86] Certainly, he and his colleagues did nothing to challenge the alignment of lesbianism with immorality. In fact, the basis of defence arguments was that Torres's novel served the public good by warning its readers, especially young women, about the dangers of lesbianism.

Allan Seiger, a professor at the University of Michigan, tried to underscore the relationship of the lesbian activity to the war: 'These women are to be regarded, I think, as much casualties of the war as other soldiers ...'[87] John Bakless, a journalism professor at the University of New York, stated that the book presented the lesbian episodes as being 'positively repulsive to any normal male or female.'[88] He also said that in 'the context of the book as a whole they clearly point out that the wages of sin is death.'[89] But, asks Mercier, is it not likely that

> a little girl who is not maybe a French woman in the same barracks, but who is in [a] convent or in a boarding school reaching the puberty age, does not know anything about these things, reads this passage from this book, wouldn't you say they would be willing to indulge in this practice to see if it is as described?
>
> A: I have read that book through, and I wouldn't want to be near a lesbian. Don't forget what happens ...
>
> Q: And you do not think they would be tempted to try lesbianism?
>
> A: No, sir, there is disaster there too plainly, and it is only with sympathy and regret that you can read it ...[90]

What happens is that Ursula, the sixteen-year-old, sleeps with Claude, the older bisexual woman, and falls in love with her. Claude 'toys' with Ursula emotionally. In her tormented state, Ursula is unable to muster feelings for a male Polish soldier who is pursuing her. Later, she tries to have sex with a male French sailor. But she is not up to it, and he ends up treating her like a little sister during the several days and nights they spend together. After this, Ursula's affections for Claude diminish. She falls in love with the Polish soldier, they plan to marry, they have sex, she gets pregnant, and he goes off to the front and is killed. In despair, she kills herself. It is a disaster, certainly. But the sequence of events is hardly caused by her one night of lesbian sex.

However, it is not Mercier's reading of the plot that stands out here; rather it is his attempt, and that of his opponent, to present the text as having powerful social consequences. What might the book do to young women in particular? Oddly, it is Mercier and his collection of expert witnesses who argue that the picture of lesbianism painted by Torres is an inviting one. Indeed, its attractiveness is what makes it dangerous. They refer several times to the passage where Ursula finds herself in bed with Claude – the only explicitly 'lesbian sex' scene in the book. (Not surprisingly, the markings in the margins of Mercier's copy of the book become quite frenzied at this point):

Ursula felt herself very small, tiny against Claude, and at last she felt warm. She placed her cheek on Claude's breast. Her heart beat violently, but she didn't feel afraid. She didn't understand what was happening to her. Claude was not a man; then what was she doing to her? What strange movements! What could they mean? Claude unbuttoned the jacket of her pajamas, and enclosed one of Ursula's little breasts in her hand, and then gently, very gently, her hand began to caress all of Ursula's body, her throat, her shoulders, and her belly. Ursula remembered a novel that she had read that said of a woman who was making love, 'Her body vibrated like a violin.' Ursula had been highly pleased by this phrase, and now her body recalled the expression and it too began to vibrate. She was stretched out with her eyes closed, motionless, not daring to make the slightest gesture, indeed not knowing what she should do. And Claude kissed her gently, and caressed her ... All at once, her insignificant and monotonous life had become full, rich and marvellous ... Ursula wanted only one thing, to keep this refuge forever, this warmth, this security. (45)

What would become of a normal teenage girl who read this passage? Adult women, surely, would have the moral strength to resist the temptation such a positive image might hold. But teenagers, their moral characters not yet fully developed, would be less able to distinguish right from wrong. According to Isabelle Finlayson – Crown witness, mother of two, and member of the Ottawa school board and numerous women's groups – teens had not had enough experience to 'be expected to form their [moral] standards, therefore, they would take it [the lesbian sexual activity] as a proper conduct, as conduct accepted generally.'[91] Finlayson seems to be saying that teens had not yet had time to bring their standards in line with socially approved ones. They were still, in a sense, moral works-in-progress who might choose pleasure over indignation and denial.

According to Rev. Terrence Findlay, another Crown witness, the danger of the seduction scene was that a young girl might read such a passage and be enticed to experiment. A young girl, he said, is only 'beginning to form within her' a knowledge and experience of sex and is, therefore, 'intensely curious.' Findlay suggested that if a girl had not already received training about the dangers of lesbianism, the book might 'have a tendency to suggest to that girl that here is a way of satisfying sexual desires without the danger of consorting with male companions.'[92] This kind of literature, he said, tended to sway normal girls towards the abnormal, by making the latter seem both attractive and possible.

Ford tried to counter Findlay's position by emphasizing the 'normality' of most teenaged readers. Is it not likely that the pleasure of the seduction scene would be annulled by the scene where Ursula finds herself unable to have sexual relations with the French sailor? For Ford, these two scenes are intimately linked – lesbian sex leads to frigidity with men. Would not a 'normal teen-age girl' with 'normal sexual reactions' be 'nauseated' by Ursula's 'abnormal relations' – the latter phrase referring both to sex with a woman and an inability to have sex with a man?[93]

Ford wanted *Women's Barracks* to be taken up as a cautionary tale that might warn young women of the dangers of lesbianism, and in this way might serve the public good. No one disagreed with him over the need for this, although Crown witnesses rejected Torres's book as appropriate to the task. But, asked Ford, were they not all better informed on the subject after having read the novel? Isabelle Finlayson, in particular, claimed she had known nothing about lesbianism before she read the book. How then, asked Ford, could she possibly have warned her daughter of lesbian dangers? Ford's argument had nothing to do with the book's effects on Finlayson herself; as an adult she was assumed to be beyond its influence, capable of reaching her own conclusions on such a vexing moral issue. Someone like Finlayson, well schooled in popular discourses about sexual deviance and perversion, would have been able to see past the pleasure of the seduction scene to the downfall which would inevitably follow. A teenaged girl, on the other hand, needed to have that downfall made explicit. According to Ford, Torres's novel did just that. It provided the context that schoolgirl gossip and curbside chatter about lesbianism might not.

Judge McDougall did not accept Ford's case. In his judgment he wrote:

[The book] deals almost entirely with the question of sex relationships and also with the question of lesbianism. A great deal of the language, and particularly the description of two incidents of unnatural relationships between women, is exceedingly frank. The argument advanced before me was that publicity should be given to the question of lesbianism in order that it might act as a deterrent influence and in this respect would be a matter of public good. The dissemination of such information is no doubt a matter that should receive proper attention from a medical and psychological standpoint, but the manner in which the material is presented in this book does not comply with those standards in any manner.[94]

The underlying assumption, on both sides, indeed the basis of the obscenity charge, was that a pulp novel could have a harmful impact on young people who read it. The test of obscenity used by Canadian courts demanded that Davis and Ford take this as their starting point.

In 1953, *Women's Barracks* was the focus of another trial in St Paul, Minnesota, where notions of the corruptibility of young people were not embedded in the definition of obscenity and therefore had no sway over the final judgment: 'In conclusion, therefore, it is the opinion of the Court that the book, *Women's Barracks*, does not have a substantive tendency to deprave or corrupt by inciting lascivious thoughts or arousing lustful desire in the ordinary reader in this community in these times. It is the finding of the Court that the likelihood of its having such a salacious effect does not outweigh the literary merit it may have in the hands of the average reader.'[95]

Notions of adolescence as a time of rapid and profound change echoed widespread fears about change in the society at large. As the progression of one's adolescence was seen to determine the shape of one's adulthood, so too the collective progress of living, breathing adolescents was thought to indicate the shape Canadian society would take in the future. In this sense, youth operated as a metaphor for the development of the society as a whole: if they turned out all right, it was assumed the nation would be fine, too. But, after two decades of turmoil, such an outcome was not guaranteed.

It is in this context that ideas about the moral and physical capacities of young people were able to help constitute the limits of sexual discourse. The desire to 'protect' youth and the future they were assumed to represent helped to motivate broad-ranging initiatives of moral and sexual regulation – such as the conviction of National News, the banning of crime comics, and the implementation of the senate special committee – that took not only youth but adults as their objects. Common-sense ideas about the nature of adolescent moral and sexual development contributed to the setting of limits on how and where sexuality could be expressed or represented and by whom. Some adults saw teenagers as being under the control of their blossoming sex drives. These adults wanted to set limits on public discussions of sexuality because they feared it would set teens off on an orgy of experimentation. Other adults were less concerned about the impulses of puberty and the exigencies of hormones than they were about teenagers' moral immaturity. They worried that boys and girls faced with sexual information or images would be unable to distinguish right from wrong and thus might 'innocently' engage in questionable activities. In both perspectives, notions of sexuality as potentially dangerous, as destabilizing and morally charged, combined with ideas about the nature of puberty and adolescent development to curtail public discussion of sex.

The relationship between discourses about sexuality and discourses about youth – especially the way these combined to conduct social anxieties around a broad range of issues – was central to the generation of the moral panic around obscenity. At stake in the furore over mass-market publications were accepted standards of sexual morality, standards that affected both young people and adults. Indecent material, in its various guises, offered competing ways of making sense of sex, morals, and relationships. Comics and trashy novels contradicted the many efforts to transform teenagers into 'fine moral citizens' that were commonplace in English Canada during the late 1940s and 1950s. The discourses made available in the pulps threatened the complex of processes through which particular forms of heterosexual expression were normalized. Comics, girlie magazines, and trashy novels suggested alternative ways of organizing sexuality, ones that might upset the dominance of a family-centred, monogamous heterosexuality. At bottom, indecent literature challenged dominant sexual and moral standards and these, as much as individual young people, were assumed to need protecting.

8
Conclusion

As a concept, heterosexuality was not yet sixty years old as the Second World War ended. Still, it had already evolved considerably: from a category of deviant sexual behaviour, to a classification of sexual object choice, to the basis of successful marriages, to a marker of the maturity and ability to conform that were critical to social reckoning at mid-century. Moreover, between the 1920s and the 1940s, definitions of heterosexuality came to encompass notions about proper gender roles, about the nature of sexualized relationships between women and men, and about the emotional and psychic development of individuals. Indeed, by the late 1940s, the meanings of heterosexuality had expanded to such an extent that its hegemonic position in Canadian culture – as represented by the number of Canadians marrying and starting families – was read as a marker of national stability.

Clearly, heterosexuality is not reducible to any type of natural or biological essence. Neither is it a simple matter of sexual attraction between women and men, nor of the particular forms of sexual behaviour women and men might engage in with each other. Heterosexuality is a discursively constituted social category that organizes relations not only between women and men, but also between those who fit definitions of heterosexuality and those who do not, and between adults and youth. Heterosexuality also helps to constitute relations of class, ethnicity, and race. It is frequently made meaningful by way of non-sexual discourses, and, in turn, these discourses are themselves sexualized.

The ability to lay claim to a definition of normality was a crucial marker of postwar social belonging. To be marked as sexually 'abnormal' in any way was to throw into question the possibility of achieving or maintaining status as an adult, as a 'responsible citizen,' as a valued contributor to the social whole. Normal sexuality, as constructed in post-war advice books, films, magazines, and sex-education curricula, in legal, medical, psychological, and popular discourses, was invariably the preserve of married, monogamous, adult heterosexual couples who produced children, and of the adolescent girls and boys who were preparing themselves to fit into that model. That young people could 'prepare for' or be prepared for normal sexuality is a central aspect of postwar sexual discourses. With the rise of developmental psychology, so-called normal sexuality was understood to be an emotional and psychic achievement. While this process played itself out on biological terrain, biology alone was not enough to guarantee one's normalness. Hence the tremendous impulse, expressed by many adults, to intervene in teenage sexual development.

Teens were assumed, in many senses, to be works-in-progress, malleable and easily influenced – characteristics that many adults thought could facilitate their turning into either delinquents or model, sexually responsible citizens. As a group, therefore, teens were often the targets of an 'ideal' sexual knowledge intended to guide them towards maturity. Youth were portrayed in popular media and sex education materials as the 'parents of the future,' a formulation which brought teen sexual development to social prominence and aligned it with the development of society as a whole. Given this, it is not surprising that teenagers were frequently the ground over which the boundaries of normative sexuality were negotiated and reinforced. But young people were not simply the targets of sexual knowledge. Notions about their moral and physical capacities also helped to constitute sexual discourse in a more general sense. The desire to 'protect' youth and the future they were assumed to represent helped to motivate broad-ranging initiatives of moral and sexual regulation that took adults and young people as their objects. Common-sense ideas about the nature of adolescent sexual and moral development contributed to the setting of limits on how and where sexuality could be expressed or represented, and by whom. Some adults saw teenagers as being under the control of their blossoming sex drives. These adults wanted to set limits on public discussions of sexuality because they feared such discussions would set teens off in an orgy of experimentation. Other adults were less concerned about the impulses of puberty and the exigencies of hormones than they were about teenagers' moral immaturity. They worried that boys and girls faced with sexual information or images would be unable to distinguish right from wrong and thus, 'innocently,' might engage in questionable activities. In both perspectives, notions of sexuality as potentially dangerous, destabilizing, and morally charged combined with ideas about the nature of puberty and adolescent development to curtail public discussion of sex – as we saw in previous chapters in debates over both sex education and indecent literature.

As a concept, 'youth' was part of what made postwar sexual discourses work. Regulatory efforts that were promoted as a means of 'protecting the children' carried a certain moral weight that both justified their existence and increased the likelihood of their success. In this framework, images and discussions of juvenile delinquency operated as the possible fate of young people who were left 'unprotected.' While delinquency had many social meanings in the postwar years, it was routinely invoked as a sexual category, as the consequence of the moral corruption of youth, or of youthful sexuality run amok. In either case, fears about delinquency contributed to calls for regulation that would control the sexual activities of young people and efforts that would steer teenage morality in the right direction.

The centrality of youth in postwar sexual discourses was a product of the particular social conditions of the era. After six years of war and the decade-long Depression that had preceded them, Canadians were not always trusting of what the future might bring. They worried about the rise of the cold war and expressed fears about the fragility of the nascent peace and prosperity. At the same time, people revelled in the allied victory over fascism and demonstrated a heightened faith in democracy. Technological change and the increasing availability of consumer goods put 'modern life' within the reach of large segments of the Canadian population. These contradictory aspects of postwar life combined to orient Canadians in a profound way towards home, family, and stability. Nuclear families would help protect Canadians against the insecurities of the age. They would also provide the base for the growing consumer economy and for the democracy that was promoted as the route to victory in the cold war. Families were understood to be the primary stabilizing influence on both individuals and the nation as a whole.

In this context, postwar youth, as the 'parents of the future,' would prove critical to Canada's success or failure in the modern age. As a collectivity, youth were represented in popular discourses as a product of both wartime disruptions and modern prosperity. The social progress of adolescents was read by many as an indication of the shape society would take in the future. While the 'youth problem' was taken up as a sign of social disarray, the confidence of 'modern' teens was seen as a sign of postwar progress. Issues of sexuality could determine which of these images was prominent or appropriate at any given time for particular groups of young people. Were they behaving 'normally' or not? If teenagers were normal – that is, if they met the social norms through which sexual normality was constituted – popular discourses suggested that the future would be normal too.

This study is primarily concerned with the way that definitions of normality – definitions under which heterosexuality was subsumed – operated as and within forms of social and moral regulation. In particular, it addresses the way that normality was not simply 'imposed' on young people but was something they came to desire, or, as Nikolas Rose puts it, the way that personal desires fell into line with the 'needs' of postwar social and political formations – the way those formations helped to 'shape the private self.'[1] I have sketched out some of the ways in which the desire to be normal was constituted in young people in the postwar period, the ways in which normality was normalized. From school curricula to legal sanctions against so-called delinquent behaviour to ostracism for teen pregnancy, we can see how sexual normality was constructed in class, gender, and race-specific ways as the path to social acceptance and future happiness. Discourses about the importance of normality were so pervasive in the postwar period that alternatives to them were hard to imagine, although, of course, some people did manage to. It's through this kind of restriction of possibility in people's lives that the process of normalization goes to work, homogenizing the social fabric, erasing differences among individuals, and encouraging conformity. Thus, postwar sex education curricula presented only a single, Anglo-Saxon, middle-class version of the family, advice books failed to account for sexual variations, and discourses about indecent literature tried to curtail the accessibility of some forms of sexual representation. Dominant versions of sexuality were thereby constructed as the only 'natural' forms of sexuality – as the normal ones.

That normality was understood to be 'natural,' to be a self-evident category, only made it more effective as a standard by which individuals were measured and categorized, as a means of moral regulation. What's natural cannot be challenged or changed. It is assumed to be inevitable. In this book I have begun to unpack 'normality' as a complex discursive construction. Future research might also try to account for how postwar young people negotiated normalizing discourses. In suggesting here the ways that these discourses achieved their power, I don't mean to con-

struct them as completely determining of teenage behaviour and iden-
tity-formation. Obviously, as lesbian and gay oral histories have shown,
not everyone was willing or able to conform to mainstream sexual standards.[2] The discussion of sexual discourses in this book offers a starting
point for oral histories which might point to the ways postwar teenagers
understood dominant notions of sexuality. How do present-day adults
feel mainstream sexual discourses affected their lives, the choices they
made, and their understanding of their own sexualities?

As a study of dominance, of a taken-for-granted category like heterosexuality, this project raises interesting methodological questions. As feminists have frequently suggested, dominant categories function as the
default categories of everyday discourse; they rarely need to announce
themselves. As with maleness, for instance, heterosexuality's dominance
over other forms of sexual expression makes its social presence obvious.
It is not surprising, then, that I had few opportunities to deal with evidence that explicitly articulates, say, a position on heterosexuality or a
definition of what it should look like. To put it in very simple terms, the
word 'heterosexuality' rarely appeared in the sources I used for my
research. My study of it has been based on the interpretation of evidence
that 'points to' heterosexuality. It has been based on the analysis of discourses through which the meanings of heterosexuality are constructed.
   Analytic strategies inspired by linguistic theories suggest the importance of looking for meaning in the spaces between social categories, in
the binary oppositions through which these categories are constituted.[3]
In these analyses, one learns, for instance, about whiteness by studying
the way it is counterposed to racialized 'others.' One learns about masculinity by analysing its relationship to femininity. While this can prove
to be an extremely useful strategy, as I have found, there are limits to its
usefulness when one is trying to analyse the dominant side of a hierarchical opposition. In my experience, one can't always draw from a well
of difference to make sense of historical concepts.
   In practice, it is not always easy or even possible to determine which
categories are in fact in opposition to each other, to determine the two
sides of any particular binary. In such cases, a historical analysis permits
one to construct meaning from the evolution of categories over time. The
category 'heterosexuality,' for instance, has undergone substantial
change over the course of a single century as it has been produced and
reproduced within shifting discursive formations and practices. The role
of the researcher is to try to identify those formations, to pull them apart,

and to suggest how meaning might have been constructed through them.

It is important not to essentialize the space of difference between categories, to dehistoricize it, to render it fixed. While I began this project wanting to know the space of difference between homo- and heterosexualities, it later became clear to me that the opposition between these categories was not a simple one in the late 1940s and the 1950s. The homosexual/heterosexual opposition was not always the most meaningful way for me to learn about heterosexuality. As either side of a binary shifts, the space between the two sides shifts as well. The relationship between the centre and the margins is a historical construction that evolves over time and in specific social contexts. It needs to be analysed in this light.

Jonathan Ned Katz suggests that the twenty years immediately after the Second World War were the climax of the consolidation of 'heterosexual hegemony.'[4] He claims that these two decades were a time in which dominant notions of heterosexual behaviour and identity were rarely challenged; I have to agree with him. We can be thankful that this episode in the history of heterosexuality was not a particularly long one. In the late 1960s, its hegemonic position was shaken by the emerging movements around feminism and lesbian and gay liberation. And while we are yet to be free of heterosexuality as a powerful social, sexual, or political institution, its grip over the population as a whole has diminished somewhat. Certainly it has ceased to be the only option as a mode of sexual expression. Moreover, definitions of heterosexuality have changed over the last few decades. In the 1990s one can engage, for instance, in extramarital heterosexual sexual activity and still conform to mainstream definitions of sexual normality; or one can stay single without fear of severe social ostracism. It seems that over the last three decades the fit between normality and social norms has grown looser. What does not seem to have diminished, however, is the importance of normality itself as a social classification.

These changes in the social definition of sexuality are, at least in part, at the root of current nostalgia for the 1950s, those good old days of the 'traditional family' and stable marriages. Present-day conservatives like to remember the postwar period as the lost era of family values. What American sociologist Wini Breines has suggested, in her study of white teenage girls in the 1950s, is that the 'family values' that are so frequently mourned by today's right wing are exactly the values that led postwar teenagers to participate in the various social-protest move-ments of the 1960s.[5] Of course, members of right-wing groups draw quite different conclusions. In recent years their speeches and deputa-tions before the Toronto Board of Education and the Metropolitan Tor-onto Council have protested the development of an anti-homophobia curriculum for Toronto schools and called for funding cuts to lesbian and gay arts groups.[6] In Ontario they helped to defeat Bill 167 which would have granted same-sex benefits and family-recognition rights to lesbians and gay men. Most recently, social/moral conservatives on the Liberal backbenches were almost successful in blocking federal support for sexual, orientation protection. It took a public tongue-lashing of the Chrétien government by Human Rights commissioner Max Yalden to move the Liberals past their fear of addressing sexual inequities. That those who are against such measures often claim to be so for the sake of their children suggests that, while discourses about sexuality have cer-tainly changed since the 1950s, there continues to be a way they can be read through discourses about youth. Future studies might point to the ways the relationship between these two sets of discourses has evolved and to the reasons for the relationship's persistence. Future studies might also speculate on the possibility of some day reaching a point when sex will no longer be able to catalyse fear and narrow-mindedness – when sex will no longer make sense as something from which young people need to be protected.

Notes

Chapter 1: Introduction

1 'The Trouble With Normal' appears on Bruce Cockburn's album of the same name, True North Records, 1983 (title used with permission). Cockburn's lyrics decry the 'normalness' of a pervasive neocolonial capitalism.

2 Stephanie Coontz gives an excellent account of this kind of 'nostalgia' in her book, *The Way We Never Were*.

3 For examples of postwar Canadian lesbian and gay history, see: Chamberland, *Mémoires lesbiennes;* Chenier, 'Tough Ladies and Troublemakers'; and Churchill, 'Coming out in a Cold Climate.'

4 Bothwell, Drummond, and English, *Canada since 1945*, 238.

5 Bumsted, 'Canada and American Culture in the 1950s,' 400.

6 Foucault, 'Questions of Method,' 10.

7 For discussions of discourse, see the following by Foucault: *Power/Knowledge; The History of Sexuality;* 'Questions of Method'; and 'The Subject and Power.' The following texts have also been useful: Belsey, *Critical Practice;* Weedon, *Feminist Practice and Poststructuralist Theory;* Henriques et al., *Changing the Subject.*

8 For discussions of the linguistic and political emergence of the homosexual, see: Weeks, *Coming Out: Homosexual Politics in Britain, from the Nineteenth Century to the Present;* Foucault, *The History of Sexuality,* vol. 1; and Jonathan Ned Katz, *Gay/Lesbian Almanac.*

9 Jonathan Ned Katz, *The Invention of Heterosexuality,* 54.

10 Ibid., 19.

11 Ibid., 86.

12 Ibid., 81.

13 Krafft-Ebing, *Psychopathia Sexualis* (numerous editions; English translations

are generally of the 12th, revised edition, originally published in the United States in 1906).

14 Chauncey, *Gay New York*, 13.

15 Ibid., 111–27; see also, Kevin White, *The First Sexual Revolution*.

16 Simmons, 'Modern Sexuality and the Myth of Victorian Repression,' 160.

17 Ibid., 162.

18 See, for early examples of this argument: Radicalesbians, 'The Woman-Identified Woman'; Rubin, 'The Traffic in Women'; Myron and Bunch, eds, *Lesbianism and the Women's Movement*.

19 As exceptions to this, see: *Resources for Feminist Research*, special issue on 'Confronting Heterosexuality'; *Feminism and Psychology*, special issue on heterosexuality; The latter was expanded and published as Wilkinson and Kitzinger, eds, *Heterosexuality: A Feminism and Psychology Reader*. George Chauncey's *Gay New York* is an excellent discussion of the emergence of heterosexuality and the influence it had on gay lives in New York City in the early part of this century.

20 Rich, 'Compulsory Heterosexuality and Lesbian Existence'. Rich has changed her position on some of the material in the article; see her essay, 'Towards a Politics of Location.'

21 Dubinsky, *Improper Advances*.

22 Michel Foucault, cited by Martin, 'Feminism, Criticism and Foucault,' 6.

23 Urwin, 'Constructing Motherhood: The Persuasion of Normal Development,' 165.

24 Henriques et al., *Changing the Subject*, 218.

25 See Reisman, *The Lonely Crowd*.

26 Hacking, 'Normal.' Thanks to Ian Hacking for sharing his notes with me and thanks, too, to James Heap for bringing the paper to my attention.

27 Ibid., 13.

28 Thanks to James Heap for pointing this out to me.

29 Corrigan and Sayer, *The Great Arch*, 4.

30 Foucault, *History of Sexuality*, 116. See also his *Discipline and Punish*.

31 Johnston, 'What Is Cultural Studies Anyway?' 23.

32 Foucault, *History of Sexuality*, 11.

33 Ibid., especially part I.

34 Frank Mort's *Dangerous Sexualities*, a study of the relationship between sexuality and public health measures during the cholera epidemics in England in the 1930s, gives excellent examples of the type of displacement I am talking about.

35 Bumsted, 'Canada and American Culture in the 1950s,' 399.

36 Ibid., 402.

37 Ibid., 405.
38 Fraser Sutherland, *The Monthly Epic*, 182.

Chapter 2: Sexuality and the Postwar Domestic 'Revival'

1 Owram, *Born at the Right Time*; Iacovetta, *Such Hardworking People*; Whitaker and Marcuse, *Cold War Canada*.
2 Meyerowitz, 'Introduction,' in *Not June Cleaver*, 4; May, *Homeward Bound*.
3 Finkel, Conrad, and Strong-Boag, *History of the Canadian Peoples*, 384.
4 For a discussion of women war workers, see Pierson, *'They're Still Women after All'*; and Joan Sangster, 'Doing Two Jobs.' For a discussion of Canadians'reluctance to accept non-northern European immigrants and refugees, see Iacovetta, *Such Hardworking People*.
5 Owram, *Born at the Right Time*.
6 Parr, ed., 'Introduction,' *A Diversity of Women*, 5.
7 Finkel, Conrad, and Strong-Boag, *History of the Canadian Peoples*, 429–30.
8 Francis, Jones, and Smith, *Destinies: Canadian History since Confederation*, 338–9 and 353.
9 Finkel, Conrad, and Strong-Boag, *History of the Canadian Peoples*, 331.
10 Dempsey, *Chatelaine* editorial, 1.
11 See, for example: Canadian Youth Commission, *Youth, Marriage and the Family*; Franks, 'A Note to Brides,' 29ff; *Marriage Today*, a film produced by McGraw-Hill Book Company, 1950.
12 Advertisement for Christian Family Week, *Toronto Daily Star*, 2 May 1947.
13 The idea that strong families are the root of social stability has been a recurring theme in the face of capitalism's rise and evolution. For a discussion of this see: Ursel, *Private Lives, Public Policy*; Dehli, 'Women and Class.'
14 May, *Homeward Bound*, 10.
15 Whitaker and Marcuse, *Cold War Canada*.
16 Finkel, Conrad, and Strong-Boag, *History of the Canadian Peoples*, 426–7.
17 Advertisement for Education Week, *Telegram*, 11 Apr. 1946.
18 Saunders, 'What's the Biggest Thing in Our New Half Century?' 6.
19 Ibid., 53.
20 Adele White, 'Let's Abolish Those Atom Bomb Blues,' 6–7ff.
21 Whitaker and Marcuse, *Cold War Canada*, chs 2–4.
22 Scher, *The Un-Canadians*, 8.
23 Ibid., 9.
24 Girard, 'From Subversion to Liberation,' 3.
25 Hannant, *The Infernal Machine*, 144. For discussion of the Security Panel, also see Whitaker and Marcuse, *Cold War Canada*, ch. 7.

26　Girard, 'From Subversion to Liberation,' 4. Also see Kinsman, '"Character Weaknesses" and "Fruit Machines."'

27　Sawatsky, *Men in the Shadows*, 116.

28　Cited in Scher, *The Un-Canadians*, 81.

29　Sawatsky, *Men in the Shadows*, 126.

30　See Girard, 'From Subversion to Liberation.'

31　Kinsman '"Character Weaknesses," and "Fruit Machines"'; also Robinson and Kimmel, 'The Queer Career of Homosexual Security Vetting in Cold War Canada.'

32　Franks, 'A Note to Brides,' 29.

33　Gölz, 'Family Matters.'

34　The quotation is from a pamphlet produced by the Canadian Youth Commission, 'Speak Your Peace: Suggestions for Discussion by Youth,' Bulletin No. Two – Youth and Family Life, NAC, MG 28 I 11, vol. 64 (Ontario Committee).

35　For an example of discussions about the family as a site of democracy, see: the National Film Board films *Family Circles*, produced in 1949, and *Making a Decision in the Family* (1957); Osborne, 'Democracy Begins in the Home.' For discussions about the family as the primary site of moral education, see newspaper debates about the introduction of sex education into school classrooms: 'Board of Education Considers Courses in Sex Education'; 'No Need for Haste.'

36　Alison Prentice et al., *Canadian Women: A History*, 323.

37　Seeley, Sim, and Loosley, *Crestwood Heights*, 3.

38　Ibid., 20 (emphasis in original).

39　Joan Sangster, 'Doing Two Jobs,' 99–100.

40　Li, *The Making of Post-War Canada*, 97.

41　Iacovetta, 'Remaking Their Lives,' 143.

42　Iacovetta, 'Making '"New Canadians."'

43　See, for example: Arnup, *Education for Motherhood*; Comacchio, *Nations Are Built of Babies*.

44　Seeley, Sim, and Loosley, *Crestwood Heights*, 4. See also, Owram, *Born at the Right Time*.

45　Seeley, Sim, and Loosley, *Crestwood Heights*, 161.

46　Ibid., 165.

47　See, for example: Owram, *Born at the Right Time*, or May, *Homeward Bound*.

48　May, *Homeward Bound*, 11.

49　*A Date with Your Family*, a Simmel-Meservey Release, produced by Edward C. Simmel and written by Arthur V. Jones (no date, appears to be mid-1950s).

50　Gölz talks about how discursive constructions of the 'happy united family' were 'interlinked with an idealized notion of the "Canadian family" as both the social foundation and the metaphorical microcosm of Canadian nation-hood.' See her 'Family Matters,' 49.

51 Starting in the late 1940s, *Chatelaine* published numerous articles about women's fate in the suburban middle-class family. Features and editorials mentioned the 'something missing' in women's lives, a sense of unease and dissatisfaction. See, for instance: 'Unhappy Wives,' 2. For discussion of *Chatelaine* as a source of material that challenged prevailing ideologies, see Korinek, 'Roughing It in Suburbia.' Also, Friedan, *The Feminine Mystique*.

52 Hutton, 'The Future of the Family: A *Maclean's* Report,' 74.

53 Owram, *Born at the Right Time*, 12.

54 Alison Prentice et al., *Canadian Women*, 311.

55 Ibid.

56 Cited by Hutton, 'The Future of the Family,' 76.

57 Nash, 'It's Time Father Got Back in the Family,' 28.

58 Cited in May, *Homeward Bound*, 80.

59 Hilliard, *A Woman Doctor Looks at Love and Life*, 94.

60 Ibid., 99.

61 Ehrenreich, *The Hearts of Men*, 20.

62 Franks, 'A Note to Brides,' 29ff.

63 Morris, 'Give the Childless Couple a Break,' 11ff.

64 Anonymous, 'I'm Not Having Any,' 14.

65 *Chatelaine* (June 1947): 6.

66 The article was 'A Note to Brides,' by Ruth MacLachlan Franks, M.D. (see above, nn11, 62).

67 Iacovetta, 'Making "New Canadians."'

68 Seeley, Sim, and Loosley, *Crestwood Heights*, 426.

69 Seidman, *Romantic Longings*, 118.

70 Marion Hilliard's book and her regular columns in *Chatelaine* frequently espoused the importance of sexual happiness in marriage.

71 For discussions of North American women's sexual dissatisfactions during the 1950s, see: Breines, *Young, White, and Miserable*; and Harvey, *The Fifties: A Woman's Oral History*.

72 Morris, 'Don't Let Your Girl Friends Ruin Your Marriage,' 26.

73 Seidman, *Romantic Longings*, 94.

74 Strong-Boag, 'Home Dreams,' 479.

75 Lautenslager, 'A Minister's Frank Talk to Brides and Grooms,' 98–9.

76 See, especially, Ehrenreich, *The Hearts of Men*.

77 Reisman, *The Lonely Crowd*.

78 Ehrenreich, *Fear of Falling*, 34.

79 Anglin, 'Who Has Won the War between the Sexes?' 12.

80 Iacovetta, 'Making "New Canadians,"' 276.
81 Ibid., 70.
82 Costello, *Love, Sex and War*, 9.
83 In the year after the war the divorce rate tripled, as hastily constructed wartime marriages withered under more prolonged consideration. But between 1947 and 1951 rates were relatively stable. Between 1951 and 1968, the divorce rate rose steadily from 88.9 to 124.3 divorces per 100,000 married persons (Alison Prentice et al., *Canadian Women: A History*, 323).
84 'Church Group Would Study Sex Education.'
85 For a discussion of the Canadian birth-control movement, see McLaren and McLaren, *The Bedroom and the State*. On excitement about the pill, see Anglin, 'The Pill That Could Shake the World,' 16–17. Letters, for and against Anglin's article appear in *Chatelaine* (Dec. 1953), 3.
86 See Kinsman, *The Regulation of Desire*, and the National Film Board film *Forbidden Love*, directed by Aerlyn Weissman and Lynne Fernie, 1992.
87 The menstruation article, 'High School Huddle,' was written by Adele White, 26–7. It was followed by both positive and negative letters. The letter complaining about 'the ungainly display of limbs' appeared in *Chatelaine* (Nov. 1952): 2. And the complaint about psychiatry, from a reader wondering why 'every issue *has* to have an article about sex,' appeared in *Chatelaine* (Oct. 1949): 14.
88 Pomeroy, *Dr. Kinsey and the Institute for Sex Research*, 265.
89 Ibid., 273.
90 Ibid., 360, 363.
91 Ketchum, 'Turning New Leaves,' 44–5; Sandwell, 'Statistical Method Applied to Sex Shows New and Surprising Results,' 12; Seeley and Griffin, 'The Kinsey Report,' 40–2; Rumming, 'Dr. Kinsey and the Human Female,' 7–8; Kidd, Review of *Sexual Behavior in the Human Male*, 45–6. For a less positive critique, see Hughes, 'Kinsey Again: Leers or Cheers?' 10ff. For a bona-fide anti-Kinsey rant, see the review by 'E.J.M.,' 50ff.
92 Dempsey, 'Dr. Kinsey Talks about Women to Lotta Dempsey,' 10–11.
93 Sandwell, 'Statistical Method Applied to Sex,' 12.
94 Irvine, *Disorders of Desire*, 54.
95 Ketchum, 'Turning New Leaves,' 45.
96 Sandwell, 'Statistical Method Applied to Sex.'
97 Hughes, 'Kinsey Again: Leers or Cheers?' 10.
98 May, *Homeward Bound*, ch. 4.

Chapter 3: Hope for the Future or Repercussions of the Past

 1 'Low Standards of Conduct Handicap Work of Schools.'

2   This point is made nicely by Constance Nathanson in the title of her book, *Dangerous Passage: The Social Control of Sexuality in Women's Adolescence*.

3   Alison Prentice et al., *Canadian Women: A History,* 311.

4   For a discussion of the relationship between mothers in the labour force and fears about juvenile delinquency, see Pierson, *'They're Still Women after All,'* 50; and, Susan Prentice, 'Militant Mothers in Domestic Times.'

5   Gillis, *Youth and History,* 182.

6   Fass, *The Damned and the Beautiful.*

7   Doherty, *Teenagers and Teenpics,* 44.

8   Ibid., 51.

9   Seeley, Sim, and Loosley, *Crestwood Heights.*

10 *The Meaning of Adolescence,* produced by McGraw Hill Books, 1953; *The Teens,* produced by Crawley Films for the National Film Board, 1957; *Who Is Sylvia?,* produced by the National Film Board, 1957.

11 G. Stanley Hall, *Adolescence: Its Psychology and Its Relations to Physiology, Anthropology, Sociology, Sex, Crime, Religion and Education.*

12 Ross, *G. Stanley Hall,* 333.

13 Kett, *Rites of Passage,* 218.

14 Ibid., 217.

15 Ross, *G. Stanley Hall,* 332.

16 Paul Axelrod notes that G.S. Hall spoke in Toronto in 1891 at a meeting of the National Education Association. Axelrod says that evidence that Hall's theories were used and influential in Canada can be found in McKee, 'Voluntary Youth Organizations in Toronto, 1880–1930,' ch. 2. See Axelrod, *Making a Middle Class,* 188 n47.

17 Ross, *G. Stanley Hall,* 329.

18 G.S. Hall, *Adolescence,* 457.

19 Calhoun, 'The Child Mind as a Social Product,' 80.

20 Landis, *Adolescence and Youth,* 51.

21 Mead, *Coming of Age in Samoa,* 2.

22 Mead, 'Adolescence in Primitive and Modern Society,' 174.

23 Rousseau, *Émile, or On Education,* 216.

24 Cited by Kett, *Rites of Passage,* 134.

25 Ibid., 134.

26 Hollingshead, *Elmtown's Youth,* 6.

27 Ibid., 6 n9. The study he referred to was by Wayne Dennis, 'The Adolescent.'

28 Landis, *Adolescence and Youth, 2nd ed.,* 47.

29 Ellis, *Psychology of Sex,* 83.

30 This combination of factors is particularly apparent in the blaming of working mothers in wartime discussions of delinquency.

31 Hebdige, *Hiding in the Light,* 17.

32 Sidney Katz, 'It's a Tough Time to Be a Kid.' Part one.
33 Tumpane, 'The Cruel World vs. Teen-agers,' 4–5.
34 Friedenberg, *The Vanishing Adolescent*, 177.
35 Ibid., 182.
36 Ibid., 177.
37 See D'Emilio, 'The Homosexual Menace'; Kinsman, '"Character Weaknesses" and "Fruit Machines"'; May, *Homeward Bound*.
38 Staff report on the work of the North Toronto Area Social Planning Council, Committee on Juvenile Delinquency, City of Toronto Archives, SC 40, Box 67, File 3. Also Minutes from a meeting on 19 Feb. 1963.
39 Ness, 'Who's Afraid of Teenage Problems?' 28.
40 See: Seeley, Sims, and Loosley, *Crestwood Heights*, esp. ch. 8; Axelrod, *Making a Middle Class*, 16.
41 'The Secret World of Our Teen-agers,' 12–13.

Chapter 4: Youth Gone Bad

1 Toronto Board of Education, *Minutes*, 19 May 1955. See also 'The Blackboard Jungle: Some Protest School Film Protest.'
2 Toronto Board of Education, *Minutes*, 17 June 1954.
3 'Delinquency Seen as Main Ill.' According to the 1955 edition of *Canadian Who's Who*, Feinberg was selected by a *Saturday Night* magazine poll as one of the seven greatest preachers in Canada. He was a frequent contributor on both local and national television and radio programs, and to the Toronto *Globe and Mail* and various religious and non-religious magazines. Throughout the 1960s, he was very active in the peace movement.
4 During the first half of this century, discussions about venereal diseases rarely focused on the transmission of micro-organisms – germs. Instead they highlighted the types of people likely to carry them or the approaches to sex such people might follow. Prostitutes especially were targeted by this type of discourse. But so were other groups assumed to be 'promiscuous,' or sexually or morally different. At various times 'foreigners,' homosexuals, single women, and the 'feebleminded' have been identified as sources of infection. For more discussion on this, see Cassel, *The Secret Plague*; Mary Louise Adams, 'In Sickness and in Health.'
5 Houston, 'The "Waifs and Strays" of a Late Victorian City'; Bennett, 'Taming "Bad Boys" of the "Dangerous Class"'; and Neil Sutherland, *Children in English-Canadian Society*.
6 For examples of this kind of argument, see 'Parents and Juvenile Delinquents,' (editorial); D.C. Draper (Chief Constable, Toronto City Police Force), 'Report on Juvenile Delinquency,' submitted to Board of Commissioners of

Police, Toronto, 13 Apr. 1944, Metropolitan Toronto Archives, RG 5.1, Box 153, File 4; Zoffer, 'Psychological Factors in Juvenile Crime,' 18.

7   For a particularly vitriolic example of anti-teenager sentiment, see Tumpane, 'The Cruel World vs. Teen-agers,' 4.

8   Hugh Wolter, 'Brief on Delinquency and Anti-social Behaviour for Community Councils and Other Groups' (Mar. 1949), 1, City of Toronto Archives, RG 283.

9   See previous chapter. Staff report on the work of the North Toronto Area Social Planning Council, Committee on Juvenile Delinquency, City of Toronto Archives, SC 40, Box 67, File 3.

10 For statistics about delinquency, see the *Reports* of the Toronto Family Court, City of Toronto Archives, RG 47, Box 135. Total number of offences committed in 1942 was 1693; in 1943 it was 1618; in 1945 it was 1055; in 1947 it was 739; in 1949 it was 844; and in 1952 (the last year available in the collection of *Reports*) it was 827.

11 Stuart Hall et al., *Policing the Crisis*, 16.

12 Cohen, *Folk Devils and Moral Panics*, 10.

13 Richardson, *The Century of the Child*.

14 'Delinquency and Schools'; 'Child Delinquency Starts in Homes.'

15 'To Combat Delinquency' (editorial); 'Parents and Juvenile Delinquents'; 'A Problem for Parents' (editorial); letter to Attorney General Blackwell from Mrs J.H. Booth, dated 25 Apr. 1944, AO RG 4-02, File 24.4; Toronto Home and School Council, 'A Survey of the Gang Problem in Toronto,' Metropolitan Toronto Archives, RG 5.1, Box 153, File 6.

16 Dorothy Sangster, 'How Much Freedom Should a Teen-ager Have?' 61.

17 United Welfare Chests, Youth Services Department, 'Bulletin,' No. 6 (May-Aug. 1947), 3, City of Toronto Archives, RG 11, Series A1, Box 2, File 3.

18 Rogers, *Street Gangs in Toronto*, 47–8.

19 Sewell, *The Shape of the City*, 66–74.

20 Welfare Council of Toronto and District, 'A Plan for the Reduction of Juvenile Delinquency in Toronto,' 15 Nov. 1943, 25, Library of the Social Planning Council of Metropolitan Toronto.

21 'Teen Trouble: What Can Recreation Do about It?' National Recreation Center (USA), no date (though the text suggests some time in 1943 or later. The copy I saw was in its sixth printing), NAC, MG 28 I 11, vol. 38, File 2 (3v).

22 Hugh Garner, 'Youth Trouble in Kitchener,' *Chatelaine* (July 1951): 12.

23 For an example of this kind of view, see the chapter titled, 'Preview' in Davis, *Sex and the Adolescent*.

24 Strange, *Toronto's Girl Problem*; Schlossman and Wallach, 'The Crime of Precocious Sexuality.'

25 Letter from C.P. Hope of the attorney general's office to Henry A. Burbidge, Family Court judge, 5 May 1952, AO, RG 4-32, 1952, File 475.

26 '6 Months, 10 Lashes for 9 at Kitchener.'

27 '12 Men Held in Delinquency of Five Girls Aged 12 to 14.'

28 'Trustees "Excuse" Girls, Give Clue to Identity; 9 Boys Get Jail, Lashes.'

29 *Chatelaine* (Sept. 1951): 72.

30 Rogers, *Street Gangs in Toronto*, 20.

31 Schwalbe, 'Negro and Partly-Negro Wards of the Children's Aid Society of Metropolitan Toronto,' 76, City of Toronto Archives, SC 1, Box 113, File 65.

32 Toronto Family Court, 'Report for the Year 1947,' City of Toronto Archives, RG 47, Reports, Box 135.

33 Toronto Family Court, 'Report for the Year 1946,' City of Toronto Archives, RG 47, Reports, Box 135. I looked at the years 1944 until 1952, the last year for which the reports are available.

34 Dubinsky, *Improper Advances*.

35 For example, see Gibson, 'Twenty-nine Delinquent Children.'

36 Maynard, '"Horrible Temptations."'

37 'Considerations to Be Presented to the Minister of National Defense for Naval Services, Regarding the Rumoured Closing of the Ontario Training School for Girls, Galt, Ontario, June 30, 1942,' City of Toronto Archives, SC 40, Box 2; File 19.

38 Schlossman and Wallach, 'The Crime of Precocious Sexuality,' 46. See also, Odem, *Delinquent Daughters*.

39 Reports by Dr F.L. Nichols included in a memo from R.C. Montgomery, Director, Hospitals Division, Department of Health to C.F. Neelands, Deputy Provincial Secretary, 11 Feb. 1944, AO, RG 10-107-0-324.

40 Scott, 'A Follow-up Study of the Experiences after Discharge of a Number of Girls Who Have Lived in Warrendale,' 58, City of Toronto Archives, SC 1, Box 113, File 65.

41 Ibid., 96.

42 See, for instance: Canadian Youth Commission, *Youth, Marriage and the Family*, 56; Welfare Council of Toronto and District, 'A Plan for the Reduction of Juvenile Delinquency in Toronto,' 15 Nov. 1943, 5, Library of the Social Planning Council of Metropolitan Toronto.

43 In 'The Crime of Precocious Sexuality,' their study of female delinquency in the progressive era in the United States, Schlossman and Wallach found that boys were far more likely than girls, even un-pregnant ones, to receive probation, the justice system's legitimate version of the second chance (63).

44 AO, RG 4-32, 1948, no. 590.

45 'Weds Girl, 14, Boy "Freed."'

46 Letter from J.R.H. Kirkpatrick to Deputy Minister of Child Welfare, 26 Jan.

1955. Reply from C.R. Magone, Deputy Attorney General to J.R.H. Kirk-patrick, 10 Feb. 1955, Archives of Ontario, RG 4-32, 1955, no. 177.

47 McGuire, 'The Age Factor in Unmarried Motherhood,' City of Toronto Archives, SC 1, Box 111, File 50.

48 Young, *Out of Wedlock*. Young's work is cited frequently in the dissertations of social work students from the University of Toronto which are on file in the City of Toronto Archives with the papers of the Children's Aid Society, SC 1, Boxes 109, 110, 111, 112.

49 Ibid., 22.

50 See Fliess, 'On the Psychology of Two Types of Unmarried Mother.'

51 Solinger, *Wake Up Little Susie*.

52 Social Planning Council of Metropolitan Toronto, 'A Report on Maternity Homes in Metropolitan Toronto,' July 1960, City of Toronto Archives, SC 1, Box 118, File 7.

53 Mair, 'Why Are More Teenage Girls "Getting into Trouble"?' 30–1ff.

54 'Report on the Welfare Council's Workshop on Toronto Street Gangs, May 26, 1949,' Appendix A of *Special Committee Minutes*, 8 July 1949, Conference re: Juvenile Delinquency and Associated Problems, City of Toronto Archives, RG 200, Box 6, Book 12.

55 AO, RG 4-32, 1951, no. 660, Transcript, 186. All five of the defendants were convicted. Their original sentences ranged from eighteen months definite/twelve months indefinite to four months definite/two months indefinite in the Ontario Reformatory in Brampton. The sentences were successfully appealed and lengthened. Howie Meeker appeared as a character witness for one of the defendants.

56 The mention of Cherry Beach flagged the immoral nature of the liaison. Cherry Beach had a tawdry reputation. It was not maintained as were the eastern and western beaches in the city. Apparently, young people used to meet there for late-night parties, while the children of working-class families went there to swim because, unlike Sunnyside or the Island beaches, they could get access to and swim at Cherry Beach for free. See letter to the editor, *Toronto Daily Star*, 6 July 1950. Toronto Harbour Commission Archives, Sunnyside Scrapbooks.

57 AO, RG 4-32, 1951, no. 660, Transcript, 341–2.

58 See Redl, 'Zoot Suits: An Interpretation.' For a more recent analysis, see Cosgrove, 'The Zoot Suit and Style Warfare.'

59 In the United States, riots broke out between servicemen and black and Hispanic zoot-suiters in Los Angeles in 1943. Subsequently, the making of the suits was prohibited. My mother remembers that young men wearing zoot-suits in Toronto were ridiculed as having avoided conscription. She also says

that boys wore the pants especially for jitterbugging and that they spent a lot of time worrying about the drape of the leg.

60 Valverde, 'Building Anti-delinquent Communities.'

61 Ibid., 29.

62 'Review and Summary of the Discussion and Thinking of the Sub-committee on Gangs to Date,' 9 Feb. 1949: brief attached to a memo from William A. Turnbull to Commissioner of Public Welfare, Metropolitan Toronto Archives, RG 5.1, Box 153, File 5.

63 McRobbie and Garber, 'Girls and Subcultures,' 213.

64 Humphries, *A Secret World of Sex*, 154.

65 Ibid., 144.

66 For fictional treatments of delinquency, see: King, 'Moment of Decision'; Peterson, 'The Runaway'; or Elson, *Tomboy*, a pulp novel about a teenage girl who is 'just one of the boys' in a gang. For films, see: *Police Club for Boys*, NFB, 1954; *Measure of a Man*, Brigham Young University Productions (date unknown); *Boy with a Knife*, Educational Film Distributors, 1956; *Borderline*, NFB, 1956; *What about Juvenile Delinquency*, 1955.

67 G. Stanley Hall, *Adolescence*, 205.

68 Strange, *Toronto's Girl Problem*, 194. See also Cavallo, *Muscles and Morals*.

69 Blatz, 'Your Child – and Sex,' 39.

70 Richardson, *Century of the Child*, 120; see also Dehli, 'Fictions of the Scientific Imagination.'

71 Social Planning Council, Recreation Section, 'Report of Meeting with Representatives of the Boys Brigade,' 15 July 1958, City of Toronto Archives, SC 40, Box 23, File 8.

72 'Report on the Investigation of the Recreational Opportunities for Teen Age Girls,' Oct. 1943, Metropolitan Toronto Archives, RG 5.1, Box 153, File 9.

73 Seeley, Sim, and Loosley, *Crestwood Heights*, 215.

74 Ibid., 330.

75 Iacovetta, *Such Hardworking People*, 152.

76 Social Planning Council, Committee to Assess the Need for Specialized Services in the Leisure-Time Field for the Negro Population, *Minutes*, 17 Nov. 1958, City of Toronto Archives, SC 40, Box 25, File 7.

77 Social Planning Council, *Report* of the Committee to Assess the Need for Specialized Services in the Leisure-Time Field for the Negro Population, 2, City of Toronto Archives, SC 40, Box 25, File 7.

78 Richards, 'So You're Starting a Teens' Canteen,' 28.

79 'Organizes Teen-age Club.'

80 'Teen Trouble,' 19, NAC, MG 28 I. 11, Vol. 38, File 2 (3v).

81 'Too Much Stress on Play.'

82 Rogers, *Street Gangs in Toronto*, 82.

83 'Community Centres an Answer' (editorial).

84 Letter from H.J. Terry to Hon. Leslie E. Blackwell, attorney general, 5 Jan. 1945, AO, RG, 4-02, File 24.4.

85 '16-Year-Old Girl Plans Dummy Hold-up with Youths Picked up in Dance Hall,' 13.

86 'Toronto Trustees Defend Students' Right to Dance.'

87 'Everyone Bewildered by City's Curfew Move.'

88 For a wartime assertion of the link between commercial entertainment and immorality, see the Welfare Council of Toronto and District, 'Crime and the Community,' 1940, 12, Library of the Social Planning Council of Metropolitan Toronto.

89 'Curfew Hour Held Unneeded in Queen City.'

90 *Toronto Daily Star*, 3 Apr. 1944.

91 'Reject Junction Club's Bid for Mixed Splash Parties.'

92 Tumpane, 'At City Hall.'

93 'Informal Discussion by Young People Representing a Cross-section of the Youth of Toronto, on Recreation Needs and Problems as They See Them, Monday, May 13th, 1946,' Part 2, City of Toronto Archives, RG 12A, Box 78, File 3.

94 Memo from B.W. Heise, acting Deputy Minister of Public Welfare to R.P. Vivian, Minister of Public Welfare, 7 Jan. 1944, AO, RG 4-02, File 22.7.

95 '"Lights Till Wee Hours" to Banish Lovers' Lanes Nip School Vandalism.'

96 'Put up Morality Lights at 2 Schools, Committee Asks.'

Chapter 5: 'Why Can't I Be Normal?'

1 See Rose, *Governing the Soul*.

2 D'Emilio, *Sexual Politics, Sexual Communities*, 16.

3 Radclyffe Hall, *The Well of Loneliness*.

4 See, for instance, the last lines of the book: 'God ... We have not denied You, then rise up and defend us. Acknowledge us, oh God, before the whole world. Give us also the right to our existence!' (ibid., 437).

5 For discussion of 'the ideology of maturity' as it was applied to adolescents in the American context, see Graebner, 'Coming of Age in Buffalo.'

6 Kinsey, Pomeroy, and Martin, *Sexual Behavior in the Human Male*; Kinsey, Pomeroy, Martin, and Gebhard, *Sexual Behavior in the Human Female*.

7 Rumming, 'Dr. Kinsey and the Human Female,' 7.

8 Kinsey et al., *Sexual Behavior in the Human Male*, 199.

9 Ibid., 202–3.

10 Ibid., 580.
11 See also Seeley and Griffin, 'The Kinsey Report,' 42.
12 Hughes, 'Kinsey Again: Leers or Cheers?' 10.
13 Kinsey et al., *Sexual Behavior in the Human Male*, 201.
14 May, *Homeward Bound*, 11.
15 Dubinsky, *Improper Advances*. See also Odem, *Delinquent Daughters*.
16 Simmons, 'Companionate Marriage and the Lesbian Threat.'
17 For the most part I gleaned the titles of books and pamphlets from bibliographies prepared by (1) teachers at the Toronto Board of Education, (2) the Canadian Youth Commission, and (3) contributors to the newsletter for Ontario public health nurses. Other titles were mentioned as worthy of attention in Canadian magazine articles. In the end I've chosen six titles that span the mid-1940s to the early 1960s. The decision to include a particular book was based on three things: first, and most practically, on its current availability; second, on the number of references made to it or its author in other sources; and third, on its representativeness in terms of the genre as a whole. It's important to note that all six were published originally in the United States.
18 Duberman, *Cures*.
19 Tyrer, *Sex, Marriage and Birth Control*.
20 *Are You Popular?* Produced by Coronet Films, first in 1947 and re-made in 1958 with a new cast and updated dialogue. Both copies are available for viewing at Prelinger and Associates, New York.
21 Landers, *Ann Landers Talks to Teenagers about Sex*, 47.
22 Davis, *Sex and the Adolescent*, 59.
23 Strain, *Teen Days*, 160.
24 Kirkendall, *Understanding Sex*, 34.
25 Davis, *Sex the Adolescent*, 63.
26 Ehrenreich, *The Hearts of Men*, 24.
27 Strain, *Teen Days*, 160.
28 Kirkendall, *Understanding Sex*, 34.
29 Duvall, *Facts of Life and Love for Teenagers*, 202–6.
30 Williams and Kane, *On Becoming a Woman*, 51.
31 Duvall, *Facts of Life and Love for Teenagers*, 274.
32 Landers, *Ann Landers Talks to Teenagers about Sex*, 81.
33 Ibid., 92.
34 Ibid.
35 Major, 'New to Our Youth,' 102.
36 Davis, *Sex and the Adolescent*, 228.
37 I am thinking particularly of sexological writings like Havelock Ellis's *Studies*

in the Psychology of Sex, vol. I, part four, and Richard von Krafft-Ebing, *Psychopathia Sexualis*. Radclyffe Hall's *The Well of Loneliness* also fits this model. An invert was, according to these writers, someone born with a bad match between their body and their *felt* gender. So Stephen, in *The Well of Loneliness*, felt she was very much a masculine soul living inside a feminine body.

38 Strain, *Sex Guidance in Family Life Education*, 142.
39 *Chatelaine* (Sept. 1948), 106.
40 Ibid.
41 Duvall, *Facts of Life and Love for Teenagers*, 22.
42 Strain, *Sex Guidance in Family Life Education*, 144.
43 Strain, *Teen Days*, 81.
44 Ibid., 75.
45 Duvall, *Facts of Life and Love for Teenagers*, 77.
46 Williams and Kane, *On Becoming a Woman*, 46 (emphasis in original).
47 See Bailey, *From Front Porch to Back Seat*; Rothman, *Hands and Hearts* D'Emilio and Freedman, *Intimate Matters*.
48 Dubinsky, *Improper Advances*, 114.
49 Peiss, *Cheap Amusements*.
50 Fass, *The Damned and the Beautiful*, 261.
51 D'Emilio and Freedman, *Intimate Matters*, 258.
52 Bailey, *From Front Porch to Back Seat*, 26.
53 Ibid., 27.
54 Ibid., 53.
55 May, *Homeward Bound*, 101.
56 Sylvia Fraser, *My Father's House*, 71.
57 Clifford R. Adams, 'Romance Isn't Easy,' 4.
58 Hilliard, 'Can You Live without Him?' 10–11.
59 Sidney Katz, 'Going Steady: Is It Ruining Our Teen-agers?' 9.
60 Ibid., 39.
61 Ibid., 38.
62 Williams and Kane, *On Becoming a Woman*, 46.
63 Strain, *Teen Days*, 130.
64 Duvall, *Facts of Life and Love for Teenagers*, 120.
65 Sidney Katz, 'Going Steady,' 10.
66 Landers, *Ann Landers Talks to Teenagers about Sex*, 19.
67 Hilliard, 'Dr. Marion Hilliard Talks to Single Women,' 48.
68 Williams and Kane, *On Becoming a Woman*, 29.
69 *Going Steady*, produced by Coronet Films, 1951.
70 *How Much Affection?*, produced by Crawley Films for McGraw-Hill Books, 1957.

71 There is obviously a point that needs to be made here about the NFB's more 'realistic' film as compared to those produced for the American market.

72 *Joe and Roxy*, produced by the National Film Board of Canada as part of the Perspective Series, 1957. The fact that Roxy and Joe are home alone, while Roxy's mother is at work, was a relatively radical statement when U.S. films were portraying mothers as forever baking, always home after school. In some American films, teens who brought friends over when their parents were out, let alone 'boyfriends' or 'girlfriends,' were portrayed as misbehaving and risking punishment.

73 Hilliard, 'Dr. Marion Hilliard Helps Teen-age Girls Meet Their Biggest Problem,' 100.

74 Williams and Kane, *On Becoming a Woman*, 28.

75 Breines, *Young, White, and Miserable*, 87.

76 Kinsey et al., *Sexual Behavior in the Human Female*, 287.

77 Ibid., 300.

78 Ibid., 233.

79 Breines, *Young, White and Miserable*, 115.

80 Alison Prentice et al., *Canadian Women: A History*, 311.

81 Williams and Kane, *On Becoming a Woman*, 149.

82 'It's a Tough Time to Be in Love,' (editorial), 1.

83 Rose, *Governing the Soul*, 11.

Chapter 6: Sex Goes to School

1 Foster, 'Penicillin Can Wipe out Canada's Number One Health Scourge,' 22.

2 B. Fraser, 'VD ... No. 1 Saboteur,' 7.

3 For a discussion of VD in Canada during the Second World War, see Pierson, *'They're Still Women after All.'*

4 'Want All Canadians Given Test for V.D.'

5 'Open VD Education Campaign for Fourth Year High Pupils.'

6 Bland, '"Guardians of the Race" or "Vampires on the Nation's Health"?' 377.

7 McLaren, *Our Own Master Race*, 74.

8 Buckley and McGinnis, 'Venereal Disease and Public Health Reform in Canada.'

9 *Sixteen to Twenty-Six* (for young women) and *Very Dangerous* (for young men), both produced by the NFB, 1945.

10 Dehli, 'Women and Class,' 217.

11 Toronto Board of Education, *Minutes*, 19 June 1941, 122.

12 Ontario, Department of Education, *Courses of Study*, Grades IX, X, XI, and XII,

Defense Training and Health and Physical Education, May 1942, 7 and 18. Reported on in the *Toronto Daily Star*, 25 Aug. 1942.

13 The total number of cases was 41,069. Health League of Canada, 'The Social Hygiene Voice,' Jan. 1945, NAC, MG 28 I 11, Vol. 35, File 1 (3d).

14 'Goldring to Report on Social Hygiene.'

15 C.C. Goldring, Report to the Management Committee of the Board of Education, 6 Mar. 1944, Toronto Board of Education, Social Hygiene File.

16 Ibid., 3.

17 'Goldring to Report on Social Hygiene.'

18 Health League of Canada, Toronto Branch, Subcommittee on Sex Education, *Minutes*, 25 July 1944, NAC, MG 28 I 11, Vol. 35, File 1 (3d).

19 'A Sound Proposal' (editorial).

20 'Trustees Approve Teaching Sex Subjects in Schools.'

21 '"Teach Young How to Live Is Obligation," Drew Says.'

22 'Problems of Sex Instruction.'

23 'Delinquency Seen as Main Ill.'

24 'Sex Education Classes Said Vital to School Health.'

25 'Women's Groups Divided on School Sex Education.'

26 'Church Group Would Study Sex Education.' There is no evidence that this proposal was ever made explicitly to any school board.

27 Letter from R.E.G. Davis to S.R. Laycock, national president of the Canadian Federation of Home and School Associations, 11 Mar. 1947, NAC, MG 28 I 11, Vol. 42.

28 Dora Wilensky (Jewish Family and Child Services, Toronto) cited in a letter from Margaret Davis to Mrs Kaspar Fraser [Lois], 11 Apr. 1947, NAC, MG 28 I 11, Vol. 42.

29 'A Challenge to the Schools' (editorial).

30 Ibid.

31 Chapin, 'Sex Instruction in the School Curriculum,' 39.

32 'Sex Education Scheme Approved by Teachers.'

33 Toronto Board of Education, *Reports* by board officials, 'Parenting School,' 8 Jan. 1945. Previous attempts by the board, in conjunction with the Home and School Council, to educate working-class and immigrant parents had resulted in failure. See Dehli, 'Women and Class,' especially ch. 7.

34 Blatz, 'Your Child – and Sex,' 7.

35 Richardson, *The Century of the Child*, 112; Dehli, 'Fictions of the Scientific Imagination.'

36 Winnifred Ashplant, secondary school health counsellor from London, Ontario, quoted in 'Sex Education Classes Said Vital to School Health.'

37 Blatz, 'Your Child – and Sex,' 38.

38 Rose, *Governing the Soul*, 4.
39 'Guiding Principles in the Presentation of the Subject of Venereal Diseases,'
    Feb. 1946, appended to C.C. Goldring's Report to the Management Commit-
    tee of the Board of Education, Toronto, 13 May 1948. Toronto Board of Educa-
    tion Archives, Sex Education File.
40 Ibid., 1.
41 Phair and Speirs, *Good Health*, 209.
42 'Guiding Principles in the Presentation of the Subject of Venereal Diseases,' 3.
43 C.C. Goldring, Report to the Management Committee of the Board of Educa-
    tion, 13 May 1948, 3.
44 The films were called: *In the Beginning* (1938), *Human Reproduction* (1947,
    McGraw-Hill), *Sex in Life*, and *Menstruation*. I have been able to watch only
    the first two of these. Neither deals with issues of conduct or sexual behav-
    iour or feelings. Their primary focus is on the fertilization of eggs, cell divi-
    sion, etc. *In the Beginning* uses rabbits to document the reproductive cycle – to
    the point of cutting open a female to extract first her uterus and then a
    twenty-eight day-old 'foetus.' *Human Reproduction* has long shots of dia-
    grams of male and female bodies, complete with arrows and labels that
    appear and disappear as needed. We also see a foetus develop and the
    changes a woman's body goes through during pregnancy.
45 Goldring, Report, 13 May 1948, 3.
46 Sidney Katz, 'The Truth about Sex Criminals,' 12.
47 May, *Homeward Bound*, 14.
48 Freedman, '"Uncontrolled Desires,"' 200.
49 Ibid., 199.
50 'Brief from the John Howard Society of Ontario' to the Royal Commission on
    the Criminal Law Relating to Criminal Sexual Psychopaths, 13 Feb. 1956,
    NAC, RG 33/131 Vol. 1.
51 'Remarks by Chief Constable John Chisholm before the Royal Commission
    on the Criminal Law Relating to Criminal Sexual Psychopaths,' 9–10 Feb.
    1956, Toronto, NAC, RG 33/131, Vol. 1.
52 The definition comes from Section 1054 A of the 1948 *Criminal Code of Canada*.
53 See 'The Sexual Psychopath'; and 'A Practical Approach.'
54 G.H. Stevenson, 'Psychiatry and Sex Offenders,' paper presented at the On-
    tario Neuropsychiatric Association, 16 Jan. 1948, AO, RG 10- 163-0-617, Box 24.
55 Letter from a private citizen to Premier Drew, 22 May 1948, complaining re
    'sex offence law enforcement,' AO, RG 4-32, 1948, no. 540.
56 Letter from Evelyn Burt (Toronto Council of Women's International Union
    Auxiliaries) and Jean Laing to Russell Kelly, Minister of Health, 24 Jan. 1948,
    AO, RG 10-107-0-224.

57 See, for instance, 'Study of Sex Perverts in Prisons Reveals Present Penal Treatment Contributes to Their Degeneration.'

58 Canadian Penal Association, 'Interim Report: Committee on the Sex Offender,' June 1948, 9, NAC, RG 33/131, Vol. 2.

59 Ibid., 22.

60 Ibid., 24.

61 Ibid., 25.

62 Ibid., 27.

63 Goldring, Report, 13 May 1948, 3.

64 'Sex Education to Be Studied by Committee.'

65 Letter to Charles Edwards from Adolf Weinzirl, 24 July 1948, Toronto Board of Education, *Minutes* of Special Committee appointed to consider and report on the matter of Sex Education in Schools, 2 Sept. 1948, App. A, Toronto Board of Education Archives.

66 Strain, *Sex Guidance in Family Life Education*, viii. Strain's work was routinely included in bibliographies on sex education prepared by Canadian organizations. See, for instance: Report of Teachers'Committee on Sex Education for Grades VII and VIII, 12: appended to *Minutes* of Special Committee appointed to consider and report on the matter of Sex Education in Schools, 22 Nov. 1948, Appendix A, Toronto Board of Education Archives; syllabus for a course on the Psychology of Adolescence, prepared by S.R. Laycock, University of Saskatchewan, College of Education, 1941, NAC, MG 28 I 11, Vol. 60; Ontario, Department of Health, Division of Public Health Nurses, 'Suggested Bibliography for Public Health Nurses in Secondary Schools,' *Bulletin* (July 1944), 5, AO, RG 10-30-A-1.

67 Strain, *Sex Guidance in Family Life Education*, 11.

68 Ibid., 319.

69 Ibid., 307.

70 Ibid., 313.

71 Report of Teachers'Committee on Sex Education for Grades VII and VIII, 1, *Minutes* of Special Committee appointed to consider and report on the matter of Sex Education in Schools, 22 Nov. 1948, App. A, Toronto Board of Education Archives.

72 Ibid., 3.

73 Ibid., 1.

74 Ibid., 4.

75 Ibid., 6.

76 Ibid., 7.

77 'Board of Education Considers Courses in Sex Education' (editorial).

78 'No Need for Haste' (editorial).

79 'Sex Education in Public Schools Report Is Tabled.'
80 Valverde, *The Age of Light, Soap and Water*, 67–76.
81 N.R. Speirs, 'Family Life Education – Introductory Lecture,' 23 Mar. 1949, appended to C.C. Goldring, Report to Management Committee of the Board of Education, Toronto, 6 Apr. 1949.
82 Ibid., 8. Frances Strain counselled the same thing.
83 Ibid.
84 'School Board Bans Sex behind Closed Doors.'
85 Toronto Board of Education, *Private Minutes*, 7 Apr. 1949.
86 'A Lesson in Sex Education.'
87 Board of Education, Management Report, No. 9, Part II, 26 Apr. 1949, Toronto Board of Education Archives.
88 Rogers, *Street Gangs in Toronto*, 20.
89 'Board Approves Sex in Very Modified Form.'
90 Ontario, Department of Education, *Courses of Study*, Grades IX, X, XI, and XII, Health and Physical Education, 1950.

Chapter 7: Manipulating Innocence

1 Letter to 'Ontario Government Censorship Bureau' (a bureaucratic entity which did not exist – the letter was directed to the Attorney General), 20 June 1949, AO, RG 4-32, 1949, no. 270.
2 Paul Guay, President of Press and Cinema Services (Canada's equivalent to the League of Decency in the United States), Ottawa Archdiocese of the Catholic Church, Brief submitted to the Senate Special Committee on Salacious and Indecent Literature; see Canada, Senate, Special Committee on Salacious and Indecent Literature (hereafter Special Committee), *Proceedings*, 3 June 1952, 10.
3 Letter to Attorney General Dana Porter from a 'citizen' in Stoney Creek, 8 Nov. 1955, AO, RG 4-32, 1955, no. 25.
4 'Notes taken at a meeting on 24 February 1956, during which a delegation representing a number of [Ontario] civic and religious groups presented a brief to the Attorney General re: salacious literature,' AO, RG 4-02, File 91.7.
5 B.C. Provincial Congress of Canadian Women, Brief submitted to the Senate Special Committee on Salacious and Indecent Literature, Special Committee, *Proceedings*, 11 Feb. 1953, 41.
6 For a discussion of the evolution of mass-produced pocket books and the various technologies that have made it possible, see Radway, *Reading the Romance*.
7 The book was *Women's Barracks* by Tereska Torres, and the distributor was

National News Company. See, *The Queen v. National News Company,* 514, AO, RG 4-32, 1953, no. 830. There are no records of how many copies were sold.

8 'Comics as Yule Gift to Clergyman-Trustee, Tely's Palooka Fan.'

9 Senate, Special Committee, *Report,* 29 Apr. 1953, 243.

10 Banning, 'Filth on the Newsstands,' 150.

11 Gilbert, *A Cycle of Outrage,* 3.

12 Barker, *A Haunt of Fears,* 6.

13 Peiss, *Cheap Amusements.*

14 Dubinsky, *Improper Advances,* 12.

15 By 1954, U.S. magazines occupied 80 per cent of Canadian newsstand space, and 74.6 per cent of the 1289 feature films that were shown in Canada in 1953 were Hollywood productions (only one was Canadian). American programming was broadcast regularly by Canadian radio and television stations (including on Canadian Broadcasting Corporation television channels). For discussions of the impact of American popular culture in Canada see: Finkel, Conrad, and Strong-Boag, *History of the Canadian Peoples; F. Sutherland, The Monthly Epic;* and Rutherford, *When Television Was Young.*

16 Barker, *Haunt of Fears.* While Communist and other left organizations, such as the Congress of Canadian Women, were involved in the anti-comics campaign, they do not seem to have been the driving force in this country. The Canadian movement was very broad-based and seems to have been given its greatest push from PTA groups.

17 Barker, *Haunt of Fears,* 87.

18 See Landis, *Adolescence and Youth,* 47.

19 Banning, 'Filth on the Newsstands,' 150.

20 Congress of Canadian Women, Submission to the Senate, Special Committee on Salacious and Indecent Literature, Special Committee, *Proceedings,* 25 June 1952, 149.

21 Resolution from the Town of Timmins, Ontario, about indecent literature, AO, RG 4-32, 1952, no. 59. Endorsed by at least thirty-two other municipalities, it urged the government to survey and censor magazines in order to eliminate 'all that which is undesirable and unfit for consumption by the children of this Province ...'

22 Canadian Preparatory Committee, International Conference in Defense of Children, Submission to Senate, Special Committee on Salacious and Indecent Literature, Special Committee, *Proceedings,* 25 June 1952, 161.

23 Christian Social Council of Canada, Brief presented to the Senate Special Committee on Salacious and Indecent Literature, Special Committee, *Proceedings,* 17 June 1952, 77.

24 Special Committee, *Report,* 246.

25 Special Committee, *Proceedings*, 25 Apr. 1953, 221.

26 Canada, House of Commons, *Debates*, 21 Oct. 1949, 1043.

27 Parsons, 'Batman and His Audience,' 68–9; Boichel, 'Batman: Commodity as Myth,' 6.

28 Bell, *Guardians of the North*, 18. Bell's booklet is the catalogue from an exhibition of the same name at the Canadian Museum of Caricature during the summer of 1992.

29 Ibid., 3.

30 For more detailed descriptions of these and other comic-book characters, see ibid.

31 Ibid., 11.

32 Ibid., 15.

33 Ibid.

34 AO, RG 4-32, 1949, no. 270.

35 'Trustee Calls "Comic" Books "Degrading and Detrimental."'

36 Cited in Brief presented to a Special Committee of the Senate by the IODE, 1952, AO, RG 4-02, File 91.7.

37 Jukes, 'Are Comics Really a Menace?' 6–7.

38 Ibid., 7.

39 *Unusual Comics*.

40 *FBI Comics*.

41 'Comic Book Study Urged for Effect on Children.'

42 'Board Debates Comic Books.'

43 Canada, House of Commons, *Debates*, 14 June 1948, 5201.

44 Canada, House of Commons, *Debates*, 9 June 1948, 4935.

45 Brannigan, 'Mystification of the Innocents,' 118.

46 Canada, House of Commons, *Debates*, 8 June 1948, 4932.

47 Statement by G.K. Fraser, MP for Peterborough West. Canada, House of Commons, *Debates*, 6 Oct. 1949, 580.

48 Canada, House of Commons, *Debates*, 4 Oct. 1949, 517.

49 Canada, House of Commons, *Debates*, 7 Oct. 1949, 624.

50 Statement by G.K. Fraser, MP for Peterborough West. Canada, House of Commons, *Debates*, 6 Oct. 1949, 580.

51 Canada, House of Commons, Bill 10, 1949.

52 Ibid.

53 'Comics as Yule Gift to Clergyman-Trustee.

54 Parsons, 'Batman and His Audience,' 71.

55 Wertham, *Seduction of the Innocent*.

56 Ibid., ch. 11: 'Murder in Dawson Creek – Comic Books Abroad.'

57 Ibid., 282.

58 Copy of letter from Fredric Wertham to Mrs T.W.A. [Eleanor] Gray, 14 Dec. 1953. The letter is appended to a letter from Mrs Gray, on behalf of the British Columbia Parent-Teacher Federation, to the attorney general of Ontario, 4 Feb. 1954, AO, RG 4-32, 1954, no. 26, Box 98.

59 Wertham, *Seduction of the Innocent*, 10.

60 Ibid., 81.

61 Ibid., 175.

62 Stainton-Rogers and Stainton-Rogers, *Stories of Childhood*, 27.

63 Ibid., 29.

64 Wertham, *Seduction of the Innocent*, 177.

65 For an example of this, see Davis, *Sex and the Adolescent*, 62.

66 Wertham, *Seduction of the Innocent*, 188.

67 Ibid., 191.

68 Ibid., 99.

69 Ibid., 34.

70 'Code of the Comics Magazine Association of America,' 26 Oct. 1954, AO, RG 4-02, File 76.12.

71 Canada, Senate, *Debates*, 8 May 1952, 186.

72 The quotations are taken from a speech given by Senator J.J. Hayes Doone in New Brunswick in 1949. Cited in Canada, Senate, *Debates*, 8 May 1952, 186.

73 Ibid., 186.

74 Senate, *Debates*, 25 June 1952, 501.

75 Special Committee, *Report*, 243.

76 'Let's Be on Guard' (editorial).

77 *Regina v. National News Company Limited*, 8 Oct. 1952, AO, RG 4-32, 1953, no. 830.

78 Torres, *Women's Barracks*. While published by a New York company, the book was printed in Canada. There is a copy of the novel, with margin notes by the crown attorney, on file with the court transcripts. AO, RG 4-32, 1953, no. 830.

79 Torres, *The Converts*. The text on the front cover of the book jacket reads, 'The autobiography of Tereska Torres, author of "Women's Barracks."'

80 Torres, *Women's Barracks*, 5.

81 Judge A.G. McDougall, 'Reasons for Judgment, re: *Tragic Ground*,' *Regina v. The National News Company Limited*, 22 Nov. 1952, AO, RG 4-32, 1953, no. 830.

82 *Rex v. Hicklin*, Law Reports, 3 Queen's Bench, 360, 1868; *Rex v. Beaver*, 9 Ontario Law Reports, 418, 1904.

83 *Regina v. American News Co. Limited*, Ontario Reports, 145, 150 (1957).

84 *R. v. National News*, 16.

85 The other two tags mark a slang reference to prostitution and a scene where a young woman loses her virginity with a man.

86 *R. v. National News*, 29.
87 Ibid., 44.
88 Ibid., 64.
89 Ibid., 54.
90 Ibid., 64.
91 Ibid., 380.
92 Ibid., 361.
93 Ibid., 365.
94 A.G. McDougall, 'Judgment re: Women's Barracks,' 22 Nov. 1952, AO, RG 4-32, 1953, no. 830.
95 Judgment from a trial in St Paul, Minnesota, 16 June 1953, quoted in Torres, *Women's Barracks*, 11th printing, June 1958, inside front cover.

Chapter 8: Conclusion

1 Rose, *Governing the Soul*.
2 See, for instance: Kennedy and Davis, *Boots of Leather, Slippers of Gold*; Harvey, *The Fifties*.
3 See, for instance, Fuss, ed., *Inside/Out*.
4 Jonathan Ned Katz, 'The Invention of Heterosexuality,' 20.
5 Breines, *Young, White and Miserable*.
6 For discussions of right-wing anti-gay organizations like CURE (Citizens United for Responsible Education) see: Pegis, 'A Sick Body of Evidence'; Jackson, 'Christians, the Right and Political Power.'

Sources

Archival Sources

Archives of Ontario (AO)

RG 2 Education
  Pamphlets, regulations, etc. (Series Q).
  Physical Education Branch Directors' Select Records. 1945–65 (Acc. 10932)
RG 4 Attorney General
  Ministers' subject/correspondence files. 1943–59 (Series 4-02).
  Committee on Obscene Literature. 1958 (Series 4-11).
  Central Registry Files. 1944–55 (Series 4-32).
  Sex Deviates. 1958 (Series 4-36).
RG 10 Health
  Ministers' Files. 1956–63 (Series 1).
  Public Health Nursing, Printed Material. 1921–59 (Series 30-A).
  Subject Correspondence, VD Control. 1943–77 (Series 63).
  Public Health Central Files. 1938–60 (Series 106).
  Mental Health Central Files. 1942–63 (Series 107).
RG 20 Correctional Services
  Minister's Advisory Council on Treatment of the Offender. 1959–73.
RG 22 Court Records
  Unmarried Parents Files, Provincial Family Court, Metro Toronto. 1942–66
    (acc. 21742 [FD1], boxes 104–10).

City of Toronto Archives

Toronto. Board of Control. *Minutes*. 1945–60.

Toronto. Council. *Minutes*. 1945–60.
RG 1 Reports
  Civic Recreation Committee. 'Youth and Recreation in Toronto, Preliminary
    Survey.' 1936.
  Welfare Council of Toronto and District. 'Crime and the Community.' 1940.
RG 9 Police
  Annual Reports of Chief Constable. 1944–55.
RG 11 Department of Public Health
  Annual Reports. 1944–60.
RG 12A Department of Parks and Recreation
  Toronto Recreation Council. Sub-committee on Recreation and Housing. 1944–
    46 (Box 68, File 2).
  Parks Department. Matters Regarding Juvenile Delinquency. 1942–6 (Box 78,
    File 3).
  Parks Department. Juvenile Delinquency. 1947–51 (Box 90, File 9).
RG 37 Public Welfare Department
  Annual Reports. 1944–60.
RG 47 Toronto Family Court
  Annual Reports. 1944–52.
RG 200 Special Committee Minutes
  Minutes of the Advisory Committee on Recreation. 1937–40.
  Private Conference re: VD Control. 1944.
  Minutes of Juvenile Delinquency Committee. 1946–9.
  Conference re: Juvenile Delinquency and Associated Problems. 1949.
RG 283 Juvenile Delinquency Committee. 1948–9.
SC 1 Children's Aid Society papers.
SC 40 Social Planning Council papers.

Library of the Social Planning Council of Metropolitan Toronto

Report of the Mayor's Citizens Committee for the Investigation of Narcotic
  Addiction and Vice in Metro Toronto. 1959.
Social Planning Council. Report on Maternity Homes in Metropolitan Toronto.
  1959.
Welfare Council of Toronto and District. 'A Plan for the Reduction of Juvenile
  Delinquency in Toronto.' 1943.

Metropolitan Toronto Archives

RG 5.1 Office of the Commissioner of Public Welfare
  Juvenile Delinquency and Youth Program. 1937–65 (Box 153).

Youth Projects. 1943–9 (Boxes 153 and 154).

National Archives of Canada (NAC)

RG 33/131 Royal Commission on the Criminal Law Relating to Criminal Sexual
   Psychopaths. 1948–58 (Vols 1–3).
MG 28 I 11 Canadian Youth Commission Papers
   Family Life Files (Vol. 42).
   Printed Materials (Vol. 60, 64, 67).
   Questionnaires and Polls (vols 45–52).
   Recreation Files (Vol. 38).

Toronto Board of Education Archives

Toronto Board of Education. Management Committee. *Minutes*. 1942–60.
Toronto Board of Education. *Minutes*, 1942–60.
Toronto Board of Education. *Reports* by board officials. 1945–60.
Toronto Board of Education. *Special Committee Minutes*. 1944–9.
Curriculum files: Sex Education, Health Education.
Vertical files: Family Life Education, Sex Education, Social Hygiene.
Scrapbooks of newspaper clippings: 1944–55.

Toronto Harbour Commission Archives

Sunnyside Scrapbooks.

Films

The following films were produced by the National Film Board of Canada and
are available for viewing at the National Archives in Ottawa.

Borderline. 1956.
Family Circles. 1949.
Forbidden Love. 1992 (available at regional NFB offices).
Joe and Roxy. 1957.
Making a Decision in the Family. 1957.
Police Club for Boys. 1954.
Sixteen to Twenty-Six. 1945.
The Teens. 1957.
Very Dangerous. 1945.
Who Is Sylvia? 1957.

I viewed the following films at the offices of Prelinger and Associates, a stock footage house and film archives in New York (430 W. 14th Street, Rm 206, New York, NY 10014)

A Date with Your Family. Simmel Meservey Release, nd.
Are You Popular? Coronet Films. 1947.
Are You Popular? Coronet Films. 1958.
Are You Ready for Marriage? Coronet Films. 1950.
Boy with a Knife. Educational Film Distribution. 1956.
Choosing for Happiness. McGraw-Hill Books. 1950.
Dating Dos and Don'ts. Coronet Films. 1952.
Emotional Maturity. McGraw-Hill Books. 1957.
Going Steady. Coronet Films. 1951.
How Do You Know It's Love? Coronet Films. 1950.
How Much Affection? McGraw-Hill Books. 1957.
How to Say No. Coronet Films. nd.
Human Reproduction. McGraw-Hill Text Films. 1947.
In the Beginning. Producer unknown. 1938.
Is This Love? McGraw-Hill Books. 1957.
Marriage Today. McGraw-Hill Books. 1950.
Measure of a Man. Brigham Young University. nd.
Molly Grows Up. Personal Products Corporation. 1953.
More Dates for Kay. Coronet Films. 1952.
Perversion for Profit. Citizens for Decent Literature. 1956.
Physical Aspects of Puberty. McGraw-Hill Books. 1953.
Social-Sex Attitudes in Adolescence. McGraw-Hill Books. 1953.
The Meaning of Adolescence. McGraw-Hill Books. 1953.
The Last Date. Mutual Casualty Company. nd.
What about Juvenile Delinquency. Young America Films. 1955.
When Should I Marry? McGraw-Hill Text Films. 1957.
Your Body during Adolescence. McGraw-Hill Books. 1954.

Books and Articles

Adams, Clifford R. 'Romance Isn't Easy.' *Chatelaine* (Sept. 1948): 4–5, 92.
Adams, Mary Louise. 'In Sickness and in Health: State Formation and Early VD Initiatives in Ontario.' *Journal of Canadian Studies* 28, no. 4 (Winter 1993–4): 117–30.
Anglin, Gerald. 'The Pill That Could Shake the World.' *Chatelaine* (Oct. 1953): 16–17, 99–103.

- 'Who Has Won the War between the Sexes?' *Chatelaine* (June 1955): 11–13, 66–70.

Anonymous. 'I'm Not Having Any.' *Chatelaine* (Apr. 1947): 14, 64, 78.

Ariès, Philippe. *Centuries of Childhood: A Social History of Family Life.* New York: Vintage 1965.

Arnup, Katherine. *Education for Motherhood.* Toronto: University of Toronto Press 1994.

Axelrod, Paul. *Making a Middle Class: Student Life in English Canada during the Thirties.* Montreal and Kingston: McGill-Queen's University Press 1990.

Bailey, Beth. *From Front Porch to Back Seat.* Baltimore: Johns Hopkins University Press 1988.

Banning, Margaret Culkin. 'Filth on the Newsstands.' *Reader's Digest* (Oct. 1952): 148–59.

Barker, Martin. *A Haunt of Fears: The Strange History of the British Horror Comics Campaign.* London: Pluto 1984.

Bell, John. *Guardians of the North: The National Superhero in Canadian Comic-book Art.* Ottawa: National Archives of Canada 1992.

Belsey, Catherine. *Critical Practice.* New York: Routledge 1980.

Bennett, Paul W. 'Taming "bad boys" of the "dangerous class": Child Rescue and Restraint at the Victoria Industrial School, 1887–1935.' *Histoire sociale – Social History* 21, no. 41 (May 1988): 71–96.

Boichel, Bill. 'Batman: Commodity as Myth.' In Pearson and Uricchio, eds, *The Many Lives of the Batman*, 4–17.

'The Blackboard Jungle: Some Protest School Film Protest.' *Globe and Mail*, 20 May 1955.

Bland, Lucy. '"Guardians of the Race," or "Vampires upon the Nation's Health"?: Female Sexuality and Its Regulation in Early Twentieth-Century Britain.' In Elizabeth Whitelegg et al., eds, *The Changing Experience of Women*, 373–88. Oxford: Basil Blackwell 1982.

Blatz, W.E. 'Your Child – and Sex.' *Maclean's* (1 Jan. 1945): 7, 37–9.

'Board Approves Sex in Very Modified Form.' *Globe and Mail*, 5 May 1949.

'Board Debates Comic Books.' *Globe and Mail*, 10 Jan. 1951.

'Board of Education Considers Courses in Sex Education.' Editorial. *Telegram*, 9 Sept. 1948.

Bothwell, Robert, Ian Drummond, and John English. *Canada since 1945.* Rev. ed. Toronto: University of Toronto Press 1989.

Brandt, Alan. *No Magic Bullets.* London: Oxford 1985.

Brannigan, Augustine. 'Mystification of the Innocents: Crime Comics and Delinquency in Canada, 1931–1949.' *Canadian Justice History* 7 (1986): 111–44.

Breines, Wini. *Young, White, and Miserable: Growing Up Female in the Fifties.* Boston: Beacon 1992.

Buckley, Suzann, and Janice Dickin McGinnis. 'Venereal Disease and Public Health Reform in Canada.' *Canadian Historical Review* 63 (1982): 337–54.

Bumsted, J.M. 'Canada and American Culture in the 1950s.' In his *Interpreting Canada's Past*, vol. 2, 398–411. Toronto: Oxford, 1986.

Calhoun, Arthur Wallace. 'The Child Mind as a Social Product.' In Calverton and Schmalhausen, eds, *The New Generation*, 74–87.

Calverton, V.F., and Samuel D. Schmalhausen, eds. *The New Generation: The Intimate Problems of Modern Parents and Children*. London: George Allen and Unwin 1930.

Canada. House of Commons. *Debates*. 1948–58.

– Senate. Special Committee on Salacious and Indecent Literature. *Proceedings and Report*. Ottawa 1953.

Canadian Youth Commission. *Youth, Marriage and the Family*. Toronto: Ryerson 1948.

– *Youth Speaks out on Citizenship*. Toronto: Ryerson 1948.

Cassel, Jay. *The Secret Plague: Venereal Disease in Canada, 1838–1939*. Toronto: University of Toronto Press 1987.

Cavallo, Dominick. *Muscles and Morals: Organized Playgrounds and Urban Reform, 1880–1920*. Philadelphia: University of Pennsylvania Press 1981.

'A Challenge to the Schools.' Editorial. *Toronto Daily Star*, 29 Nov. 1944.

Chamberland, Line. *Mémoires lesbiennes: Le lesbianisme á Montréal entre 1950 et 1972*. Montreal: Les éditions remue-ménage 1996.

Chapin, Miriam. 'Sex Instruction in the School Curriculum.' *Saturday Night* (15 Apr. 1944): 39.

Chauncey, George. 'From Sexual Inversion to Homosexuality: The Changing Medical Conceptualization of Female "Deviance."' In Peiss and Simmons, eds, *Passion and Power*, 87–117.

– *Gay New York: Gender, Urban Culture and the Making of the Gay Male World, 1890–1940*. New York: Basic 1994.

Chenier, Elise. 'Tough Ladies and Troublemakers: Toronto's Public Lesbian Community, 1955–1965.' MA thesis, Queen's University 1995.

'Child Delinquency Starts in Homes.' *Telegram*, 22 Sept. 1948.

'Church Group Would Study Sex Education.' *Globe and Mail*, 9 Mar. 1944.

Churchill, David. 'Coming out in a Cold Climate: A History of Gay Men in Toronto during the 1950s.' MA thesis, University of Toronto, Ontario Institute for Studies in Education 1995.

Cohen, Stanley. *Folk Devils and Moral Panics: The Creation of Mods and Rockers*. London: MacGibbon and Kee 1972.

Comacchio, Cynthia R. *Nations Are Built of Babies*. Montreal and Kingston: McGill-Queen's University Press 1993.

'Comic Book Study Urged for Effect on Children.' *Globe and Mail*, 11 Aug. 1950.

'Comics as Yule Gift to Clergyman-Trustee, Tely's Palooka Fan.' *Telegram*, 13 Dec. 1950.

'Community Centres an Answer.' Editorial. *Globe and Mail*, 3 Jan. 1946.

Coontz, Stephanie. *The Way We Never Were: American Families and the Nostalgia Trap.* New York: Basic Books 1992.

Corrigan, Philip. 'On Moral Regulation: Some Preliminary Remarks.' *Sociological Review* 29, no. 2 (1981): 313–35.

Corrigan, Philip, and Derek Sayer. *The Great Arch: English State Formation as Cultural Revolution.* Oxford: Blackwell 1985.

Cosgrove, Stuart. 'The Zoot Suit and Style Warfare.' In Angela McRobbie, ed., *Zoot Suits and Second-hand Dresses: An Anthology of Fashion and Music*, 3–22.Boston: Unwin Hyman 1988.

Costello, John. *Love, Sex and War: Changing Values, 1939–1945.* London: Collins 1985.

'Curfew Hour Held Unneeded in Queen City.' *Telegram*, 14 Apr. 1944.

Davis, Maxine. *Sex and the Adolescent.* New York: Permabooks 1960.

Dehli, Kari. 'Fictions of the scientific imagination: Researching the Dionne Quintuplets.' *Journal of Canadian Studies* 29, no. 4 (1994): 86–110.

– 'Women and Class: The Social Organization of Mothers' Relations to Schools in Toronto, 1915 to 1940.' PhD diss. University of Toronto, Ontario Institute for Studies in Education, 1988.

'Delinquency and Schools.' *Toronto Daily Star*, 30 Mar. 1944.

'Delinquency Seen as Main Ill.' *Globe and Mail*, 13 Mar. 1944.

D'Emilio, John. 'The Homosexual Menace: The Politics of Sexuality in Cold War America.' In Peiss and Simmons, eds, *Passion and Power*, 226–40.

– *Sexual Politics, Sexual Communities: The Making of a Homosexual Minority in the United States, 1940–1970.* Chicago: University of Chicago Press 1983.

D'Emilio, John, and Estelle B. Freedman. *Intimate Matters: A History of Sexuality in America.* New York: Harper and Row 1988.

Dempsey, Lotta. 'Dr. Kinsey Talks about Women to Lotta Dempsey.' *Chatelaine* (Aug. 1949): 10–11, 59–60.

– Editorial. *Chatelaine* (Aug. 1952): 1.

Dennis, Wayne. 'The Adolescent.' In Leonard Carmichael, ed., *Manual of Child Psychology*, 633–66. New York: John Wiley and Sons 1946.

Doherty, Thomas. *Teenagers and Teenpics: The Juvenilization of American Movies in the 1950s.* Boston: Unwin Hyman 1988.

Donzelot, Jacques. *The Policing of Families.* New York: Pantheon 1979.

Duberman, Martin. *Cures.* New York: Dutton 1991.

Dubinsky, Karen. *Improper Advances: Rape and Heterosexual Conflict in Ontario, 1880–1929.* Chicago: University of Chicago Press 1993.

Duvall, Evelyn Millis. *Facts of Life and Love for Teenagers.* New York: Association Press 1950.

Ehrenreich, Barbara. *Fear of Falling: The Inner Life of the Middle Class.* New York: Harper Collins 1989.

– *The Hearts of Men: American Dreams and the Flight from Commitment.* New York: Anchor/Doubleday 1983.

'E.J.M.' Review of *Sexual Behavior in the Human Male. Canadian Doctor* (July 1948): 50–6.

Ellis, Havelock. *Psychology of Sex.* New York and Toronto: New American Library 1933.

– *Studies in the Psychology of Sex.* New York: Random House 1936.

Elson, Hall. *Tomboy.* New York: Charles Scribner's Sons 1950.

'Everyone Bewildered by City's Curfew Move.' *Globe and Mail,* 5 Apr. 1944.

Fass, Paula. *The Damned and the Beautiful: American Youth in the 1920s.* New York: Oxford 1977.

FBI Comics No. 2 (Oct./Nov. 1946). Bell Publishing.

Feminism and Psychology. Special issue on heterosexuality. Vol. 2, no. 3 (1992).

Finkel, Alvin, and Margaret Conrad, with Veronica Strong-Boag. *History of the Canadian People.* Vol. 2. *1867–Present.* Toronto: Copp Clark Pitman 1993.

Fliess, Robert. 'On the Psychology of Two Types of Unmarried Mother: A Psychoanalytic Postscript.' Postscript to Young, *Out of Wedlock,* 243–9.

Foster, Ann. 'Penicillin Can Wipe Out Canada's Number One Health Scourge.' *Saturday Night* (21 July 1945): 22–3.

Foucault, Michel. *Discipline and Punish: The Birth of the Prison.* New York: Vintage 1979.

– *The History of Sexuality.* Vol. 1. Translated by Robert Hurley. New York: Pelican 1981.

– *Power/Knowledge.* Edited by C. Gordon. New York: Pantheon. 1980.

– 'Questions of Method: An Interview with Michel Foucault.' *Ideology and Consciousness* 8 (1981): 3–14.

– 'The Subject and Power.' *Critical Inquiry* 8 (1982): 777–95.

Francis, R. Douglas, Richard Jones, and Donald B. Smith. *Destinies: Canadian History since Confederation.* 2nd ed. Toronto: Holt, Rinehart and Winston 1992.

Franks, Ruth MacLachlan. 'A Note to Brides: Don't Delay Parenthood.' *Chatelaine* (May 1946): 29, 44, 100.

Fraser, B. 'VD ... No. 1 Saboteur.' *Maclean's* (15 Feb. 1944): 7, 43–5.

Fraser, Sylvia. *My Father's House: A Memoir of Incest and Healing.* Toronto: Doubleday 1987.

Freedman, Estelle B. '"Uncontrolled Desires": The Response to the Sexual Psychopath, 1920–1960.' In Peiss and Simmons, eds, *Passion and Power*, 199–225.

Friedan, Betty. *The Feminine Mystique*. New York: Dell 1963.

Friedenberg, Edgar Z. *The Vanishing Adolescent*. New York: Dell 1959.

Fuss, Diana, ed. *Inside/out: Lesbian Theories, Gay Theories*. New York: Routledge 1991.

Garner, Hugh. 'Youth Trouble in Kitchener.' *Chatelaine* (July 1951): 12–13, 58–60.

Gibson, Barbara. 'Twenty-nine Delinquent Children.' Unpublished research report, University of Toronto, School of Social Work 1955.

Gilbert, James. *A Cycle of Outrage: America's Reaction to the Juvenile Delinquent in the 1950s*. New York: Oxford 1986.

Gillis, John. *Youth and History*. New York: Academic Press 1974.

Girard, Philip. 'From Subversion to Liberation: Homosexuals and the Immigration Act 1952–1977.' *Canadian Journal of Law and Society* 2 (1987): 1–27.

'Goldring to Report on Social Hygiene.' *Toronto Daily Star*, 12 Feb. 1944.

Gölz, Annalee. 'Family Matters: The Canadian Family and the State in the Postwar Period.' *Left History* 1, no. 2 (Fall 1993): 9–49.

Graebner, William. 'Coming of Age in Buffalo: The Ideology of Maturity in Postwar America.' *Radical History Review* 34 (1986): 53–74.

Hacking, Ian. 'Normal.' A discussion paper prepared for the 'Modes of Thought' Workshop, Toronto, Sept. 1993.

Hall, G. Stanley. *Adolescence: Its Psychology and Its Relations to Physiology, Anthropology, Sociology, Sex, Crime, Religion and Education*. New York: Appleton 1907.

Hall, Radclyffe. *The Well of Loneliness*. New York: Permabooks 1951.

Hall, Stuart. 'The Toad in the Garden: Thatcherism among the Theorists.' In Cary Nelson and Lawrence Grossberg, eds, *Marxism and the Interpretation of Culture*, 35–73. Urbana and Chicago: University of Illinois Press 1988.

Hall, Stuart, Chas Chrichter, Tony Jefferson, John Clarke, and Brian Roberts. *Policing the Crisis: Mugging, the State, and Law and Order*. London: Macmillan 1978.

Hannant, Larry. *The Infernal Machine*. Toronto: University of Toronto Press 1995.

Harvey, Brett. *The Fifties: A Woman's Oral History*. New York: Harper Collins 1993.

Hebdige, Dick. *Hiding in the Light*. London: Routledge 1988.

Henriques, Julian, Wendy Hollway, Cathy Urwin, Couze Venn, and Valerie Walkerdine. *Changing the Subject: Psychology, Social Regulation and Subjectivity*. London: Methuen 1984.

Hilliard, Marion. 'Can You Live without Him?' *Chatelaine* (Mar. 1958): 10–11.

– 'Dr. Marion Hilliard Helps Teen-age Girls Meet Their Biggest Problem.' *Chatelaine* (Oct. 1956): 11, 100–3.

- 'Dr. Marion Hilliard Talks to Single Women.' *Chatelaine* (Feb. 1956): 17, 47–52.
- *Problems of Adolescence: A Woman Doctor's Advice on Growing up.* London: Macmillan 1961.
- *A Woman Doctor Looks at Love and Life.* New York: Doubleday 1956.
- *Women and Fatigue: A Woman Doctor's Answer.* New York: Doubleday 1960.

Hollingshead, A.B. *Elmtown's Youth: The Impact of Social Class on Adolescents.* New York, John Wiley and Sons 1949.

Houston, Susan E. 'The "Waifs" and "Strays" of a Late Victorian City: Juvenile Delinquents in Toronto.' In Joy Parr, ed., *Childhood and Family in Canadian History,* 129–42. Toronto: McClelland and Stewart 1982.

Hudson, Barbara. 'Femininity and Adolescence.' In McRobbie and Nava, eds, *Gender and Generation,* 31–53.

Hughes, Perry. 'Kinsey Again: Leers or Cheers?' *Saturday Night* (20 June 1950): 10, 15.

Humphries, Steve. *A Secret World of Sex. Forbidden Fruit: The British Experience, 1900–1950.* London: Sidgwick and Jackson 1988.

Hutton, Eric. 'The Future of the Family: A *Maclean's* Report.' *Maclean's* (26 May 1956): 12–15, 74–9.

Iacovetta, Franca. 'Making "New Canadians": Social Workers, Women and the Reshaping of Immigrant Families.' In Iacovetta and Valverde, eds, *Gender Conflicts,* 261–303.
- 'Remaking Their Lives: Women Immigrants, Survivors and Refugees.' In Parr, ed., *A Diversity of Women,* 136–67.
- *Such Hardworking People: Italian Immigrants in Postwar Toronto.* Montreal and Kingston: McGill-Queen's University Press 1992.

Iacovetta, Franca, and Mariana Valverde, eds. *Gender Conflicts: New Essays in Women's History.* Toronto: University of Toronto Press 1992.

Irvine, Janice. *Disorders of Desire.* Philadelphia: Temple University Press 1990.

'It's a Tough Time to Be in Love.' Editorial. *Chatelaine* (May 1954): 1.

Jackson, Ed. 'Christians, the Right and Political Power.' *Xtra* (16 Apr. 1993): 1.

Johnston, Richard. 'What Is Cultural Studies Anyway?' *Anglistica* 26, nos 1, 2 (1983): 1–81.

Jukes, Mary. 'Are Comics Really a Menace?' *Chatelaine* (May 1949): 6–7.

Katz, Jonathan Ned. *Gay/Lesbian Almanac.* New York: Harper and Row 1983.
- 'The Invention of Heterosexuality.' *Socialist Review* 20, no. 1 (1990): 7–34.
- *The Invention of Heterosexuality.* New York: Dutton 1995.

Katz, Sidney. 'Going Steady: Is It Ruining Our Teen-agers?' *Maclean's* (Jan. 1959): 9–11, 37–9.

- 'It's a Tough Time to Be a Kid.' Parts 1,2,3. *Maclean's* (15 Dec. 1950; 1 Jan. 1951; 15 Jan. 1951): 7–9, 33, 35; 10–11, 40; 14–15, 44–5.
- 'The Truth about Sex Criminals.' *Maclean's* (1 July 1947): 12, 46–8.
Kennedy, Elizabeth Lapovsky, and Madeline D. Davis. *Boots of Leather and Slippers of Gold: The History of a Lesbian Community.* New York: Routledge 1993.
Ketchum, J.D. 'Turning New Leaves.' *Canadian Forum* (May 1948): 44–5.
Kett, Joseph. *Rites of Passage: Adolescents in America, 1790 to the Present.* New York: Basic Books 1977.
Kidd, J.R. Review of *Sexual Behavior in the Human Male*. *Food for Thought* (Feb. 1949): 45–6.
King, Violet. 'Moment of Decision.' *Chatelaine* (June 1951): 18–19, 26, 30–4, 39.
Kinsey, Alfred, Wardell B. Pomeroy, Clyde E. Martin, and Paul H. Gebhard. *Sexual Behavior in the Human Female.* New York: Pocket Books 1965 (originally published 1953).
Kinsey, Alfred, Wardell B. Pomeroy, and Clyde E. Martin. *Sexual Behavior in the Human Male.* Philadelphia: W.B. Saunders 1948.
Kinsman, Gary. '"Character Weaknesses" and "Fruit Machines": Towards an Analysis of the Anti-homosexual Security Campaign in the Canadian Civil Service.' *Labour / Le Travail* 35 (Spring 1995): 133–61.
- *The Regulation of Desire*. Rev. ed. Montreal: Black Rose 1996.
Kirkendall, Lester A. *Understanding Sex.* Life Adjustment Booklet. Rev. ed. Chicago: Science Research Associates 1957 (originally published 1947).
Korinek, Valerie. 'Roughing It in Suburbia: Reading *Chatelaine* Magazine, 1950–1969.' PhD diss., University of Toronto 1996.
Krafft-Ebing, Richard von. *Psychopathia Sexualis.* New York: Paperback Library 1965 (originally published 1892).
Krich, Aron, ed. *Facts of Love and Marriage for Young People.* New York: Dell 1962.
Landers, Ann. *Ann Landers Talks to Teenagers about Sex.* Englewood Cliffs, NJ: Prentice-Hall 1963.
Landis, Paul. *Adolescence and Youth.* New York: McGraw-Hill 1947.
- *Adolescence and Youth: The Process of Maturing.* 2nd ed. New York: McGraw-Hill 1952.
- 'Dating Days.' In Krich, ed., *Facts of Love and Marriage for Young People*, 28–43.
- *Understanding Teenagers.* New York: Appleton-Century-Crofts 1955.
Lautenslager, E.S. 'A Minister's Frank Talk to Brides and Grooms.' *Chatelaine* (May 1954): 18–19, 96, 98–100.
'A Lesson in Sex Education.' *Globe and Mail*, 11 Apr. 1949.
'Let's Be on Guard.' Editorial. *Vancouver Sun*, 23 Mar. 1953.
Li, Peter S. *The Making of Post-War Canada.* Toronto: Oxford University Press 1996.

'"Lights Till Wee Hours" to Banish Lovers' Lanes Nip School Vandalism.' *Globe and Mail*, 19 June 1947.

'Low Standards of Conduct Handicap Work of Schools.' *Toronto Daily Star*, 17 Apr. 1948.

McGuire, Joan. 'The Age Factor in Unmarried Motherhood.' Unpublished paper, University of Toronto, School of Social Work, Aug. 1954 (filed with the Children's Aid Society papers, City of Toronto Archives).

McKee, Leila Mitchell. 'Voluntary Youth Organizations in Toronto, 1880–1930.' PhD diss., York University 1982.

McLaren, Angus. *Our Own Master Race: Eugenics in Canada, 1885–1945*. Toronto: McClelland and Stewart 1990.

McLaren, Angus, and Arlene Tigar McLaren. *The Bedroom and the State*. Toronto: McClelland and Stewart 1986.

McRobbie, Angela, and Mica Nava, eds. *Gender and Generation*. London: Macmillan 1984.

McRobbie, Angela, and Jenny Garber. 'Girls and Subcultures: An Exploration.' In Stuart Hall and Tony Jefferson, eds. *Resistance through Rituals: Youth Subcultures in Post-war Britain*, 209–22. London: Birmingham Centre for Contemporary Cultural Studies and Hutchinson, 1976.

Mair, Shirley. 'Why Are More Teenage Girls "Getting into Trouble"?' *Chatelaine* (Nov. 1959): 30–1, 58, 60.

Major, Ralph H. 'New to Our Youth.' *Coronet* (Sept. 1950): 101–8.

Manual of Hygiene for Father and Son. Toronto: Canadian Hygienic Productions 1947.

Martin, Biddy. 'Feminism, Criticism and Foucault.' In Irene Diamond and Lee Quinby, eds, *Feminism and Foucault: Reflections on Resistance*. Boston: Northeastern University Press 1988.

May, Elaine Tyler. *Homeward Bound: American Families in the Cold War Era*. New York: Basic Books 1988.

Maynard, Steven. '"Horrible Temptations": Sex, Men, Working-class Male Youth in Urban Ontario, 1890–1940.' *Canadian Historical Review* (forthcoming 1997).

Mead, Margaret. 'Adolescence in Primitive and Modern Society.' In Calverton and Schmalhausen, eds, *The New Generation*, 169–88.

– *Coming of Age in Samoa*. New York: Morrow Quill 1968 (originally published 1928).

Menninger, William. *Growing up Emotionally*. Chicago: Science Research Associates 1957.

Meyerowitz, Joanne. *Not June Cleaver: Women and Gender in Postwar America, 1945–1960*. Philadephia: Temple University Press 1994.

Modell, John. *Into One's Own: From Youth to Adulthood in the United States, 1920–1975*. Berkeley and Los Angeles: University of California Press 1989.

Morantz, Regina Morkell. 'The Scientist as Sex Crusader: Alfred C. Kinsey and American Culture.' *American Quarterly* 29 (1977): 563–89.

Morris, Eileen. 'Don't Let Your Girl Friends Ruin Your Marriage.' *Chatelaine* (Oct. 1954): 26, 50–1, 55, 58–9.

– 'Give the Childless Couple a Break.' *Chatelaine* (May 1955): 11, 76, 78, 80–1.

Mort, Frank. *Dangerous Sexualities: Medico-Moral Politics in England Since 1830*. London: Routledge and Kegan Paul 1987.

Moscovitch, Allan, and Jim Albert, eds. *The Benevolent State: The Growth of Welfare in Canada*. Toronto: Garamond 1987.

Mother and Daughter: A Digest for Women and Growing Girls. Toronto: Hygienic Productions 1946.

Myron, Nancy, and Charlotte Bunch, eds. *Lesbianism and the Women's Movement*. Baltimore: Diana Press 1975.

Nash, John. 'It's Time Father Got Back in the Family.' *Maclean's* (12 May 1956): 28–9, 82–5.

Nathanson, Constance. *Dangerous Passage: The Social Control of Sexuality in Women's Adolescence*. Philadelphia: Temple University Press 1991.

Ness, Margaret. 'Who's Afraid of Teenage Problems?' *Saturday Night* (13 Mar. 1951): 28–9.

'No Need for Haste.' Editorial. *Globe and Mail*, 26 Jan. 1949.

Odem, Mary. *Delinquent Daughters: Protecting and Policing Adolescent Female Sexuality in the United States, 1885–1920*. Chapel Hill: University of North Carolina Press 1995.

'Open VD Education Campaign for Fourth Year High Pupils.' *Globe and Mail*, 12 June 1946.

'Organizes Teen-age Club.' *Toronto Daily Star*, 2 Jan. 1945.

Osborne, Ernest. 'Democracy Begins in the Home.' In Krich, ed., *Facts of Love and Marriage for Young People*, 306–20 (article first published in 1953).

Owram, Doug. *Born at the Right Time: A History of the Baby Boom Generation*. Toronto: University of Toronto Press 1996.

'Parents and Juvenile Delinquents.' Editorial. *Toronto Daily Star*, 6 Apr. 1944.

Parr, Joy, ed. *A Diversity of Women: Ontario, 1945–1980*. Toronto: University of Toronto Press 1995.

Parsons, Patrick. 'Batman and His Audience: The Dialectic of Culture.' In Pearson and Uricchio, eds, *The Many Lives of the Batman*, 66–89.

Pearson, Roberta E., and William Uricchio, eds. *The Many Lives of the Batman: Critical Approaches to a Superhero and His Media*. New York and London: Routledge and the British Film Institute 1991.

Pegis, Jessica M. 'A Sick Body of Evidence.' *Xtra* (3 Sept. 1993): 17.

Peiss, Kathy. *Cheap Amusements: Working Women and Leisure in Turn-of-the- Century New York*. Philadelphia: Temple University Press 1986.

Peiss, Kathy, and Christina Simmons, eds. *Passion and Power: Sexuality in History*. Philadelphia: Temple University Press 1989.

Peterson, Phyllis Lee. 'The Runaway.' *Chatelaine* (Feb. 1955): 14–15, 36–40, 42–3.

Phair, J.T., and N.R. Speirs. *Good Health*. Toronto: Ginn nd.

Pierson, Ruth Roach. *'They're Still Women after All': The Second World War and Canadian Womanhood*. Toronto: McClelland and Stewart 1986.

Pomeroy, Wardell B. *Dr. Kinsey and the Institute for Sex Research*. New York: Harper and Row 1972.

'A Practical Approach.' *Globe and Mail*, 10 June 1948.

Prentice, Alison, Paula Bourne, Gail Cuthbert Brandt, Beth Light, Wendy Mitchinson, and Naomi Black. *Canadian Women: A History*. Toronto: Harcourt, Brace Jovanovich 1988.

Prentice, Susan. 'Militant Mothers in Domestic Times: Toronto's Postwar Childcare Struggles.' PhD diss., York University 1993.

'A Problem for Parents.' Editorial. *Globe and Mail*, 3 Aug. 1945.

'Problems of Sex Instruction.' *Globe and Mail*, 22 Mar. 1946.

'Put up Morality Lights at 2 Schools, Committee Asks.' *Globe and Mail*, 30 Mar. 1950.

Radicalesbians. 'The Woman-Identified Woman.' In Anne Koedt, Ellen Levine, and Anita Rapone, eds, *Radical Feminism*, 240–5. New York: Quadrangle 1973.

Radway, Janice A. *Reading the Romance*. London: Verso 1984.

Redl, Fritz. 'Zoot Suits: An Interpretation.' *Survey Midmonthly* (Oct. 1943): 259–62.

Reisman, David. *The Lonely Crowd*. New Haven: Yale University Press 1950.

'Reject Junction Club's Bid for Mixed Splash Parties.' *Globe and Mail*, 18 Jan. 1949.

Resources for Feminist Research. 'Confronting Heterosexuality,' a special issue. Vol. 19, nos 3, 4 (1991).

Rich, Adrienne. 'Compulsory Heterosexuality and Lesbian Existence.' In Snitow, Stansell, and Thompson, eds, *Powers of Desire*, 177–205.

– 'Towards a Politics of Location.' In her *Blood, Bread and Poetry*. London: Virago 1987.

Richards, Allison. 'So You're Starting a Teens' Canteen.' *Chatelaine* (Apr. 1945): 28, 30, 61–2.

Richardson, Theresa R. *The Century of the Child: The Mental Hygiene Movement and Social Policy in the United States and Canada*. Albany: State University of New York Press 1989.

Robinson, Daniel J., and David Kimmel. 'The Queer Career of Homosexual Security Vetting in Cold War Canada.' *Canadian Historical Review* 75, no. 3 (Sept. 1994): 319–45.

Rogers, Kenneth. *Street Gangs in Toronto*. Toronto: Ryerson 1945.

Rose, Nikolas. *Governing the Soul: The Shaping of the Private Self*. London: Routledge 1990.

Ross, Dorothy. *G. Stanley Hall: The Psychologist as Prophet*. Chicago: University of Chicago Press 1972.

Rothman, Ellen S. *Hands and Hearts: A History of Courtship in America*. New York: Basic Books 1984.

Rousseau, Jean-Jacques. *Émile, or On Education*. Translated by Allan Bloom. New York: Basic Books 1979 (originally published 1762).

Rubin, Gayle. 'The Traffic in Women: Notes on the "Political Economy of Sex.' In Rayna R. Reiter, ed., *Towards an Anthropology of Women*, 157–210. New York: Monthly Review Press 1975.

Rumming, Eleanor. 'Dr. Kinsey and the Human Female.' *Saturday Night* (15 Aug. 1953): 7–8.

Rutherford, Paul. *When Television Was Young: Primetime Canada, 1952–1967*. Toronto: University of Toronto Press 1990.

Sandwell, B.K. 'Statistical Method Applied to Sex Shows New and Surprising Results.' *Saturday Night* (21 Feb. 1948): 12.

Sangster, Dorothy. 'How Much Freedom Should a Teen-ager Have?' *Chatelaine* (Dec. 1951): 12–13, 61–3.

Sangster, Joan. 'Doing Two Jobs: The Wage-Earning Mother, 1945–1970.' In Parr, ed., *A Diversity of Women*, 98–134.

Saunders, Bryne Hope. 'What's the Biggest Thing in Our New Half Century?' Editorial. *Chatelaine* (Jan. 1950): 6.

Sawatsky, John. *Men in the Shadows: The RCMP Security Service*. Toronto: Doubleday 1980.

Scher, Len. *The Un-Canadians*. Toronto: Lester 1992.

Schlossman, Steven, and Stephanie Wallach. 'The Crime of Precocious Sexuality: Female Juvenile Delinquency and the Progressive Era.' In D. Kelly Weisberg, ed., *Women and the Law: A Social Historical Perspective*, vol. 1. Cambridge: Schenkman 1982.

'School Board Bans Sex behind Closed Doors.' *Globe and Mail*, 8 Apr. 1949.

Schwalbe, Lenore. 'Negro and Partly-Negro Wards of the Children's Aid Society of Metropolitan Toronto.' Unpublished paper, University of Toronto, School of Social Work, Dec. 1958 (filed with the Children's Aid Society papers, City of Toronto Archives).

Scott, Lorraine M. 'A Follow-up Study of the Experiences after Discharge of a Number of Girls Who Have Lived in Warrendale, a Residential Treatment

Centre.' Unpublished paper, University of Toronto, School of Social Work, Jan. 1959 (filed with the Children's Aid Society papers, City of Toronto Archives).

'The Secret World of Our Teenagers.' *Chatelaine* (Sept. 1955): 12–13, 59–61.

Seeley, John R., and J.D.M. Griffin. 'The Kinsey Report.' *Canadian Welfare* (15 Oct. 1948): 40–2.

Seeley, John R., R. Alexander Sim, and Elizabeth W. Loosley. *Crestwood Heights: A Study of the Culture of Suburban Life*. Toronto: University of Toronto Press 1956.

Seidman, Steven. *Romantic Longings: Love in America, 1830–1980*. New York: Routledge 1991.

Sewell, John. *The Shape of the City: Toronto Struggles with Modern Planning*. Toronto: University of Toronto Press 1993.

'Sex Education Classes Said Vital to School Health.' *Globe and Mail*, 4 May 1945.

'Sex Education in Public Schools Report Is Tabled.' *Globe and Mail*, 8 Dec. 1948.

'Sex Education Scheme Approved by Teachers.' *Globe and Mail*, 23, Jan. 1945.

'Sex Education to Be Studied by Committee.' *Telegram*, 25 May 1948.

'The Sexual Psychopath.' *Toronto Daily Star*, 9 June 1948.

Simmons, Christina. 'Companionate Marriage and the Lesbian Threat.' *Frontiers* 4, no. 3 (1979): 54–9.

– 'Modern Sexuality and the Myth of Victorian Repression.' In Peiss and Simmons, eds, *Passion and Power*, 157–77.

'6 Months, 10 Lashes for 9 at Kitchener.' *Telegram*, 16 Feb. 1951.

'16-Year-Old Girl Plans Dummy Hold-up with Youths Picked up in Dance Hall.' *Justice Weekly* (5 Jan. 1946): 13.

Snitow, Ann, Christine Stansell, and Sharon Thompson, eds. *Powers of Desire: The Politics of Sexuality*. New York: Monthly Review Press 1983.

Solinger, Rickie. *Wake up Little Susie: Single Pregnancy and Race Before Roe v. Wade*. New York: Routledge 1992.

'A Sound Proposal.' Editorial. *Toronto Daily Star*, 10 Feb. 1944.

Stainton-Rogers, Rex, and Wendy Stainton-Rogers. *Stories of Childhood: Shifting Agendas of Child Concern*. Toronto: University of Toronto Press 1992.

Steedman, Carolyn, Cathy Urwin, and Valerie Walkerdine, eds. *Language, Gender and Childhood*. London: Routledge and Kegan Paul 1985.

Strain, Frances Bruce. *Sex Guidance in Family Life Education: A Handbook for the Schools*. New York: Macmillan 1942.

– *Teen Days: A Book for Boys and Girls*. New York: Appleton-Century-Crofts 1946.

Strange, Carolyn. *Toronto's Girl Problem*. Toronto: University of Toronto Press 1995.

Strong-Boag, Veronica. 'Home Dreams: Women and the Suburban Experiment in Canada, 1945–1960.' *Canadian Historical Review* 72, no. 4 (1991): 471–504.

'Study of Sex Perverts in Prison Reveals Present Penal Treatment Contributes to Their Degeneration.' *Globe and Mail*, 22 Apr. 1948.

Sutherland, Fraser. *The Monthly Epic: A History of Canadian Magazines, 1789–1989.* Toronto: Fitzhenry and Whiteside 1989.

Sutherland, Neil. *Children in English-Canadian Society: Framing the Twentieth-Century Consensus.* Toronto: University of Toronto Press, 1976.

'"Teach Young How to Live Is Obligation," Drew Says.' *Telegram*, 11 Apr. 1944.

'To Combat Delinquency.' Editorial. *Globe and Mail*, 12 Feb. 1944.

'Too Much Stress on Play.' *Telegram*, 30 Apr. 1946.

'Toronto Trustees Defend Students' Right to Dance.' *Telegram*, 1 May 1948.

Torres, Tereska. *The Converts.* London: Rupert Hart-Davis 1970.

– *Women's Barracks.* New York: Fawcett 1950 (Gold Medal Book No. 132).

'Trustee Calls "Comic" Books "Degrading and Detrimental."' *Globe and Mail*, 26 Sept. 1945.

'Trustees Approve Teaching Sex Subjects in Schools.' *Toronto Daily Star*, 11 Apr. 1944.

'Trustees "Excuse" Girls, Give Clue to Identity; 9 Boys Get Jail, Lashes.' *Globe and Mail*, 17 Feb. 1951.

Tumpane, Frank. 'At City Hall.' *Globe and Mail*, 11 Jan. 1948.

– 'The Cruel World vs. Teen-agers.' *Chatelaine* (May 1950): 4–5, 98–9.

– '12 Men Held in Delinquency of Five Girls Aged 12 to 14.' *Toronto Daily Star*, 5 Feb. 1951.

Tyrer, Alfred Henry. *Sex, Marriage and Birth Control.* Toronto: Marriage Welfare Bureau 1943 (originally published 1936).

'Unhappy Wives.' Editorial. *Chatelaine* (Apr. 1948): 2.

Unusual Comics (Sept./Oct. 1946). Bell Publishing.

Ursel, Jane. *Private Lives, Public Policy: 100 Years of State Intervention in the Family.* Toronto: Women's Press 1992.

Urwin, Cathy. 'Constructing Motherhood: The Persuasion of Normal Development.' In Steedman, Urwin, and Walkerdine, eds, *Language, Gender and Childhood*, 164–202.

Valverde, Mariana. *The Age of Light, Soap and Water: Moral Reform in English Canada, 1885–1925.* Toronto: McClelland and Stewart 1991.

– 'Building Anti-delinquent Communities: Morality, Gender and Generation in the City.' In Parr, ed., *A Diversity of Women*, 19–45.

'Want All Canadians Given Test for V.D.' *Toronto Daily Star*, 5 Apr. 1944.

'Weds Girl, 14, Boy "Freed."' *Kitchener-Waterloo Record*, 20 Jan. 1955.

Weedon, Chris. *Feminist Practice and Poststructuralist Theory.* Oxford: Blackwell 1987.

Weeks, Jeffrey. *Coming Out: Homosexual Politics in Britain, from the Nineteenth Century to the Present.* London: Quartet 1977.

– *Sex, Politics and Society: The Regulation of Sexuality Since 1800.* London: Longman's, 1981.

Wertham, Fredric. *Seduction of the Innocent.* New York and Toronto: Rinehart 1954.

Whitaker, Reg, and Gary Marcuse. *Cold War Canada: The Making of a National Insecurity State, 1945–1957.* Toronto: University of Toronto Press 1994.

White, Adele. 'High School Huddle.' *Chatelaine* (Sept. 1947): 26–7, 48.

– 'Let's Abolish Those Atom Bomb Blues.' *Chatelaine* (Jan. 1950): 6–7, 53.

White, Kevin. *The First Sexual Revolution: The Emergence of Male Heterosexuality in Modern America.* New York: New York University Press 1993.

Wilkinson, Sue, and Celia Kitzinger, eds. *Heterosexuality: A Feminism and Psychology Reader.* London: Sage 1993.

Williams, Mary McGee, and Irene Kane. *On Becoming a Woman.* New York: Dell 1958.

'Women's Groups Divided on School Sex Education.' *Globe and Mail,* 22 Mar. 1946.

Young, Leontine. *Out of Wedlock.* New York: McGraw-Hill 1954.

Zoffer, Gerald. 'Psychological Factors in Juvenile Crime.' *Saturday Night* (26 Jan. 1946): 18.

Illustration Credits

Index

Adams, Clifford R., 100
adolescence, discovery of, 43–4; and puberty, 44
adolescent, as term, 40
adolescents, 4; as primitive, 44; sexual development of, 46. *See also* teenagers; youth
advice literature, 86–106, 169
Anglican Church, 112
Are You Popular? (film), 90

Bailey, Beth, 98, 99
Bakless, John, 161
Barker, Martin, 137, 139
Batman, 154
Bell, John, 143–4
Bernhardt, Karl, 119
Big Brothers, 57, 74, 109, 133
Big Sisters, 65
Bill 10, 149–50
Bill 167, 172
black youth, 62–3, 76–7
Blackboard Jungle (film), 53
Bland, Lucy, 109
Blatz, W.E., 75, 116, 120
Boys' Brigade, 75
Brando, Marlon, 53

Brannigan, Augustine, 148
Breines, Wini, 34, 104, 171
Britain, 56; campaign against horror comics in, 137, 139; gangs in, 73
British Columbia Parent–Teacher Federation, 150
Bumsted, J.M., 6, 17

Cabbagetown, 58
Calhoun, Arthur Wallace, 45
Canada, Department of Justice, 74
Canadian Broadcasting Corporation, 5, 24
Canadian Council on Mental Hygiene, 125
Canadian Forum, 36, 37
Canadian High News, 102
Canadian National Council for Combatting Venereal Disease, 109
Canadian National Exhibition, 70
Canadian Penal Association, 123–4, 128
Canadian Social Hygiene Council, 109, 110
Canadian Teachers' Federation, 112
Canadian Welfare, 36
Canadian Youth Commission, 59, 113

Catholic Church, 113
Central Neighbourhood House, 70
Chambers, Frank, 110
Chapin, Miriam, 115
Chatelaine, 5, 21, 22, 29, 30, 33, 34, 35, 36, 49, 51, 57, 59, 62, 68, 77, 88, 93, 96, 100, 102, 106, 145
Chauncey, George, 8
Cherry Beach, 71
childlessness, 30–1
childrearing, 28
Children's Aid Society, 63, 65
Children's Protection Act, 79
Christian values, 142
class, 50, 55, 56, 57–9, 67, 72–3, 75–7, 80–1; construction of middle class, 90–1; and dating patterns, 98–9; of high school students, 119; and parenting, 115; representations of working-class youth, 90; and sex education, 133
Cockburn, Bruce, 3
Cockburn, C.J., 159
Cockburn, W.R., 77, 144
Cohen, Stan, 56
cold war, 21–5, 138, 141, 152
Comic Magazine Association of America, 155
comics, 136, 137, 138; American, 143; Canadian, 143–4; crime, 139, 142–50; and delinquency, 145, 148, 150; and girls, 153; and homosexuality, 153–4
Committee on Juvenile Delinquency, 74
Communism, 22, 23, 50, 121, 139, 141, 152
consumption, 28, 34
Coronet, 95
Corrigan, Philip, 14

Crawley Films, 89, 103
Crestwood Heights (Seeley, Sim, and Loosley), 26, 28
Criminal Code, 122, 139, 149, 150, 159
Cures (Duberman), 88
curfew, 79–80

dance halls, 78–9, 80
dancing, 79
Date with Your Family, A (film), 28
dating, 88, 89; evolution of, 98–100; going steady, 99–102; as heterosexual practice, 98–106; petting, 105; as sign of normal heterosexual development, 101
Davie, Jean, 119
Davis, J.C., 142
Davis, Maxine, 91, 92, 95
Davis, R.E.G., 113
delinquency, 41, 42, 49, 54, 156, 168; charges, 63, 64; and comics, 145, 148, 150; explanations of, 56–9; gender aspects, 60, 63, 64; and girls, 64–70; and heterosexual conduct, 66; institutional response to, 73–5; and male sexuality, 62; and middle-class youth, 59; as national issue, 55; and normal sexuality, 60; rates of, 148; recreation as solution to, 74–5; and sex education, 112; and social change, 54–9; and urban spaces, 77–82
democracy, 141, 157; and moral standards, 23–5
Dempsey, Lotta, 21, 36
Depression the (of 1930s), 20
Dionne quintuplets, 116
discourse, as analytic tool, 6
divorce rates, 26
Doherty, Thomas, 43

domesticity, 9, 19–21, 121, 130, 168; and cold war, 21–3
Doone, J.J. Hayes, 142, 156, 157
Duberman, Martin, 88
Dubinsky, Karen, 11, 63, 87, 98, 138
Duvall, Evelyn, 93, 98, 102

Edmison, J. Alex, 128
Edwards, Charles, 125
effeminacy, 8
Ehrenreich, Barbara, 30
Ellis, Havelock, 47
Elmtown's Youth (Hollingshead), 46
Émile (Rousseau), 46, 151
eugenics, 44, 109
expert discourse, 31

Factory Act, 81
family, 121, 129–30, 133; and the cold war, 21–5; and consumption, 28; and democracy, 28; middle-class, as norm, 26–7; norms and ideals of, 28–32; and patriotism, 25
family life education, 119, 125–35
Fass, Paula, 98
fatherhood, 30
FBI Comics, 146
Federated Women's Institutes, 142
Federation of Home and School Associations, 142
Feinberg, Abraham, 54
Feminine Mystique, The (Friedan), 29
feminism, 171
feminists, 4
films, 103–4; sex education, 119; teen guidance, 89–91
Findlay, Terence, 162–3
Finlayson, Isabel, 162–3
Ford, G.W., 160, 163

Foucault, Michel, 6, 12, 13, 16, 134
Fowler, Orson, 46
Fraser, Sylvia, 100
Freedman, Estelle, 121–2
Freud, Sigmund, 10, 45
Freudian theory, 84, 85
Friedan, Betty, 29
Friedenberg, Edgar, 49–50
Fruit Machine, 24
Fulton, E. Davie, 142, 144, 145, 147–50, 155, 156

Galton, Francis, 14
gangs, 70, 72, 73; clothes and, 71–2; girls and, 70–3
Garner, Hugh, 59
Garson, Stuart, 148
gay liberation, 4, 11, 171
gay men, 4
gender: ideology, 118; roles, 102, 127, 166; and sexuality, 8
gender identity, 97–8
Gillis, John, 41
Girard, Philip, 23
Girl Guides, 76
Globe and Mail, 49, 62, 78, 112, 117, 130, 131, 132–3
Going Steady (film), 103
Goldring, Charles, 57, 110, 115, 119, 124–5, 128, 132, 133
Gölz, Annalee, 25
Gouzenko, Igor, 22
Gray, Eleanor, 150
Green, Howard C., 149
Griffin, J.D.N., 128

Hacking, Ian, 13
Hall, G. Stanley, 43–7, 74
Hall, R.K., 39–40, 41
Hall, Radclyffe, 83–4

Health League of Canada, 5, 107, 111;
    Social Hygiene Committee, 54
Hebdige, Dick, 47–8
Henriques, Julian, et al., 13
heterosexual norms, 3
heterosexuality: category, 7, 166, 170;
    as developmental process, 10, 87–8;
    identity, 10; invention of word, 8; as
    natural, 95, 102, 126, 166; as normal
    4, 91–5, 124, 169; as perversion, 8;
    research about, 11
Hicklin test, 159–60
high school, 99
Hilliard, Marion, 30, 88, 100–1, 102,
    104
Hincks, C.M., 147
History of Sexuality, The (Foucault), 14,
    134
Hollingshead, A.B., 46
Holy Blossom Temple, 54
homosexual behaviour, 13
homosexual/heterosexual binary, 8,
    84–5, 171
homosexuality, 7, 30, 49, 153; as
    abnormal, 91–5; as adolescent
    phase, 93, 153; as adult condition,
    92; causes of, 92–3; and comics,
    153–4; and Communism, 50; inven-
    tion of word, 7; inversion, 83; mar-
    ginalization of, 16; as practice for
    heterosexuality, 93; same-sex
    crushes, 93; sissies, 95–8; as threat
    to youth, 92, 94–5; tomboys, 95–8.
    See also lesbians
homosexuals: in the civil service, 24–
    5; and immigration laws, 24
How Much Affection? (film), 103
Hughes, Perry, 38
Humphries, Steve, 73
Hutton, Eric, 29–30

Iacovetta, Franca, 18, 27, 76
illegitimate births, 68
Ilsley, J.L. 147–8
immigrant families, 27
immigrants, 20, 58, 101, 115
Imperial Order Daughters of the
    Empire (IODE), 142–5
indecency, 138, 139–42; campaigns
    against, 140; definitions of, 139
Institute for Child Study, 75, 116,
    119
inversion, 83
Irvine, Janice, 37
Italians, 76

Jewish youth, 76
Joe and Roxy (film), 90, 103
Johnston, Richard, 16
Jukes, Mary, 145
Junior Chamber of Commerce, 111
Justice Weekly, 78

Katz, Jonathan Ned, 7, 11, 171
Katz, Sidney, 48, 101, 102, 121
Kellogg's, 96–7
Kertbeny, Karl Maria, 7
Kett, Joseph, 44, 46
Kiernan, James, 9
King, William Lyon Mackenzie,
    143
Kingsway, the, 78
Kinsey, Alfred, 14, 85–6, 95, 104,
    130
Kinsey reports, 35–8, 132
Kirkendall, Lester, 92
Kitchener, Ont., youth sex scandal,
    59–62
Kiwanis Club, 123
Knight, Robert P., 86
Koch, Erich, 24

Krafft-Ebing, Richard von, 8

Lady Chatterley's Lover (Lawrence), 160
Laidlaw, J.A., 159
Landers, Ann, 91, 93–4, 102
Landis, Paul, 45, 46
lesbian and gay history, 4, 170
lesbian pulp novels, 83
lesbianism, 158–64
lesbians, 24, 140, 154
Lonely Crowd, The (Reisman), 34

McAree, J.A., 160
McCarthyism, 24
McDougall, A.G., 158, 163
McIvor, Daniel, 149
McLean, J.M., 160
Maclean's, 5, 29, 48, 75, 101, 116, 121
McRobbie, Angela, and Jenny Garber, 73
Mair, Shirley, 69
marriage, 32–5, 89, 121, 129, 140, 166; average age of, 29, 105–6; companionate, 9, 87; and gender roles, 34; preparation for, 87; and sex, 32–3
marriage manuals, 89
masculinity, 8, 33–4, 154
mass-market publications, 136, 138, 156
Massey Commission, 17
maternity homes, 68, 69
May, Elaine Tyler, 18, 22, 38, 99, 121
Mead, Margaret, 45
Meaning of Adolescence (film), 43
mental hygiene, 31–2, 113
Mercier, Raoul, 159, 160, 161–2
Meyerowitz, Joanne, 18
middle-class sexuality, 8
moral panic, 56, 121, 158, 165

moral regulation, 14–15, 81, 126, 137, 164, 167, 169; and recreation, 73–7; and sex education, 120
morality lights, 81–2
morals offences, 63

National Committee on Mental Hygiene, 147
National Film Board, 43, 89, 90, 103, 109
National News Company, 158, 159
'New Canadians,' 27
Nichols, F.L., 65
normal, as descriptive term, 13–14, 84
normal/abnormal binary, 84–5, 94
normality, 83; as conformity, 87, 166; definitions of, 85–6; and gender, 95–8; as heterosexuality, 91–5
normalization, 12–16, 107, 130, 141, 169
North Toronto Committee on Juvenile Delinquency, 50

obscenity, 138, 157, 159, 160, 164
On Becoming a Woman (Williams and Kane), 93, 98
Ontario, Department of Education, 110–11, 113, 117, 125
Ontario, Department of Health, 65, 111, 134
Ontario, Department of Labour, 81
Ontario, Department of Public Welfare, 69
Ontario Educational Association, 112, 113
Ontario, Select Committee on Reform Institutions, 74
Ontario Teachers' Federation, 142
Ontario Training School Advisory Committee, 78

Ontario Training School for Girls, 64, 65

Owram, Doug, 18, 20, 19

Parent–Teacher Associations, 81
Parent–Teacher Federation, 142
parenting classes, 115
Parents' Action League, 122
Peiss, Kathy, 98, 99
physical education, 111, 117, 119, 120, 134
Pierson, Ruth Roach, 41
Playboy, 137
Pomeroy, Wardell, 36
popular culture, 139
popularity, 90, 99
postwar Canada, 18–38; economy, 19, 20–1; scholarship on, 19; social conditions, 19
premarital sex, 104
Prentice, Susan, 41
prescriptive literature, 88
prostitution, 109, 153
psychiatry, 31–2
psychoanalytic theory, 9, 68
psychology, 84
puberty, 46, 47, 62, 165
pulp novels, 136–8, 140, 156, 159; lesbian, 83

queer, 8, 93

race: whiteness, 90
rape, court case, 70–1
Reader's Digest, 17, 137
Regent Park, 58
Regina v. American News, 159
Reisman, David, 34
Rich, Adrienne, 11
Robb, C.W., 125

Rogers, Kenneth, 123, 128
Rose, Nikolas, 116, 169
Ross, Dorothy, 44
Ross, Isabel, 81–2, 131
Rothman, Ellen, 98
Rousseau, Jean-Jacques, 44, 46, 151
Roxborough, E.L., 109, 120
Royal Canadian Mounted Police, 22, 30; security investigations, 22–5
Royal Commission on Criminal Sexual Psychopaths, 122
Rumming, Eleanor, 85, 86

Salvation Army, 69
same-sex crushes, 93
same-sex sexual behaviour, 93
Sandwell, B.K., 37
Sangster, Joan, 27
Saturday Night, 36, 37, 38, 50, 85, 86, 115
Sawatsky, John, 24
Sayer, Derek, 14
Schlossman, Steven, and Stephanie Wallach, 65
Second World War: social conditions, 19
Seduction of the Innocent (Wertham), 150–6
Seidman, Steven, 32
Seiger, Allan, 161
Senate Committee on Salacious and Indecent Literature, 122, 138, 140, 141, 156–8
sex advice, 88–106
Sex and the Adolescent (Davis), 91
sex crime, 121–5, 153; and sex education, 123–5
sex delinquency, 59–64, 79, 129, 132, 157
sex education, 88, 90, 96, 107, 169; as

family life education, 125–8; films, 119; and juvenile delinquency, 112; London, Ont., 108, 111; and moral regulation, 120; and parents, 115–16; and provincial curriculum, 112; and sex crime, 123–5; and the state, 120; and venereal disease, 114. *See also* family life education

Sex, Guidance and Family Life Education (Strain), 126

sex magazines, 137

Sex, Marriage and Birth Control (Tyrer), 89

sexologists, 7

sexual behaviour, 37, 93, 102–6; masturbation, 63, 132, 153

sexual deviance, 23, 87, 92, 107, 121, 123, 153, 166

sexual discourses, 16–17; and power, 12

sexual identity, 10

sexual normality, 3, 38

sexual perversion, 121, 131, 140

sexual psychopaths, 122–3

sexuality: and gender, 95–8; social constructions of, 12; sublimation of, 45; teenage, 10

Sher, Len, 22

Simmons, Christina, 9

Sinatra, Frank, 75

sissies, 95–8

social hygiene, 54, 109–13, 125, 126

Social Planning Council of Metro Toronto, 68, 76. *See also* Toronto Welfare Council

Solinger, Rickie, 68

Speirs, N.R., 128, 131–2

Stainton-Rogers, Rex, 151–2

Stainton-Rogers, Wendy, 151–2

Stanley Gardens, 70

Strain, Frances Bruce, 92, 97, 101, 126

Strange, Carolyn, 75

subjectivity, 15–16

Sunday closing laws, 80–1

teen clubs, 76–7

teen culture, 42

Teen Days (Strain), 92

teen market, 42, 49

teenagers: hostility towards, 49–50; as problem, 48–50; and prosperity, 50–1; as social category, 49; as symbol, 167; as term, 40, 42–3. *See also* adolescents; youth

Teens, The (film), 43

Time magazine, 17, 36

tomboys, 95–8

Toronto Board of Education, 107–35, 137, 172; film protest, 53–4, 77; Management Committee, 110–11, 115, 125, 130, 133, 144

Toronto Board of Trade, 74

Toronto Daily Star, 61, 80, 111, 114–15

Toronto Home and School Council, 74, 110

Toronto Juvenile Court, 79, 116

Toronto Local Council of Women, 75

Toronto Mayor's Committee on Juvenile Delinquency, 74

Toronto Playground Association, 75

Toronto Police Commission, 78

Toronto Teachers' Council, 115

Toronto Telegram, 61, 77, 125, 130, 134

Toronto Welfare Council, 58, 70, 72, 74, 76. *See also* Social Planning Council

Torres, Tereska, 158

Trevor, Mrs E.C., 77

Tumpane, Frank, 49, 80

Tyrer, Alfred Henry, 89

United States: Americanization of
  Canada, 6, 17; liberal sex reform, 9;
  as moral threat to Canada, 138;
  popular culture, 139; postwar
  scholarship, 11; sex crime in, 121–2
United Welfare Chest, 57, 74
Unusual Comics, 146
unwed mothers, 66–9, 105; illegitimate births, 68; maternity homes,
  68; and sex delinquency, 68
urban space, 77–82; regulation of
  access to, 77–82
Urwin, Cathy, 13

Valverde, Mariana, 72
Vanishing Adolescent, The (Friedenberg), 49
venereal disease, 47, 107–8; prevention, 109, 112, 113–17, 120; and provincial curriculum, 120; rates of,
  110; and sex education, 114, 117;
  teachers' guide about, 117; as youth
  problem, 108

Waller, Willard, 99
Warrendale, 66
Webb, Mary, 69
welfare state, 6, 25, 101
Well of Loneliness, The (Hall), 83
Wertham, Fredric, 150–6
Whitaker, Reg, and Gary Marcuse, 18,
  22
Who Is Sylvia? (film), 43
Wild One, The (film), 53, 70
Williams, J.P.F., 110
Williams, Mary McGee, and Irene
  Kane, 93, 98, 101, 106

Winzerl, Adolf, 125
Woman's Christian Temperance
  Union, 74
women and work, 20, 33
Women's Barracks (Torres), 137, 158–64
Women's College Hospital, 119
Women's Law Association, 74
women's liberation, 11
Wonder Woman, 154
working mothers, 27

Yalden, Max, 172
Young, Leontine, 68
Young, White and Miserable (Breines),
  104
Young Women's Christian Association, 5, 76
youth: and class, 50, 55, 56, 57–9, 67,
  72–3, 75–7, 80–1, 90; as corruptible,
  137, 148; and innocence, 41–2, 137,
  140, 151–2; as metaphor, 40–1, 42,
  164; as sexual category, 60, 140, 165,
  168; sexuality, 120; social despair
  about, 39–40; as symbol, 50–1, 87;
  as term, 40; trouble, 42, 60; in wartime, 41; and work, 41, 81, 119. *See
  also* adolescents; teenagers
Youth, Marriage and the Family (Canadian Youth Commission), 113
youth problem, 41, 47–8, 54; and biology, 47; and puberty, 46; solutions
  to, 73–82
Youth Takes a Stand (television program), 103

zoot suits, 71–2

STUDIES IN GENDER AND HISTORY

General editors: Franca Iacovetta and Craig Heron

1 Suzanne Morton, *Ideal Surroundings: Domestic Life in a Working-Class Suburb in the 1920s*

2 Joan Sangster, *Earning Respect: The Lives of Working Women in Small-Town Ontario, 1920–1960*

3 Carolyn Strange, *Toronto's Girl Problem: The Perils and Pleasures of the City, 1880–1930*

4 Sara Z. Burke, *Seeking the Highest Good: Social Service and Gender at the University of Toronto, 1888–1937*

5 Lynne Marks, *Revivals and Roller Rinks: Religion, Leisure, and Identity in Late-Nineteenth-Century Small-Town Ontario*

6 Cecilia Morgan, *Public Men and Virtuous Women: The Gendered Languages of Religion and Politics in Upper Canada, 1791–1850*

7 Mary Louise Adams, *The Trouble with Normal: Postwar Youth and the Making of Heterosexuality*